1

A
Companion
to
John

REV. NOEL F. MOHOLY, O.F.M.

A Companion to John

Readings in Johannine Theology
(John's Gospel and Epistles)

EDITED BY MICHAEL J. TAYLOR S.J.

ALBA · HOUSE   NEW · YORK

SOCIETY OF ST. PAUL, 2187 VICTORY BLVD., STATEN ISLAND, NEW YORK 10314

Library of Congress Cataloging in Publication Data

Main entry under title:

A Companion to John.

Includes bibliographical references.
1. Bible. N.T. Johannine literature--Theology--
Addresses, essays, lectures. I. Taylor, Michael J.
BS2601.C56   230   77-7042
ISBN 0-8189-0348-1

Nihil Obstat:

William B. Smith, S.T.D.
Censor Librorum

Imprimatur:

✠ James P. Mahoney, D.D.
Vicar General, Archdiocese of New York
May 11, 1977

*Designed, printed and bound in the United States of
America by the Fathers and Brothers of the Society of St. Paul,
2187 Victory Boulevard, Staten Island, New York, 10314,
as part of their communications apostolate.*

1 2 3 4 5 6 7 8 9 (Current Printing: first digit).

ACKNOWLEDGMENTS

Grateful acknowledgment is made to the following authors and publishers for use of material under their copyright:

"John and the Synoptics" by John Marsh. From John Marsh: **The Gospel of St. John** (1968), pp. 44-71. Copyright © John Marsh, 1968. Reprinted by permission of Penguin Books, Ltd., London. Citations in this essay from **The Fourth Gospel** by Edwyn Hoskyns and F. Noel Davey, reprinted with permission of Faber and Faber, Ltd., Publishers, London.

"The Johannine Logos Doctrine" by T. W. Manson. Reprinted from **On Paul and John** by T. W. Manson (London: SCM Press, Ltd., 1963; distributed in the U.S.A. by Alec R. Allenson, Inc., Naperville, Ill.), pp. 136-160 with permission of the publisher.

"Word and Wisdom in St. John" by Basil De Pinto. Reprinted from **Scripture,** the Quarterly of the Catholic Biblical Association of Great Britain, Vol. 19, No. 45 (January, 1967), pp. 20-27, with permission of the publisher.

"The Qumran Scrolls and the Johannine Gospel and Epistles" by Raymond E. Brown. Reprinted with permission of Macmillan Publishing Co., Inc., from **New Testament Essays** by Raymond E. Brown. © 1965, The Bruce Publishing Co., pp. 102-131, issued in paperback in 1968, and available from Image Books, Garden City, New York.

"The Signs: Jesus and the World" by W. D. Davies. From **Invitation to the New Testament,** copyright © 1966 by W. D. Davies, pp. 440-465. Used by permission of Doubleday & Co., Inc.

"Egō Eimi—I Am," by Raymond E. Brown. From **The Gospel According to John** (Anchor Bible Series), translated and edited by Raymond E. Brown, pp. 533-538. Copyright © 1970 by Doubleday & Co., Inc. Used by permission of the publisher.

"Theology of Man according to John" by Karl Schelkle. Reprinted from **Theology of the New Testament,** Vol. 1, pp. 141-155,

CONTENTS

INTRODUCTION

Most Christians, even in an age that identifies comfortably with the human Christ, seem to have a special fondness for the Johannine Jesus. This is paradoxical in a way because John's Jesus, though man, is clearly more than man. He is, as the gospel tells us, the Word made flesh, an earthly manifestation of heavenly glory, one sent by the Father to reveal the mystery of God himself. Yet such a *divine figure* is eagerly embraced by Christians who regard Jesus as brother also.

John's Jesus is indeed "different." When we compare him to the synoptic Christ we almost wonder at times if John is talking about the same person. The synoptics are filled with a multitude of incident, parable, didactic one-liners, where John is selective in incident and hesitant to use parable, preferring longer discourses to convey the meaning and teaching of Jesus. His chronology differs, Jesus' style, his manner of teaching differs, even the overall theme of his gospel seems to differ, as his version speaks more about the coming of God's life than his kingdom. His gospel has often been called the book of life, eternal and everlasting.

Nevertheless, few Christians find themselves uneasy with John; not many label him dangerous or heterodox. The Church certainly has accorded him as much respect as the synoptics, finding in him much content and inspiration for her life and preaching. Difference there may be, but it is not irreconcilable or incompatible. John paints his distinct picture not because he contemns the synoptic view of Jesus or because he thinks it inadequate or naïve. His difference lies in his special viewpoint, in his singular manner of interpretation, in his particular theological emphasis. Each evangelist may seem to paint a different Christ; but really it is the background and angle of the portrait that makes it different. John's angle is indeed striking, and it is a challenge to define and explain it precisely.

Theories abound, but scholars generally feel that John's uniqueness can be accounted for if we place him within the context
of the religious and philosophical currents circulating in the
Mid-East in the latter part of the first century, when most agree
the gospel reached its final form.

First we know he[1] wrote in Greek and thus must have been
more than casually familiar with the cultural and religious
values of the Graeco-Roman world. His work seems intentionally to use terms that even the secular man of that time would
find meaningful, as for example, when we see Jesus claiming
to be "the way", "the truth", "a new life." His work even more
so manifests an insider's knowledge of the Old Testament.
Though he quotes it much less than the other evangelists, he
refers to various parts of it explicitly and by allusion. He can,
for instance, use quotes from Isaiah like "the blinded eyes . . .
hardened hearts" text familiar to other New Testament writers
(Is 6:10; Jo 12:40). He can also use bold biblical imagery such
as the bronze serpent on the staff (Nb 21:9) to symbolize the
crucified and exalted Christ (Jo 3:14). No evangelist is more

---

1. We should make clear at the outset that the authorship of the fourth
gospel and the epistles is much disputed and perhaps must ever remain so.
In the second century the anonymous work came to be attributed to "John"
but it is only Irenaeus late in the century who clearly equates the Apostle
John with the evangelist. The arguments for or against Irenaeus' position
cannot be restated here and are inconclusive anyhow. It might be best to
say we simply do not know for sure who the author is. Still, an attractive
theoretical reconstruction of authorship is that of a number of recent commentators who hold that the "beloved disciple" spoken of in the gospel is
indeed John the Apostle and that the tradition contained in the gospel and
the epistles is ultimately rooted in his experience and insight. In the course
of many years of development within the Johannine church, these traditions
took on oral and later written expression. Finally this tradition was formulated into the gospel and epistles by a Christian or Christians of a later
generation than that of the Apostle, probably undergoing several stages of
editing as the Writings came to final form. But John the Apostle can rightly
be considered to be the author of the gospel and the epistles since it is concluded by these scholars that it was he who "authored" and influenced the
shaping of the earlier stages of the Johannine tradition that later developed
into the written gospel and epistles. Most of the essays in this book simply
refer to the evangelist as *John,* even though most of the authors would
admit the identity of *John* is still an unresolved question.

knowledgeable in the festal and cultic life of Israel. A number of scholars further note John's reliance on the Old Testament Wisdom literature, where he seems to find biblical precedent and analogy for the "divine" dimension he discovers in Jesus. Many exegetical studies support the position that John was thoroughly intimate with this tradition, a tradition incidentally that other New Testament Christians found helpful in drawing out the divine-human measure of Christ.

Another first-century Jewish movement that may possibly have influenced John is discovered when we compare his writings with those of the Essene sect of Qumran, the now famous Dead Sea Scrolls. Though the documents antedate John's gospel by some years there are striking similarities between the language of the scrolls and key Johannine expressions, e.g., the use of an ethically dualist "light-darkness" terminology or phrases such as "witnessing to the truth", "loving the brethren" and others which have distinct Johannine parallels. Some think the evangelist may once have been a follower of John the Baptist, who himself may have been an Essene.

And the Johannine Writings suggest that still other religious and philosophical forces of his time may have had some influence on the evangelist and the way he expressed himself. Many scholars for instance find in John a gnostic flavor and terminology. Gnosticism is dualistic, stressing man's radical desire for psychic fulfillment while distrusting if not contemning his earthly components; it is a mythological system that believes a heavenly revealer has come to save man from worldly bondage and limitation by communicating to him a special knowledge (*gnosis*) of his heavenly origin and destiny. Certain similarities to Johannine thought and expression are impressive. Other scholars see a similarity between key Johannine notions, such as the *Logos*, and the speculations of the hellenist Jewish philosopher Philo. The question of gnostic or Jewish philosophical influence on John is still admittedly controversial. One of the troubles is that many scholars assumed gnosticism came on the scene later than John and thought his more traditional Jewishness had little affinity with the syncretistic Judaism of Philo. Thus it was assumed that at least in the case of gnosticism John could have possibly influenced it and not the other way around. Recent studies, however, think there is a stronger case for positing gnosticism as an earlier movement than supposed and see in its primitive form a strong Jewish influence. If so, then John in his "gnostic" and "philosophical" terminology could well have been attempting to show advocates of these schools that Jesus among other things was truly the *Logos* and *gnosis*-revealer postulated by these systems.

No one maintains we are close to discovering the full and precise background that would explain John's "difference", but at least from this brief inspection we must admit that he has written a remarkable work that finds so many resonant parallels with the different religious and philosophical movements of his day. John above all lived in a hellenistic world, profoundly interested in religious syncreticism and universalism. He seems well versed not only in the Bible, its traditional Jewish interpretation, and the new Christian tradition developing around Jesus as Messiah, but also in the religious tendencies and aspirations of other contemporaries beyond his own tradition, Jewish and non-Jewish. He seems to have chosen to present Jesus in an idiom that would reflect these many interests, especially to emphasize the appeal of Jesus for *all* men, both Jew and Gentile. Such a reflection by no means exhausts the way John speaks of Jesus, but it helps us to realize his religious and cultural frame of reference may be much wider than we earlier assumed.

And if we seek further reason to show that John seems to have a wider religious audience in mind we discover it as we read the stated purpose of his gospel. He tells us in chapter 20, verse 21: "These things are written that *you* may believe that Jesus is the Christ, the Son of God, and that believing *you* may have life in his name." The *you* seems to refer to all interested people: Jews, Greeks, Christians, non-Christians. His use of *Logos* in the very first sentence seems to imply this. *Logos* or Word is an uttered thought. The Stoic philosophers spoke to the Greeks of the *Logos* as the soul of the universe, the divine thought and rational principle that prevaded all things, and as John proceeds he makes clear that the whole of creation is a revelation of the thought and purpose of God and that the fullest word God ever spoke, the fullest revelation he ever gave to man about himself and the world was in the Word made flesh. This kind of beginning would surely appeal to many Greeks. And Jews, moreover, had learned from their Scriptures that the "Word of God" was not just Yahweh having conversation with men; it meant he was revealing himself, in a way giving himself to the world in power, wisdom, and love. When John began his preface by telling us the Word became flesh, it seems he was informing *all* his readers that in the upcoming story of Jesus they would find the ultimate truth about God, man, and the world, for God was speaking out, revealing the fullest meaning of every life in terms of this one special life.

And as John unfolds the story of Jesus he stresses his value for *all* men. He says that embodied in Jesus is the salvation God wants for every one. He says that the blessing which the gospel offers is mainly fullness of life—real life, divine life, eternal life, and it is available to all men through Christ. He says that Jesus before his departure to the Father promised his disciples and through them the world, another advocate, a "Spirit" to be his "other self", guiding men to the truth and light that would lead them to fullness of life. And moreover John makes clear that this Jesus who had been crucified half a century ago remains incontrovertibly alive and active everywhere in the present world to give his life to any and all who would believe. No wonder this book has so influenced the faith and life of Christians. It is John who writes: "God so loved the world that he *gave* it his only Son, that all who believe in him may not perish but have eternal life" (Jo 3:16). In short, John's Christ is not just the subject of an ancient and edifying story that would appeal to a few; his Jesus is God's ever contemporary gift of life and love to every man. Nor is he to be found only in a distant period-time of Palestine; rather it is in the *here and now* of our lives that we discover Christ and hear his challenge.

Having briefly indicated the uniqueness of John's writings and the varied forces that may possibly have contributed to that uniqueness, we must add that should one want to undertake a deeper study of the evangelist, his style, purpose, background, etc., the amount of literature available is simply overwhelming. And so we come to this present collection of essays. It seems, to the editor at least, that the vast complex of specialized works and commentaries on John, because of their format, technical scholarship, sheer size and cost, are not always suitable for use by student-novices of John, i.e., by individuals, study groups, seminary, college, and high school students who are studying John for the first time. It might be wiser for those just beginning a more serious investigation of the fourth gospel and the epistles to start learning about John from essays which have proved to be informative, illuminating, and readable treatments of the general meaning of John, his themes, special problems, etc. Once we become familiar with John and his "difference" in this basic way, we can, I think, with greater profit advance to more specialized studies.

This book, then, is an anthology of essays which presents readers with examples of modern critical studies on the Johannine Writings.[2] Because of John's unique way of setting forth the Christ-event, such selections could be multiplied of course. And experts will think of other essays that should have been included. But choices and reasonable limits had to be made and they were usually made on the grounds that the particular essay chosen, as well as addressing itself to an important Johannine question, did so in a way that combined acceptable scholarship with an easier readability and clarity of expression than is normally found in essays on the subject.[3] No one denies that John's unique interpretation of Christ needs explanation

---

2. Since the Book of Revelation as it relates to the gospel and the epistles presents many unresolved problems, that particular book is not given any lengthy, specific treatment in this reader. It is close to the Johannine tradition, for there are in it many similarities in terminology and theological theme. But the difference is great and it was thought that the Apocalypse and the other Johannine writings should not be grouped together as constituting a single testimony to the Church's tradition.

3. These essays contain only the footnotes essential to an understanding of the topic under discussion. For the author's complete footnote references the original articles should be consulted; they are specified in the acknowledgements.

and commentary; unfortunately professional biblical scholars as we have noted elsewhere often explain texts with such technical nuance that the ordinary reader can easily end up bewildered. And in the present case, looking to scholars to provide coherent commentary on a Johannine symbol, episode, or discourse, with some effort to relate the point to the overall thought of John, one can experience much disappointment and frustration. Accordingly, this collection of essays is offered as a way a student of John can be given an *understandable* as well as a *critical* explanation of some of the more important questions that surround the Johannine Writings. The authors are respected interpreters of John. The pieces they are submitting here have been judged to be significant and informative steps toward the understanding of the gospel and the epistles. As earlier readers have found their essays instructive, it is hoped present readers will find them helpful also.[4]

Scripture scholars as we know can probe and clarify, analyze and synthesize; they cannot, however, substitute for reading and re-reading the words of John himself. Like all the New Testament writers, he sets forth his picture of Christ and explains it best. For those who seek an understanding of the Johannine Christ, the most salutary advice can only be to take up and read the Johannine Writings themselves. If the essays in this book in some manner help to throw light on the meaning of John's Christ and prompt the reader to return again and often to the text of John to meet his Christ first hand, this volume will have fulfilled its purpose as a companion to John.

Michael J. Taylor, S.J.

---

4. John does not normally set forth his themes and then move on convinced that he has done a complete job with only one look at his subject. He returns often to already expressed themes, images, and ideas, deepening our understanding of them as he proceeds. And thus it is with many of the essays in this book. When treating a Johannine topic many authors feel it is not possible to discuss the topic without referring to other Johannine themes. John develops his material by working new meanings into previously developed ideas. Similarly many of the authors in their essays when speaking to their particular subjects often recall themes and topics discussed and developed by others. It is the *cumulative* treatment and analysis that helps us awaken fully to the meaning of Christ.

A
Companion
to
John

JOHN: A VERY DIFFERENT GOSPEL?

John Marsh

No reader of the New Testament can for long refrain from asking himself questions about John and the Synoptics. After all the first three gospels tell what is recognizably the same story in approximately the same way. If the inquiring reader begins to study the New Testament not only more closely, but with the aid of modern manuals of introduction, he will discover that the first impressions of similarity are abundantly confirmed. Mark's narrative turns out to be basic, and all but thirty-one verses of Mark are reproduced in either Matthew or Luke, or both. But when the fourth gospel is read, a very different impression is created. There is none, or very little, of the verbal identity as between Mark and the other two synoptic gospels; and while the fourth gospel is clearly telling the story of the same person known as Jesus the Messiah, the presentation of material, and even the material itself differs widely from that of the synoptics. Even more puzzling is that at some points, notably the cleansing of the Temple and the Last Supper, John seems clearly to be at variance with the united testimony of the other three gospels. This would in any event be strange, but if the testimony of Irenaeus is to be believed or can be substantiated, that John's gospel was written *after* the other three, then some explanation has to be offered of the discrepancies between John and the Synoptics.

Many scholars would affirm that Irenaeus' statement that John wrote his gospel after the other three is one that can be substantiated. The view was for long accepted, if not on the authority of Irenaeus, at least out of some respect for a very ancient tradition. This assumption was challenged in 1938 by Gardner-Smith (*St. John and the Synoptic Gospels*), who argued that John had not read any of the synoptic gospels, but drew upon

the same sources of Christian tradition. His views have found
some acceptance, and Professor Dodd adopts a similar position
in his great work. It is therefore significant that a later scholar,
C. K. Barrett, has attempted to restate the case of John's knowledge and indeed use of at least some of the synoptics. He
claims that John knew and used Mark; possibly, if not probably,
Luke, and with much less certainty, Matthew as well. His argument runs thus: There are at least ten passages which occur in
the same order (Barrett's italics) in Mark and John. (There is
a slight modification necessary since Barrett cites the entry into
Jerusalem and the Anointing of Jesus as one Marcan passage,
with elements transposed in John!) Further, within those passages there are several instances of close verbal resemblance.
Barrett is honest enough a scholar to admit that the evidence
adduced does not *prove* that John knew and used Mark as a
source; but he does claim that it gives plausibility to the view
that John had read Mark, and echoed the earlier gospel in
writing his own, even if, at times, he be found amending or correcting a tradition found in Mark (e.g. Mk 1:14f. compared
with Jn 3:24; Mk 15:21 compared with Jn 19:17).

But need it be assumed that John knew and had read Mark
to account for the phenomena detailed by Barrett? Could they
not equally well be explained by assuming that John had access
to the same or even similar tradition about Jesus that lay behind Mark? A good many of the verbal resemblances which
Barrett notices are almost inevitable if some particular story
is to be told. It would be difficult to tell the story of the feeding
of the five thousand without having a verse including a statement that five loaves and two fishes were available. So identity
or near identity of language is not necessarily a sign of dependence. It is interesting that Dr. Dodd should have followed
the lead given by Gardner-Smith rather than attempt to sub-
stantiate an Irenaean implication of John's knowledge of the
synoptics.

What can be concluded about John's relationship to the
synoptics? First a recognition, dependent upon the evangelist
himself, that his material is drawn from a much more copious
mass of evidence than his own book could hold (20:30f.; 21:25).

Whether the material upon which he drew included one or more of the synoptic gospels as we now possess them is something that cannot be determined with certainty. It would seem that John did rely upon the Gospel of Mark, or some work or works very like it. In either case it is possible to suppose that in presenting the material derived from the synoptic or synoptic-like sources, John had some clear purpose in his mind as he fused his materials with his own testimony to produce the gospel that bears his name.

John's Purpose

John's avowed purpose in writing his gospel was that his readers might 'believe that Jesus is the Christ, the Son of God, and believing, have life in his name' (20:31). But this purpose is really no different in any fundamental way from that envisaged by Mark, or that detected in Mark by an early editor; for the gospel now begins with the programmatic statement: 'The beginning of the gospel of Jesus Christ, the Son of God' (Mk 1:1). There was a time, not long ago (and possibly not yet over for some), when it was generally supposed that the synoptics in general and Mark in particular told the simple historical story of the life and death of Jesus of Nazareth; and that John, though telling substantially the same story, told it with new and different theological overtones. But it is now generally recognized that Mark is as thoroughgoingly theological as John, even if the implications of this revolutionary conviction are not always perceived. The difference between John and the synoptics is not that John is theological and the synoptics not, but that they are theological in different ways. The consequences of this recognition are extensive and important, and it will be necessary to deal with some of them in the rest of this introduction. But the chief implication is that both synoptics and John, like Paul and other New Testament writers, are concerned to deal neither with mere history (what took place) nor mere mysticism (escape from what takes place) but rather with a reality which partakes both of *what takes place* and of *what goes on,* which is another formulation of the statement that John and the synoptics are all theological. They tell the story of *what took place* (the so-called "historical") in order to convey to their readers *what went on*. The purpose of the exercise is that the gospel readers should come to have belief in Jesus of Nazareth as Son of God and Savior, and in that belief find the life that is life indeed.

All this has been excellently stated in Hoskyns and Davey's profound commentary.[1] Before an examination of John and the synoptics is undertaken it is worth quoting the following passage from the end of their long Introduction (pp. 133f.):

> The test that we must in the end apply to the Fourth Gospel, the test by which the Fourth Gospel stands or falls, is whether the Marcan narrative becomes more intelligible after reading the Fourth Gospel, whether the Pauline Epistles become more transparent, or whether the whole material presented to us in the New Testament is breaking up into unrelated fragments. If the latter be the case, we must then go back to speak of Johannine and Pauline theology. Once again we should be compelled to speak of the simplicity of the synoptic gospels, of the complexity of the Pauline ideas, and of the unhistorical mysticism of the Fourth Gospel.

And a little later:

> A commentary on the Fourth Gospel can therefore be no more than a preliminary work. It leads on to further study of the Pauline Epistles and of the synoptic gospels. For the Fourth Gospel should not be regarded merely as an appendix to other biblical work, as though it lay altogether on the periphery of the Bible. The Fourth Gospel ought to be regarded as a necessary prolegomenon to the understanding, not only of the other books of the New Testament, but of the Old Testament as well. At any rate, we have no right to rule out this possibility *a priori*.

---

1. Hoskyns, E. and Davey, F., ed. *The Fourth Gospel*, London, Faber & Faber, 1947.

The present writer believes that this is a true estimate of the significance of the fourth gospel.

The Synoptics, John, and History

In spite of all that has been so wisely written by Hoskyns and Davey, it must be freely admitted that for any reader of John, particularly the modern reader, it is almost fatally easy to suppose that the notable thing about their relationship consists of their differences about certain historical data. If, as many scholars believe, John's is the last gospel, and if, as any reader rapidly observes, there are at least two important and undeniable differences about chronology, then it is easy to understand why the problems of John and the synoptics have been fairly consistently seen as "historical". John says that the Temple Cleansing took place near the beginning of the Ministry: The synoptics agree in placing it very near the end. Surely this is the plainest of indications that the difference between them is "historical". The conclusion does not follow.

The perception of the difference as historical would be valid if the two sets of documents were historical, but they are not. They are both theological. Or, to put the same point in another way, both synoptics and John are concerned to relate *what took place* so that men may learn thereby *what was going on*. Long ago Bishop Butler said that "each thing is what it is, and not another thing" and were that maxim observed in dealing with the four gospels the relationship between the synoptics and John would not be so widely misconceived as it is today. There was a time when it was held critically respectable to believe that the synoptic gospels, particularly Mark as the allegedly first of them, provided something approaching a chronological framework for a "life of Jesus". That was possible in the days of source criticism. But with the advent of form criticism and the analysis of the synoptic narrative into individual elements of different kinds such a view was no longer tenable. Instead of chronology being the thread upon which the pearls of gospel stories were strung in narrative sequence, it became clear that each pearl was a theological counter, and that chron-

ology had much less to do with selection or place than source
criticism could ever have imagined. But if even Mark is not
constructed chronologically but theologically (not concerned
simply to report what took place but always to make plain
what was going on), then any correction of Mark made by
John could not, in the nature of things, be simply chronological.
Any "correction" would primarily be concerned with theology,
with meaning, with *what was going on* and only secondarily
by implication, as it were, with chronology, with *what took
place*. This is not to deny that some plausible chronological
deductions can be made from Mark and the other synoptics.
Clearly some chronological order is embedded in Mark. The
baptism of Jesus and the calling of the disciples are bound
to have taken place before the public ministry really began.[2]
There had to be some indication of opposition before Jesus
took farewell of the Galilean crowds on the hill of the miraculous feeding. The crucifixion could not come elsewhere than at
the end. A minimal outline of this sort, for what it is worth,
can be detected. The point that needs to be made is that
even among the synoptics themselves, where dislocations of
an apparently chronological kind are made, there is always a
theological point being made, in and through the chronological
change. One or two examples may be quoted by a comparison
of the first five incidents in Jesus' career in Mark with their
treatment and placing in Luke. Mark's incidents in his order,
are: 1. The baptism (1:9-11); 2. The Temptation (1:12-13);
3. The return to Galilee with the good news of fulfillment (1:
14-15); 4. The calling of Simon and Andrew, and of James
and John (1:16-20); and 5. The authoritative preaching and the
healing in the synagogue at Capernaum (1:21-28). Luke bases
his own narrative to some extent upon Mark. He tells in some-

---

2. Though even here there may be theological motives behind the place
given to the calling of the disciples in Mark; the evangelist may find his
present placing of the calling of the disciples (Mk 1:16-20) a convenient
way of indicating in the very account of what took place that there is no
real activity of the Messiah without the prior inauguration of the people of
the Messiah. The first miracle is not related until the Messianic community
has begun to be formed (Mk 1:21-28).

what different terms of the baptism (Lk 3:21-22); he then inserts a genealogy which traces the ancestry of Jesus back to "Adam, the son of God" (Lk 3:23-38). This follows the baptism where a voice from heaven had declared that Jesus was the son of God. By the device of the genealogical tree inserted here Luke is on the one hand trying to avoid the false inference that some in fact drew from the baptismal voice—that Jesus did not assume his divine nature and status until the day of his baptism: the son of God did not come into existence on that day! On the other hand Luke is indicating that it was not only a new Israel (or Son) of God that was begun when Jesus was born, but a new humanity. The genealogical tree is thus skillfully placed to make a theological comment on the narrative; it is a means of pointing to what was going on, in the baptism and throughout the ministry. Luke resumes the Marcan order, giving, like Matthew, a somewhat longer story of the temptation, with a shift of theological emphasis to the question, 'If you are the son of God'. But when Luke reports the return to Galilee, he does not simply report a general proclamation of the arrival of fulfillment time. Instead he follows the report of Jesus' entry into Galilee (Lk 4:14-15) with the story of the preaching in the synagogue, not at Capernaum, but at Nazareth, according to Luke, his "patris" or "native city". In this story Luke brings out even more vividly than Mark (1:21-28) the astounding character of the good news of fulfillment. For in Luke it is no longer possible to detect a theme about the arrival of a new age, but instead the reader must grapple with the highly particular claim that the new age is to be identified with the person of Jesus himself. "The spirit of the Lord is upon *me*," says Jesus, quoting Isaiah (Is 61:1-2); and then adds: "Today this scripture has been fulfilled in your hearing." Luke has thought it right to indicate at the very start of the gospel that his theological convictions about the new era are focused upon and center in this particular historical person. Thereafter Luke seems to desert his Marcan model for a time; for though teaching and exorcism in Capernaum follow (as in Mark) and these are followed by the account of the healing of Peter's mother-in-law, and of the healing of the many sick persons at sunset, followed in turn by Jesus' retreat to solitude for the renewal of prayer, and a Johannine-like report of preaching in Judea, it is not until Luke has reached his eleventh incident of the ministry (in contrast to Mark's fourth) that he relates the call of any disciple. He then records the "call" of Peter. This is a narrative different from Mark's, and much more is involved than in the simple "call" of Mark. Indeed the response of Peter to the Lord's injunction to "put out into the deep and let down your nets for a catch" could be taken to presuppose the story of the "call" recorded in Mark, for Peter replied to Jesus: "Master, we toiled all night and took nothing." In this skillful and artistic resetting of Peter's "call" Luke is trying to make plain to his readers that the bond between the Master and his disciples (for the sons of Zebedee figure at the same time in Luke as in Mark) was from the very beginning rooted in a recognition of something supernatural in the person of the Lord. Such a point is made even more forcefully in John, where the very first approach of any disciple to Jesus follows the witness of the Baptist that Jesus is *the Lamb of God, who takes away the sins of the world* (1:29). Thus it can be shown that important theological points are, or always may be, involved in dislocations or transpositions of incidents, or in the insertion of new material into the narrative. The wise reader will remain alert to these clues to *what was going on* in *what was taking place*.

Displacement and transposition of order in the synoptics can thus be seen as a means of theological comment. The same point needs to be made in respect of changes of order and content as between the synoptics and John. The gospels read so very much like historical narratives of what took place (as indeed to some extent they are) that it requires effort not to treat them exclusively as such, but to understand them as much more concerned to indicate *what was going on* in the narrative provided. It is natural and understandable for any man of any century confronted with the evidence to suppose that John has consciously sought to correct the synoptics in two major points, the position of the Temple Cleansing in the ministry of Jesus, and the date of the Last Supper and the crucifixion. The differences are quite clear. John tells of the cleansing of the Temple at the very start of the ministry (2: 13-22); the synoptists place it at the beginning of the last week of Jesus' life (Mk 11:15-19). For the fourth evangelist the Last Supper took place before the Passover, and Jesus was crucified while the Passover Lambs were being slain in the temple; for the synoptists the last supper was an eating of the Passover by Jesus and the Twelve. It must then freely be granted that a chronological question arises in each instance, and much scholarly care has gone into the understandable attempt to decide which of the two chronologies—Johannine or synoptic— is the more likely in each case. The recognition of the question and the attempt to find a convincing answer are quite proper human enterprises. But it is fatal to suppose that in deciding for one chronology or author, or by producing some reconciliation of the two, the critic has really penetrated to what his text has really affirmed. If the gospels are to be treated "for what they are, and not for another thing", the synoptic narrative must be seen, no less than the Johannine, as a theological document in which what was going on is made clear in the narrative of what took place.

Take, for example, the story of the cleansing of the Temple. Its "chronological" position in Mark may be right, and John's placing wrong. But even if Mark be right, the chronological position bestows a theological meaning (something is *going on* in *what takes place*). In the context it is plain that the Temple cleansing was the occasion of the decision of the authorities to *destroy him* (Mk 11:18). There is a swift chronological sequence from Temple cleansing to crucifixion. But the chronological sequence involves a theological point. The affront to authority consisted in the open condemnation of the chief priests and scribes as those who, while anxious to preserve their own knowledge and worship of God, were unwilling to fulfill God's demands to make his temple a house of prayer for all nations. What was thus being denied by all the paraphernalia to keep the Temple worship specifically Jewish was the access of the Gentiles to Yahweh, a denial symbolized by the presence of money-changing and animal-selling in the very court where the

Gentiles were permitted, but where they could read at the entry
to the holy place "No Gentile is to enter on penalty of death."
But when Jesus comes he comes to the temple to make the
religion of the people of God, embodied in himself and his
community, as universal as the prophet's vision which saw
all the nations sharing in the worship of Yahweh. And the
substantive link with the crucifixion is then at once apparent,
for it was by his self-offering in death that Jesus fulfilled his
destiny as the savior of the world.

In the Johannine placing of the story there is a greater historical space between the cleansing and the cross. But the theological proximity to the death and resurrection is no less. As
in Mark, those who preserve the Jewish paraphernalia of worship by selling animals and changing money are expelled;
what is significant is that, in John, the animals to be used in
the sacrifices of Judaism are also driven out (2:15), leaving
Jesus, the one true sacrifice, in the temple. The old temple of
animal sacrifices must yield to the new temple and the one
sacrifice. John tells how the authorities ask Jesus what sign
he has to show for his action; he replied by identifying the
sign with the destruction of *"this temple"*, and of his raising
it up in three days (2:19). That is to say what has really been
enacted that day, when the one who is to become the sufficient
sacrifice for the sins of the world expels all inadequate sacrifice
and its signs, is precisely an affirmation of the reality of Jesus
as the perfect sacrifice, which he is only as he gives his life
in death for all mankind. By somewhat different accounts of
what took place John and Mark have given common and united
witness to *what was going on*. But what of the chronological
difference? Does it have any theological point? John is indicating by the changed chronological point that the theological
depth manifest in the Temple cleansing in Mark was not reached
for the first time only a few days before Jesus died: it was there
from the beginning of the ministry. The underlying significance
of this answer has been admirably stated in Hoskyns and
Davey (p. 126):

The true understanding of the history of Jesus—and consequently of all observable history—therefore springs from that God-given perception of which the apostles who *beheld his glory,* and those who share their apprehension (17:20), can confidently speak, and it cuts right across the chronological understanding of history. For this reason, in the interests of that history which has been seen to bear witness to God, it has to be detached from its chronological context and narrated non-historically since only so can justice be done to its theological significance. Even the chronological movement of Jesus from His Baptism to the Cross, which in itself, as a chronological movement, is theologically significant, since it bears witness to the return of Jesus whence he came, and to the requisite movement of man to God, has to be rid of any semblance of evolution, lest God should be thought of as an historical end, or His action continued to a distant future.

Put in other words: John is trying to tell his readers that Jesus was "near the cross" not only at the beginning of the last week of his life, but at the very beginning of his ministry. And it is this "nearness" which is important. A modern, though lesser, parallel might help. How near, it might be asked, was the Third World War in 1962 when President Kennedy defied Russia over Cuba? The answer could come in two forms—one chronological, and no precise answer can be given yet, for the third world war has not yet come. But whether a third world war comes or not the world was very near it in 1962. John is saying, in effect, that the cross was "very near" even from the day when the Baptist first saw Jesus and hailed him with the words *"Behold the lamb of God, who takes away the sin of the world".* And if such theologizing at the start of the gospel be thought un-synoptic and therefore unhistorical, the reply must be made that Mark's work begins with the theological word: "The beginning of the gospel of Jesus Christ, the Son of God" and that as early as Chapter 2, in the saying about the wedding guests not fasting while the bridegroom is with them, there is some "nearness" of the cross at a considerable chronological distance from the crucifixion.

The second "displacement" can perhaps be more quickly evaluated. John is absolutely unambiguous in his evidence that the Last Supper recorded in 13:1ff. was not a Passover meal, for the simple reason that in 18:28 he reports that the Jews did not enter the praetorium, *so that they might not be defiled, but might eat the passover;* again, in telling the story of the crucifixion he says that *since it was the day of Preparation* (19:31) for the Passover, the Jews asked Pilate that the legs of the crucified might be broken. In contrast (or conflict?) with this the synoptic tradition is equally unambiguous that the Last Supper was a Passover meal. 'On the first day of Unleavened Bread, when they sacrificed the passover lamb, his disciples said to him, "Where will you have us go and prepare for you to eat the passover?"' (Mk 14:12). As has already been observed it is possible to ask the chronological question: when did the Last Supper, the crucifixion take place? Very many learned books have grappled with the problem, but certainty has not even so been reached. What the two different chronologies have in common is not just the eating of a meal and the crucifixion of Jesus, which for some unknown reason they place at different chronological points. Also common is the reference to the Passover and the consequent setting of the death of Jesus in a paschal perspective. Whether the paschal significance of the death of Jesus is brought out by means of the story of the Last Supper, or by the incidents recorded by John at the crucifixion, where Jesus, like a passover lamb, did not have one of his legs broken: what matters is that the paschal theology be made available to the Church so that Christians might be able to understand what God did in giving his son to die for the world. But why should John offer the Church a perspective different from that of the synoptics? The present writer's guess is that it was linked with the eucharistic experience of the Church. The eucharist was, and still is, a rite to be performed "in memory of" Christ. But what occasion is remembered? Is it the first eucharist after the resurrection, when in a mysterious trinity of wonder, doubt and joy, the earliest disciples were admitted to a new and indestructible communion and community with their Lord? Is it the Last Supper, where before the passion and death Jesus pre-enacted his self-offering for men? Is it the actual event of crucifixion and death itself? It would seem that both John and the synoptics share in the inheritance of the first eucharist. The one whom they remember does not come from it; for he came to it. That being so, it appears that the synoptists have chosen to see the eucharist as the re-enactment of the Last Supper, the pre-enactment; while John sees it as the re-presentation of the act itself. And this is quite in keeping with his whole attitude to history and eschatology. He so writes his story that God, or his coming to men, is not something still to be enacted, but something which happened once for all when Jesus was crucified and so glorified.

The conclusion to be drawn from all this is that it is important for the modern reader to be aware of the differences between modern historiography and that of the evangelists. It is not the case that the first records of Jesus were written down as modern historiography would suppose and require, in a chronologically accurate order, and that later John made some important corrections for sound chronological reasons. Rather the very first order is as theological as the last; and while chronological questions may be quite properly raised, it must always be remembered that chronology was itself a theological tool in the hands of the evangelists. Difficult as it is for the modern reader to realize, there are more important things, even about chronology, than correct chronological order. It is more important to understand why John can say that Jesus' hour has come (12:23; 13:1; 17:1) than to determine with irrefutable accuracy the date of the month on which it came!

Historiographical Tools: 1. Typology

John like the synoptists is trying to convey to his readers not only an impression of what took place in the life of Jesus (observable history as Hoskyns and Davey describe it) but also what went on. One tool they shared in common is called typology, which has the dictionary definition: 'the doctrine that things in the Christian dispensation are symbolized or prefigured by things in the Old Testament, as the sacrifice of Christ and the Eucharist by the sacrifice of the Paschal Lamb'. The word doctrine is an exalted description for an historian's tool, and it may well explain why modern historians view the very word with suspicion. Quite unjustifiably!' An approach to a better understanding of typology may be facilitated by a modern hypothetical example. If a third world war were to break out between Russia and the Western Powers, and once again large numbers of British troops were to be pushed back to the beaches of north-west France; and if at that time there were to be staged a saving operation akin to that which took place in 1940, it is almost certain that the British press, and possibly the press of the whole Western Alliance, would feature the story with a banner headline: "Another Dunkirk". No one would denigrate such journalism (which is the "contemporary history") as misleading typology; and yet it is precisely this procedure which is followed by the evangelists when they employ an Old Testament saying, person, or even idea to throw light on the story of the New. The phrase "Another Dunkirk" does no more—and no less—than to use a past incident whose "meaning" or "significance" or even "outcome" is well known, and which conveys a whole complex of suggestion, in order to inject into the account of an event not yet so clearly established in its meaning, the significance already established by and attached to the incident from the past. This is precisely what John and the synoptists do as they use the Old Testament typologically. They assume, of course, as any user of typology must, that the meaning of the "type" they apply is well known— as the Old Testament was to many of the first readers of the gospels. They then invite their readers to see the story they are telling in the light of the meaning the type brings. In another way of putting it they use an accepted witness to what went on in the past to point to what is going on in the story they narrate.

This being so, it is misleading to regard typology as valueless historically. Rather it is an historiographical tool of great value. All history involves meaning: and how can meaning in history be identified better than by recognition of similarities with meanings accepted from the past? It is important to note that typology differs completely from allegory; for typology is a means of being anchored to an historical occasion and to detect the meaning in it, while allegory takes the hearer out of a particular occasion in order to enunciate some universal propositions or rules.

Thus when Augustine deals with the story of the Good Samaritan he sees the injured man as the symbol of humanity; the Good Samaritan as standing for Jesus; the wine and oil as the two dominical sacraments etc. etc. But that is to abstract from the specific situation and seek quite general theological truths. But if Mark's description of John the Baptist in Mark 1:6 be seen as a typological presentation, then the reader, at each recognition of the type to be applied, is able to enter into that particular situation with a greatly enhanced understanding. He learns, by the quite simple and brief descriptions, that John the Baptist is "another Elijah" and that therefore the Messiah himself is near (though not identifiable with John); he learns that like Jonathan of old, the new John is gifted with a prevision that in a time of real darkness and defeat can sense an impossible-seeming victory very close at hand.

Typology is thus not a forced literary convention. Quite the contrary! For the evangelist of the first and the journalist of the twentieth century it is a most natural instrument to use. But it has limitations. Its usefulness is confined to those who know the significance of the type. In the imagined third world war situation the headline "Another Dunkirk" would be either unintelligible or unacceptable to a Russian newspaper reader; and a Tibetan who chanced upon the headline would have no clue from his own nation's history with which to make use of the type. But the Jew of the first century (and many a Gentile convert to the Church) was steeped in the story of the Old Testament and the rich allusiveness of the four evangelists would be most meaningful to him. In any case it is small wonder when the Christian Church came to write about the most important person and the most important event in the whole of human history that it should turn to the Old Testament for types by means of which the account they had to give of what took place should also give something like a worthy account of what went on. Shakespeare wrote of a "Daniel come to judgment". The evangelists, using the same device, have tried to say that what went on when Jesus was here could be nothing less than a recital of the mighty acts of God.

Historiographical Tools: 2. Symbolism

The author of the fourth gospel had an eye for the symbolic. Again and again he notes some little detail that is full of rich symbolism, and so again a depth of meaning is added to his narrative. One example will illustrate the point. John says that at the wedding in Cana, six jars of water were provided for the customary Jewish rites of purification. Why six? There was no requirement of Jewish law demanding just this number. So why six? Either because six were there, or John chose the number to make a point—or six were there and John saw—and made his point. What point can be made? Six was, for the Jew, near to but short of the "perfect" number seven; and John is trying to say that Judaism and its rituals is near to but short of the perfection of religion. By its purificatory rites Judaism sought to keep God's people in proper relationship with him, and with its closely guarded marriage regulations tried to secure a proper transmission of that relationship. But Judaism has signally failed. Yet, in the advent of Jesus it could now be said that Judaism could and would be replaced by the only "purificatory rite" that could make, maintain and transmit a true life for the people of God: the self-offering of Jesus in death, symbolized for ever in the wine of the Christian sacrament. John is richly endowed with this theologically sensitive, almost poetic insight. He is happily unafraid, and unashamed to use it.

John and the Synoptics: Examples and Episodes

One of the most remarkable things about the fourth gospel is that though its author and/or appendicist recognizes that there are very many stories about Jesus that he did not tell, he managed to find room for only seven miracles and very little else by way of incident. This contrasts strongly with the synoptic gospels, where no reference is made to the many stories not published, but where even the shortest gospel greatly surpasses John in the number of stories told. It is worth while quoting Hoskyns and Davey again (pp. 65-6):

> The synoptic gospels consist of a large number of disconnected or semi-disconnected fragments, incidents, episodes, put together by the Evangelists within a broad, roomy framework, capable, without serious disturbance to the general plan of the books, of being expanded to hold additional material or contracted in order to render the material more manageable. In the midst of this rich varied gallery the reader can wander about. He is magnificently free. He can pause and admire where he will. He can select an incident, visualize it, meditate upon it, and then preach about it, allegorize it, interpret it, symbolize it, apply it to his own circumstances, use it to pillory his enemies or to encourage himself and his friends. . . . And in doing all this he can pride himself that he is acting in obedience to the highest authority, that of the authentic teaching of Jesus of Nazareth, and that he is a true disciple of the "Jesus of History" because he has heard him speak and seen him act. [But] to the reader of the Fourth Gospel no such magnificent freedom is permitted. The selection of incidents has already been made, not at all as we should have made it. The interpretation has been given, and it is in form the interpretation of Jesus Himself, in substance the interpretation of the Holy Spirit of Truth (14:26; 16:12-16). The Fourth Gospel records not primarily what the crowd of eye-witnesses saw and heard of the Jesus of History, but what the disciples saw of the *glory* of the Word of God (1:14); what they apprehended, as believers, when Jesus *was risen from the dead* (2:22). The Fourth Gospel is less an apostolic witness to history than an apostolic witness to that which is beyond history, but which is, nevertheless, the meaning of the "Jesus of History", and therefore the meaning of all history.

One important qualification appears necessary to the present writer. It is this: if the comments of Hoskyns and Davey suggest that the synoptists did not set out to do what the fourth Evangelist (in their view) set out to do, and John's work must therefore be taken as in some sense 'correcting' theirs, a seriously false impression is given. For it seems clearer, the more the two traditions, synoptic and Johannine, are studied together, that what John was trying to do was to enable the readers of the synoptic gospels not to go back to them and read them in a Johannine perspective, but to show them that the synoptists' perspective was substantially identical with his own.

In Hoskyns and Davey's terms the synoptics can be termed "episodic"; so by contrast John can be aptly described as "exemplary", i.e., he takes a very limited number of incidents and subjects them to a long and penetrating analysis. But the incidents have not ceased to be episodes by being fewer in number or analysed at length. Nor is it in the end possible to maintain a clear distinction between the 'historical' character of the synoptics and the 'theological' character of the fourth gospel. One illustration may suffice: In Mark 3:1-6 the story is told how Jesus on a certain sabbath day healed a man who had a withered hand. The miracle was performed in a suspicious and hostile environment, and once it was done Pharisees and Herodians planned to destroy Jesus. The fourth gospel does not incorporate this actual story: as will be seen characteristic of it, it selects a typical miracle of this sort and treats it as an example of others. So in John is told the story of the cripple who could not reach the waters of healing, but was brought to locomotive power by the word of Jesus on a sabbath day. John passes in his characteristic way from miracle to discourse expounding it, and in the course of a long analysis it becomes clear that what Jesus had done at the Pool of Bethzatha on that sabbath day was far more than to restore locomotion to impotent limbs: he had given new life to a "dead" man. Has this not therefore been a grossly exaggerated Johannine theologizing of a plain Marcan fact? Not at all: for in Mark, before Jesus heals the man in the synagogue he eyes his critical audience and asks them 'Is it lawful on the sabbath to do good or to do harm, to save life or to kill?' (Mk 3:4). Properly understood the synoptic narrative says, and was intended to say, the same things as John's. The fourth evangelist brings no new meaning to the synoptics but he knows that when a reader of his own gospel turns back to the synoptics he cannot but fail to penetrate more closely the very heart of their message, which like his own is concerned to proclaim Jesus as both Messiah and son of God.

The synoptic gospels recount many more "miracles" than John, and the undiscerning reader might well see the picture of Jesus which emerges as that of a uniquely powerful thaumaturgist. If so, a reading of John might well put him right, and he could return to the synoptics and realize that his previous interpretation was wrong. For the synoptists, no less than John, saw Christ's miracles, and intended their readers to see them, as evidence for the divine nature of the Lord. First it is made clear that the miracles are a sign that with Jesus' activity in miracles the age of fulfillment has at last arrived. What Isaiah foretold, "In that day the deaf shall hear the words of the book, and out of their gloom and darkness the eyes of the blind shall see. The meek shall obtain fresh joy in the Lord, and the poor among men shall exult in the Holy One of Israel" (Is 29:18f.), is taken up into Jesus' own account of his mission: "Go and tell John what you hear and see: the blind receive their sight and the lame walk, lepers are cleansed and the deaf hear, and the dead are raised up, and the poor have good news preached to them" (Mt 11:5). The great messianic age has dawned in fulfillment of its promise in the life and actions of Jesus. Further, it is evident to observant readers of the synoptics that many of the wonders done by Jesus are really activities peculiar to God alone. That Jesus of Nazareth performed such deeds of divinity was itself a testimony to his divine nature. Thus it was Yahweh who "made the storm be still, and the waves of the sea were hushed" (Ps 107:29); and it was Jesus who said "Peace! be still!" and the winds ceased and there was a great calm (Mk 4:39). Again, Jesus took it upon himself to proclaim the forgiveness of sins, a prerogative that every Jew believed to belong to God alone: and even Christ's adversaries recognized this: 'When Jesus saw their faith he said to the paralytic, "My son, your sins are forgiven". Now some of the scribes were sitting there, questioning in their hearts, "Why does this man speak thus? Who can forgive sins but God alone?"' (Mk 2:5-7). And while the Pharisees could number among themselves those who could exorcize demons, Jesus claims that he exorcizes them 'by God's finger', and that therefore the Kingdom of God had come upon men (Lk 11:14-20). Similarly for the Jew it was God who gave or permitted health or disease, life or death; that Jesus so manifestly had powers both to restore diseased bodies to health and even to quicken those that were dead is eloquent testimony to the synoptists' intention that he should be regarded not as a mere miracle worker, but rather as the embodiment in one personal human life of a worthy bearer of the name Immanuel, God is with us.

John's purpose is in the end the same. He uses different methods, notably in his treatment of miracles. Indeed John does not talk of "miracles" but of *signs*. It has already become clear that to use such a word of the miracles of Jesus even as reported in the synoptic gospels would not be an entirely inappropriate thing: no doubt John was aware of this kind of consideration. But for John the works of Jesus are signs in a special way. It is possible to draw a distinction between "external" and "internal" signs; an "external" sign would be something almost arbitrary, as, for example, the color red as the sign on the hoods of some graduates of Oxford University that their degree is in the faculty of arts: any other color, historical antecedents apart, would serve equally well. An "internal" sign is not arbitrary, but in some way an actual part of the thing signified: for example, a candidate's examination paper is taken to be a "sign" of the quality and extent of his knowledge. The miracles in John are signs in this latter sense. They bring into the particular occasions of Jesus' ministry the reality they represent, which is always the same—his victorious self-offering on the cross. This can be seen in the very first sign, when the water of Jewish purification was changed by Jesus' presence into the wine, which in its sacramental significance stated that in self-offering on the cross there would be provided the one means of real purification which Judaism had sought, but failed, to provide. The working of the miracles is an "impossibility" for the modern mind, but what most needs to be said is that however baffling to human reason the story of water into wine may be, the reality of that which is but a sign is even more amazing and 'impossible'—that the Word, creative, divine, eternal, should become flesh, and give himself in suffering and death to make manifest in history the love and the glory of God.

Yet the modern reader may persist, "Did it really happen like that? Were 120 gallons of water really changed into wine?" or, in relation to another sign, "Was Lazarus really brought back to life after four days dead in the tomb?" To be an understanding interpreter of John means, in the present writer's view, an unwillingness to give an immediate yes or no to these two (or similar) questions. For if either answer is given the questioner may well think his inquiry not only satisfactorily answered, but adequately concluded: whereas to have the question answered without facing the further question of what the author believes history to be, and whether his view of it is justified, is really to treat the record for what it is not, a plain account of "observable history". To take the story of Lazarus. Unless careful note is taken of what is said in 11:23-26 about resurrection the whole episode is deprived of an indispensable interpretative clue. Jesus met Martha and to her statement that had he been in Bethany her brother would not have died (i.e., Jesus' power was adequate to keep his friends in the historical life-in-the-flesh), Jesus replied that her brother would "rise again" (11:23). Martha then answered that she knew he would rise in the resurrection at the last day, and to which Jesus replied, giving the interpretative clue for the sign to follow: *"I am the resurrection and the life; he who believes in me, though he die, yet shall he live, and whoever believes in me shall never die."* Two other scriptures play an interpretative role. Certainly the saying in 5:25 that *"the hour is coming, and now is, when the dead will hear the voice of the Son of God, and those who hear will live".* And less certainly Luke 16:31 where Jesus ends the story of the rich man and Lazarus with the words: *"If they do not hear Moses and the prophets, neither will they be convinced if someone should rise from the dead."* The general import of all this on the sign of Lazarus' *resurrection* is that the real transition from life to death is not to be looked for at the point where men pass from "physical" existence to bodily non-function, but at the point where they turn away from, reject or deny the coming of the word made flesh to bring divine life to men;

and the real transition from death to life, if any, is not to be looked for at the point where the dead may be raised in some general resurrection at the last day, for that after all is only an historicization of the essential resurrection, it is to be looked for at the point where men turn to Christ and accept him in faith as God's gift to them of life that is imperishable, unconquerable. The emergence of Lazarus from the tomb is thus much more than a uniquely marvellous resuscitation; it is an enacted confession that Christ holds in his own undying life all those who believe in him, whether physically alive or not. In this context the "modern" question can be put without making a Christian response impossible.

But if the "awkward" question be faced: did the impossible occur?, the answer has to be that the central part of the Christian gospel to which every part of the gospels refers is itself impossible! The impossible went on in what took place: God was in Christ, reconciling the world to himself. The word became flesh and dwelt among us, and we beheld his glory. He came that we might have life, and have it abundantly. If that central "impossibility" be believed, then it is less difficult to suppose that even in what took place there would be some uniquely remarkable signs of what was going on. The universe as men know it today is not a perdurable reality linked throughout its history by uninterruptible sequences of causes and effects, governed everywhere by unchangeable and unbreakable laws. It is rather a universe where pattern and probability are the categories to be used in understanding the world. If so, then instead of having to say of a miracle that it 'breaks the laws of nature' (a notion equally repugnant to the critical inquiring mind and to the Christian understanding of God) it is possible to think that it simply goes outside the familiar pattern that men know, but only for the sake of the ultimate pattern, which is the whole purpose of God. God, that is to say, has a pattern for his world. The existence of evil, itself a mystery to man, creates distortions of that divine pattern. What God has done in Jesus Christ, and this includes the so-called miracles, is to restore the over-all pattern by some further departure from its familiar regularities.

It is quite possible for a man to accept the witness of John and the synoptics to the person and mission of Jesus, and not to wish to assert that any miracles took place. It is by no means necessary to make belief in Jesus Christ rest upon an acceptance of the miracles as "observable history". Indeed the contrary is true: truly Christian belief in the gospel miracles is possible only to those who have a belief in Jesus as Son of God and Savior, for only those see the miracles as "signs" of his real nature and mission. There is however no necessary intellectual dishonesty in believing in Jesus and denying the miracles, even if a previous acceptance of the miraculous led to a belief in Christ. The attainment of direct personal relationship with Jesus Christ by any means is so satisfying and self-authenticating that the instruments by which the relationship might be begun or explained cease to be of decisive importance.

The Order of The Signs in John

John names only two miracles as *signs*, though this does not mean that only these two are rightly to be so called. Each reader, and each commentator, must therefore make his own judgments as to other signs in John. The present writer believes there are seven signs in all, six being acts performed by Jesus before the crucifixion, and the seventh being the crucifixion itself, which is the mystery of the Word-made-flesh, both sign and thing signified together, and which is both something which Jesus 'suffered' (*there they crucified him,* 19:18) and something which he did (*"No one takes it—my life—from me, but I lay it down of my own accord"* 10:18). All that can be 'seen' at the moment of crucifixion is a man being put to death; but what is really going on is the final victory of God over all the sin and evil of the world. Thus to count seven signs in John involves regarding the walking on the water (6:16-21) as part of the sign of the loaves.

John's first sign is a comprehensive introduction to the whole body of signs. He uses the sign of water becoming wine by the act of Jesus to indicate that the whole religion of Israel as an attempt to keep the people of God pure and acceptable to him is wholly outmoded and transcended since all its inadequacy is overcome by the presence and action of the Word-made-flesh as he gives his life in death for the whole world. For the future the only adequate means for a man to be acceptable to God will be the sacrifice which the Son makes in laying down his own life. John then recounts five signs which echo, and in one instance repeat, signs already familiar to those acquainted with the synoptic or synoptic-like tradition. A Gentile's sick boy is healed; a lame man walks; the hungry are fed; a blind man receives sight; a dead man is raised. It is impossible to write these sign titles without being reminded of Jesus' answer to the inquiry from John: "The blind receive their sight, the lame walk, lepers are cleansed, and the deaf hear, the dead are raised up, the poor have good news preached them" (Lk 7:22). John does not slavishly follow that synoptic catalogue of signs, but the testimony he advances is clearly of the same order and cogency as that thought proper by the synoptists. Not least is the position given to the sign of the raising of the dead, which in John, as in the synoptics, is given in double form in the raising of a dead person by Jesus (Jairus' daughter, the widow's son at Nain, Lazarus) and, in the end, the raising of Jesus himself. John has brought these twin signs close together as the climax of all the signs. It was not until Jesus had been glorified that the spirit can be given and the good news, therefore, be preached to the poor.

The Discourse in John

The impressiveness of John's gospel or "book of the signs" does not however lie in the mere fact that he has told six or seven miracle stories; the synoptists did that, and more! What gives John's gospel its characteristic impressiveness is undoubtedly his usual practice of joining the miracle story with a discourse of great profundity, whether that be given (as normally) after the relating of the miracle, or whether before it, as in the case of the cross and glorification. But it must not be too readily assumed that in this John is entirely an innovator. There are miracle stories in the gospels which contain sayings of the Lord, and there have not been lacking critics who believe that the miracle would not have been preserved in the gospel were it not for its conjunction with the saying. With that admitted, it is quite plain that John's use of the discourse is entirely distinctive, and indeed it has been one of the constant difficulties for the critically minded reader, since there is no real parallel to a discourse in any of the synoptic gospels, and since the content of the discourses appears to the judgment of many to leave their "historicity" very much in doubt. Professor Bultmann is one modern scholar who believes that John drew upon a "sign source" for his gospel, and, having made his selection, expounded the signs in discourses attached. The hypothesis may in fact be true, but a close scrutiny of the text of John does not enable a confident judgment to be made. The truth is that the signs and the discourses are so closely knit together as to defy any confident separation into material from two sources. Miracle story plus discourse constitutes sign-narrative for John. John is not interested in signs merely as "miracles" or "wonders" but only as actions embodying as they anticipate the reality of the one great decisive miracle of God's action to redeem his world.

But not all the discourses in John are linked with miracle. Some sections of the gospel (chs. 3, 4, 7, 8, 10) are discourse or discourse-like material, yet contain no miracle. Yet even this judgment needs some modification, for in 3:2 Nicodemus says to Jesus *"No one can do these signs that you do, unless God is with him,"* and the subsequent discourse can properly be taken to bear upon the nature of *signs.* The dialogue with the woman at Samaria is conducted from a starting point where she was expecting what she thought to be a miracle (4:12, 14). The brothers of Jesus, in ch. 7, want him to go to Judea and "do his works there"; and when Jesus is in Jerusalem the crowd asked *"When the Christ appears, will he do more signs than this man has done?"* In ch. 10, the question is asked about Jesus *"Can a demon open the eyes of the blind?"* On the other hand there seem to be two miracles with no accompanying discourse; viz, the story of the healing of the official's son, and the report of the walking on the water. The latter miracle is regarded by the present writer as part of the sign of the loaves, in which it plays a subordinate but very important role; for it emphasizes, in a way quite concrete and inescapable, that what Jesus had to give to man is neither food nor political leadership, but himself, which is the heart of the 'eucharistic' discourse of ch. 6. As for the story of the official's son, it closes with a saying linking it with the sign at Cana. Evidently two things were intended: first to indicate that the self-offering of Jesus in his death not only provides for Jews the fulfillment they had hoped for, but also brings to the Gentiles what they long for. Second, that the deed was no mere thaumaturgy, but a veritable manifestation of the giving of life for which the Son had come into the world. This is embodied in the final word of Jesus: *'Your son will live'* (4:53). What Jesus brought was not recovery from disease, or renewal of bodily vigor; it was *life*. The story of the healing of the official's son comes between the stories of Nicodemus and the Samaritan woman on the one side, and the lame man being healed on the other. To Nicodemus Jesus speaks of being *born again;* to the woman at the well he promises living water preventing all thirst; the paralytic's new condition he analyses as living instead of dying or dead. It is unreasonable to suppose that, in so richly allusive a context, John should have forgotten all that he sought to do in his gospel, and on this one occasion simply told a story exhausted in thaumaturgy and not therefore pointing through it and beyond it to the divine event of the coming of the Word-made-flesh in glory that could be seen by those whose eyes were opened.

Are The Discourses Historical?

The discourses, peculiar to John, so greatly contrasting with the forms of teaching in the synoptics makes it necessary to ask about them, as about the signs they often elucidate, are they historically reliable? Bultmann supposes a special 'discourse source' from which John drew his material, but in general the homogeneity of theme and language in both signs and discourse has not led a large body of scholars to agree with him. What sort of teacher was Jesus? Did he, as the synoptics suggest, make brilliant use of short parables and telling metaphor, being apt and quick in repartee and controversy; or was he, as the fourth gospel suggests, a much more methodical expositor of ideas, passing his thoughts on by a profound examination of man's world and his own presence and activity in it? The answer first needs to be made in reference to the gospels themselves. The synoptics recount many deeds; John selects six (or seven), including at least three unrecorded by the synoptists. The parallel statements about teaching could well be: the synoptists recount many parables, similitudes, etc. and even extensive blocs of teaching are not homogeneous pieces; John may have a parable, but in the main his teaching is given in different form entirely. The two sets of statements bear interpretatively on each other. It means that, with the teaching as with the actions, the first formulation of modern man's question needs refashioning. The proper question is not "Did Jesus ever really teach like this?", for to that there may be no possible answer! The better form is: "Does this matter of presenting the works and words of the Lord really help men to see who he is, and to understand what he did?" If then the question be put "But did Jesus teach in discourse or parables?" the answer is that both pieces of evidence are before the reader, but that unless both forms of teaching are seen to be means for the disclosure of the truth about Jesus the question of mere historicity is unimportant. It is generally assumed that Jesus would more naturally have used parable rather than discourse. This cannot but be an *a priori* assumption and it would be perfectly possible to argue that one and the same person could do both.

But the form of discourse apart, is it a reasonable assumption that Jesus could have said the kind of things that John reports in the great discourses? Here again, no positive solution is possible: each reader and commentator must decide for himself. But, so it seems to the present writer, the believer who has been persuaded that Jesus is the Christ, the Son of God, will be aware that he cannot state with complete confidence what was and what was not possible to him in the days of his flesh. But believing him to be the Word incarnate, it is possible to suppose that just as his "omnipotence" was equally consistent with both "mighty works" and impotence on the cross, so his omniscience could be consistent with utter ignorance of some things (Mk 13:22) and yet with confident knowledge about others. The language of Jesus as reported in the fourth gospel may not have been so inaccessible, in the light of the scrolls, as once was thought.

Thus while the discourse form is peculiar to John among the evangelists and while it must be granted that the compilation of speeches and discourses was a common task of ancient historians, the gospel reader is not precluded from supposing that Jesus used a discourse even if at the same time he admitted that no surviving discourse is likely to be in his exact words. But again, to ask for the *ipsissima verba* of Jesus, even to ask for certainty about the form of his teaching, is really to turn the gospels from being what they are into being what they are not. The discourses stand to the synoptic parables very much as the selected signs stand to the synoptic miracles —they are meant to ensure that when the reader of the discourses goes back to the synoptic records, he will no longer be tempted to treat them as "observable" (or "audible"!) history, but will see them as witnesses to the presence among men of the eternal Word, manifesting his divine glory in the flesh.

A brief consideration of the content of the teaching is needful. Not even a casual reader can fail to be struck by the absence of synoptic themes in John, and Johannine themes in the synoptics. In the synoptics there is considerable teaching about the Kingdom of God, about repentance, and about some future occasion when God's ways with men would be finally vindicated. But in John all this is virtually missing. Only in the conversation with Nicodemus does the *Kingdom of God* find mention (3:3, 5) and at the trial of Jesus he himself refers to his 'Kingdom' (*Kingship* in R.S.V., 18:36). Repentance receives no mention at all, and the eschatological terms found in the synoptics are so rare that when they occur, as they do in ch. 6 (*"raise up at the last day"* 6:39, 40, 44, 54), a scholar like Professor Bultmann has to suggest that they do not really belong to John! What has John done? Has he really distorted the message of the synoptics for something really different? Not at all. The present writer believes that what he has done is to enable the reader of the fourth gospel to move from it back to the synoptics and there to perceive what the synoptic message is. This is done by keeping his readers firmly with the historical Jesus, for it is in him that they can really meet the past, the present and the future. The past means him, that is the real theological justification for typology. If some event in the past, like the exodus from Egypt, throws light (as it does) through the Passover feast on the destiny and death of Christ, it is then seen that as the fulfillment (the achievement once for all in history) of what God sought to do in the Passover is at the cross, the cross itself sheds light back to the exodus. What is going on in the exodus helped many to see what was going on on the cross; but once it is seen what is going on in the event of the cross, then it is seen as what is going on all the time. The cross becomes the meaning, the one event of all history. The future means Jesus Christ too; that is the real essence of eschatology. It is not that the cross was a penultimate act of God, which at some future date will be followed by an ultimate act. Rather the cross is the ultimate act of history. For it is there, and not at some future moment, that men have found the ultimate judgment on the world and the ultimate assurance of the wonder and power of God's love.

So past, present, future, all play their part in the Johannine record, as they do in the synoptic story. But in John they are all linked with the great affirmation *"I am"*. *"Before Abraham was, I am"* (8:58); *"I am the light of the world"* (8:12); *"I am the resurrection and the life"* (11:25). This expounds rather than distorts the whole tenor of the synoptic record. For the synoptics it is typology that focuses the past upon Jesus. As for the future, its reality in him finds statement in two movements—of his own historical person being in the future: the one who is to come and fill the role of the Judge of Jewish apocalyptic is not a new figure but precisely himself as son of man. And during his earthly life the veil of his presence is partly lifted in the strange event known as the transfiguration, which, significantly for this theme, has been called by some critics a "displaced" resurrection appearance. In fact both John and the synoptics use devices to make it quite plain that the "historical Jesus" and the risen Lord are not twain but one, the future in the present, the eternal in the temporal, the divine in the human, God become man.

THE JOHANNINE JESUS AS LOGOS

T. W. MANSON

I must preface what I have to say on this difficult problem by stating that all the Christology of the primitive Church is based on the experience of the primitive Christians. The early Church did not begin by having a theory of divinity, incarnation, salvation—a dogmatic formula all cut and dried—and then look round for some fairly solid point in history to which they could attach it. A great deal of what passes for up-to-date critical method proceeds on these lines. The dogmas of the early Church are supposed to be derived from all kinds of sources—pagan mystery cults, late Greek philosophy, Alexandrian Hellenistic Judaism, Iranian redemption mysteries, and so on. The early Church having selected one or other of these theories, then fitted Jesus into it, or if we take account of more radical formulations of this scientific theory, created the Jesus of the Gospels out of a few fragments of tradition and its own vivid imagination playing on its own life-situation, problems, social needs, behavior patterns, and I know not what besides.

On this theory and on all theories of this sort I think it sufficient to say that they explain fairly successfully almost everything except how there came to be a Church to perform these theological feats, and why the Church pitched upon Jesus of Nazareth as the hero of its saga. If you can get over these two little difficulties there is no reason why you should not be perfectly at home with the extreme Form-critics or the Chicago School—or anywhere else *except* in the ministry of the Gospel.

It still seems more likely, and if we accept the New Testament as reliable evidence for what went on in the early Church and read it with ordinary common sense, tolerably certain that

the Church began with the picture and tried to find a frame
for it rather than that the Church first built an elaborate frame
and then painted the portrait to suit. In other words the first
Christians were Christians in the sense that they knew in their
hearts that they owed their life to Christ, that he had done for
them something that they could not do for themselves and
something that no other man, no institution, could do for them.
That is the common voice of the New Testament writers. Hear
Paul: What the Law could not do God has done in Christ.
Hear the author to the Hebrews: What the Temple and its
ritual could not do Christ has done. And the message of John
is no different. Into a world where ignorance, darkness, hatred,
sin and death had undisputed possession God sent the Logos
and this meant life and light and love and salvation. All alike
start with an experience of God's saving power. This saving
power has come into the world in the person of Jesus of Nazareth. The Church is built on the *fact* and not on a theory.
The theories that we meet in the New Testament and in later
doctrines are attempts to explain the fact. The fact is not an
invention to suit the theories. That is why, while in different
books of the New Testament we have different lines of explanation, they are at one in the fact that they set out to explain.
Their problem is "What are we to say about him who has done
for us this most godlike thing?"

This does not mean that we are to accept their explanations
without question. It does not mean—and ought not to mean—
that the High-Priestly Christology of Hebrews and the Logos
Christology of John should satisfy us completely as theology.
We are at liberty to frame a better if we can. What it does
mean is that it is only in the light of those early attempts at
explanation that we can properly see the magnitude of the fact
that had to be explained and still has to be explained by any
theory that we may frame.

The man who, as I think, was responsible for the composition of the Fourth Gospel in the form in which it has come
down to us, and who was also the author of the First Epistle,
chose the term as the best available to explain the fact of
Christ. We have now to try to discover what he meant by Logos.

At once we are faced by a bewildering maze of possible

interpretations of the term as used by John. In the books with which we are concerned it is to be noted that it occurs only in a prefatory kind of way. In the Gospel it is confined to the opening verses of the first Chapter and in the Epistle it occurs for the first and last time there in the first verse. This method of introducing the term suggests that it is one with which the author can assume that his readers are already familiar either as part of the common theological or philosophical stock of the age, or as something characteristic of his own point of view and already made familiar to them in the course of his teaching and preaching. I incline to the latter alternative: and think that the Logos idea was, somewhere about the end of the first century, what it still is in the twentieth—the trademark or hall-mark of John himself, as characteristic of his ways of thinking as the High-Priestly notion was of the author of the Epistle to the Hebrews.

If that be so our question becomes: whence did John derive the idea? And what has he made of it that stamps it as peculiarly his own? The several possible sources we must now consider.

1. *The Logos Idea in Greek Philosophical Thought*

'The conception *Logos*, word or speech, had . . . a peculiarly distinguished history among the Greeks. It was the word spoken: it was the power of language; it was the word which implies reason, persuasion, interpretation, and which settles differences instead of the armed hand; it was thus the word which mediates between the soul of man and man, or, in theological language, between man and God; to the philosopher it was the silent but eternal word upon the lips of Nature, the speech by which the Cosmos expressed its inborn reason'.[1]

It is this last sense that is important for our present purposes. In the later Greek philosophy it is, to borrow words from M. Aurelius (iv. 46), the λόγος ὁ τὰ ὅλα διοικῶυ, 'the reason that governs the universe'. How far this goes back in Greek thought is a matter of dispute. Marcus in the passage from which

---

1. Cf. G. Murray, *The Rise of the Greek Epic,* p. 92.

I quote seems to find it in Herakleitos: but Burnet maintains that the λόγος in Herakleitos is nothing but 'the discourse of Herakleitos himself; though, as he is a prophet, we may call it the "Word". It can neither mean a discourse addressed to Herakleitos nor yet "reason"... The Stoic interpretation given by Marcus Aurelius ... must be rejected altogether. The word λόγος was never used like that till post-Aristotelian times.' However that may be, it is, at least, certain that the point at which we meet this notion of λόγος as the guiding and directing power in the world in full force, is in the Stoic philosophy, and that in its earliest forms, e.g. Diogenes Laertius VII. 134, §493: 'They [Zeno, Cleanthes and Chrysippus] are of the opinion that there are two ἀρχαί of the universe, the active [τὸ ποιοῦν] and the passive [τὸ πάσχον]. As for the passive element it is undifferentiated being [ἄποιον οὐσίαν i.e., that which merely is there but has no attributes or qualities of its own: the Greek equivalent of tohu wabohu or matter]; the active element is the reason [λόγον] which is in it [the matter] or God.'

Here λόγος and Θεός mean much the same thing. It is not necessary to go into details so long as we bear in mind that the primary Stoic antithesis is between this divine λόγος and the undifferentiated ὕλη. The λόγος as active element is the cause of all subsequent differentiation. It is the creative element if we use 'creative' in the artistic sense. It does not produce something out of nothing, but gives form and purpose to what is formless and purposeless: it arranges and disposes the shapeless ὕλη into an ordered universe, a κόσμος.

This Stoic λόγος stands in the same relation to the world as the human soul does to the body. It is the soul of the world, the generative and ordering principle of all that exists in the κόσμος. It is thus a metaphysical principle. And this is important as we shall see presently.

Further, in the Stoic doctrine the λόγος is not an emanation or hypostasis of God—it is God. It is the supreme principle. The Stoic does not have a God, one of whose attributes is λόγος. He has one God who can be called indifferently νοῦς, εἱμαρμένη, Ζεύς, and many other names including λόγος. These are just names for one and the same being.

These two points form the real objection to the theory, which has been pretty widely held, that John borrowed his Logos doctrine from the Stoic philosophy either directly or through the medium of the writings of Philo. For:

(i) the Johannine interest is not metaphysical, but, like that of the rest of the New Testament, primarily historical. He is not concerned to explain the λόγος in terms of first principles, but to show how God so loved the κόσμος that he intervened in history for its redemption from the power of evil and death. It is an historical event and not a metaphysical theory that is being explained.

(ii) Whereas in the Stoic view λόγος is just another name for Θεός, in John the λόγος though divine is not identical with God. Λόγος is not a synonym for Θεός. So far as the Johannine λόγος is synonymous with anything at all it is synonymous with Jesus Christ. This is a conception which would have been absolutely impossible either to the Stoics or to Philo. For Philo cared nothing about history, as we can see from his exposition of the Old Testament and for the Stoics history reduced itself in the last resort to an "endless recurrence leading nowhere".

There are, however, elements in Philo which are not derived from Greek Philosophy and which may suggest a possible origin for the Logos doctrine of John in Jewish rather than Greek thought. Philo is eclectic and his work is a curious mixture of material inherited from his religious forebears and/or acquired from his Greek teachers. Now, there are moments when Philo becomes un-Greek and rather unphilosophical. When, for example, he calls angels the λόγοι Θεοῦ, when he calls the Old Testament ὁ ἱερὸς λόγος, when he compares the High Priest to the divine word, he is not thinking of λόγος in the Stoic sense of the immanent universal Reason, but rather of the word of God, the speech of God, 'the manifestation in the Torah of the supramundane God, a manifestation that stands high above all human reason'. That is to say, he is here thinking of the Revelation (in the strictest sense) of a transcendent God. Ultimately it may be urged that this side of Philo's doctrine of the Logos goes back to the Old Testament itself, however much it may have been modified on the way. So Walter Scott says (*Hermetica* II, pp. 24 f.): "Philo's notion of the divine Logos was based partly on the Mosaic account of the creation, partly

on the Stoic use of the word λόγος to describe the God who per-
vades the *kosmos* and operates in it. Philo's Logos may be regarded as the Stoic God dematerialized, with a supracosmic
God [the God of Platonism] set up above him."

Here it is clear where Philo differs from the Stoic doctrine.
For them there are only two principles involved, λόγος = Θεός
and ὕλη: for Philo there are three, Θεός the first cause and
creator, ὕλη the raw material of creation, and as an intermediary between the two λόγος. It is obvious that the influence of
the Old Testament has been at work here and perhaps also
another factor which we must next consider.

2. The Personification of Wisdom

We find in the late Jewish literature a tendency to speak
of the attributes of God as if they had a separate existence.
This tendency is specially marked in the Wisdom literature.
The passages that are specially relevant to our present problem
are those in which the wisdom of God is to some degree personified. How far these passages are to be taken literally as
implying a strict doctrine of the separate existence of Wisdom,
and how far they must be regarded as a kind of poetic licence
(like say Wordsworth's *Ode to Duty*) is a matter concerning
which we can probably never attain to certainty: and in a
sense it does not matter. For the point is not what the original
authors of these pieces strictly meant, but what they might
have been taken to mean in the first century A.D. Neither Philo
nor John was in any better position than we are to determine
whether Ben Sira or the author of Proverbs 8 was writing strict
theology or poetry, and meant his words literally or only "in
a manner of speaking". What is important is that in the first
century A.D. there were these documents which would without
straining the language lend themselves to the kind of doctrine
that we find in John 1 and, to a degree, in Philo.

The principal passages are Proverbs 8, especially verses 22-31;
Sirach 24; Wisdom 7-9.

a) *Pr* 8:22-31, cf. *Sirach* 1:1-10

'The Lord created me at the beginning of his work, the first of his acts of old. Ages ago I was set up, at the first, before the beginning of the earth. When there were no depths, I was brought forth; when there were no springs abounding with water. Before the mountains had been shaped, before the hills I was brought forth. Before he had made the earth with its fields, or the first of the dust of the world. When he established the heavens, I was there: when he drew a circle on the face of the deep: When he made firm the skies above: when he established the fountains of the deep: When he assigned to the sea its limit, so that the waters might not transgress his command: when he marked out the foundations of the earth: Then I was beside him, like a master workman; and I was daily his delight, rejoicing before him always; Rejoicing in his inhabited world; and delighting in the sons of men.'

In this passage Wisdom is speaking in the first person. She claims (i) pre-existence, (ii) creative activity.

(i) The pre-existence is real pre-existence: Wisdom was there before the world or any part of it was formed. But Wisdom is not identical with God. She is prior to all other created things, but is herself created. And this on the most probable rendering of 8:22: 'The Lord created me at the beginning of his work, the first of his acts of old.'

(ii) This pre-existent Wisdom, the first creation of God, then cooperated with God in the Creation of the world; 8:30:

"Then I was by him, as a master workman: and I had delight continually [in the work]".

b) Ben Sira

(i) The pre-existence of Wisdom is reasserted in Si 1:4: "Wisdom was created before all things" [i.e. the heavens and the earth]. So 1:9: "The Lord himself created wisdom; he saw her and apportioned her, he poured her out upon all his works." 24:9: "From eternity, in the beginning, he created me." From the unique position of Wisdom follows her eternity in one direction at least.

(ii) The creative activity is not heavily stressed though it is perhaps implied in 1:9.

(iii) What is made of prime importance in Sirach is the vital part which Wisdom plays in human life. Wisdom takes up her abode among men (1:15; 24:19f.). Also 24:7, 8, 12.

"Among all these [i.e., every people and nation] I sought a resting place;
I sought in whose territory I might lodge.
Then the creator of all things gave me a commandment
And the one who created me assigned a place for my tent.
And he said: 'Make your dwelling in Jacob,
And in Israel receive your inheritance . . .
So I took root in an honored people,
In the portion of the Lord who is their inheritance".
(Cf. the word became flesh and *dwelt among us.*)

(iv) Along with this goes the other important feature in Sirach—the identification of Wisdom with the Law, which, of course, carries with it the notion of the pre-existence and divine character of the Law, a dogma which subsequently became a primary tenet of Rabbinical Judaism. 15:1:

"He that takes hold of the Law finds it [i.e., Wisdom]."

c) *The Wisdom of Solomon*

In this book the influence of Greek thought is still more marked, and in the doctrine of God contained in it many resemblances have been found to Platonic and Stoic tenets. So far as Wisdom is concerned, the writer seems to combine ideas drawn from Stoicism with ideas taken from Proverbs 8. It would probably be rash to say that what our author has to say about Wisdom is just Proverbs 8 rewritten in the light of the Stoic doctrine; but it would not be so far off the mark.

(i) It will hardly do to say that pre-existence of Wisdom is asserted. Rather it is the eternity of Wisdom in such passages as Wis 7:25f.

For she is a breath of the power of God

and a pure emanation of the glory of the Almighty,
therefore nothing defiled gains entrance into her.
For she is a reflection (ἀπαύγασμα) of eternal light,
a spotless mirror of the working of God,
and an image of his goodness.

(ii) The place of the picture of Wisdom as master-workman
toiling with God at the job of creating the universe is taken
by the more Stoic notion of Wisdom as a spirit or ethereal substance pervading and penetrating all things: a spirit that informs rather than creates—an immanent power.

8:1: She reaches mightily from one end of the earth
       to the other
    And she orders all things well.

In 8:4 Wisdom appears as the determining factor in creation
in the sense, it would seem, of choosing between various possibilities.

She is an initiate in the knowledge of God
And an associate in his works.

(iii) Like Wisdom in Sirach she seeks to be with man and
when she enters into human spirits she produces all theoretical
knowledge (8:6, 8) especially theological (8:4), where she
is the medium of prophetic inspiration (8:8; 9:17). She also
teaches history (8:8), astronomy, chronology, natural science
(7:17-21) and art (7:16). She gives counsel to men in the
practical affairs of life (8:9) and from her comes the knowledge of duty and the good life (1:4f.; 7:25; 8:7-9).

It is easy to see the difference here between Wisdom and
Sirach. It is the difference between Judaism and Hellenism,
between Torah and φιλοσοφία. What is significant is the fact
that for both it was possible to personify Wisdom.

What is the common ground? Perhaps we should say the
idea of Revelation—the self-revelation of God. It is God's wisdom that is revealed in Creation, in the Law, even in the
intellectual achievements of man. And this manifestation of the
Divine Wisdom is, in part at any rate, a manifestation of God.

3. The Word of God in the Old Testament

This line of explanation depends on the fact that in the Old Testament the divine word or utterance plays a great and decisive part. The creation takes place by the word of God: "And God said, Let there be light: and there was light." The word of God is the medium of prophetic inspiration: "The word of the Lord came to . . ."

This way of speaking seems to us nowadays so much poetry; but it is to be remembered that originally it was regarded as sober fact. The writer of Genesis really believed that God gave the word of command and the world sprang into being: and the readers of Genesis 1 continued to believe it centuries after the beginning of the Christian era. This way of thinking about the 'word' is not philosophical. It belongs to a much more antique stage of human life than the philosophical. It belongs to the stage where the word is a thing and a thing which does things. This view of the spoken word is not peculiar to Hebrew ways of thinking. It would seem to be wellnigh universal (cf. Ernest Crawley's *Essay on Oath, Curse and Blessing*). In Homer the "winged words" are not words of special eloquence or epigrammatic point. They are simply words that are released by being uttered and so directed on their course to the hearer. The word flies like a bird or an arrow from speaker to hearer. And the word thus released may be the cause of good or evil. The spoken word is a sort of half-way stage between a mere wish and the thing wished for. When you express the wish— especially if in the form of blessing or curse—you have already set in motion a process which may lead to its fulfillment. The mere word itself, without any conscious wish behind it, may become incalculably effective. For example, in the *Agamemnon*, 235 ff.

> στόματός τε καλλιπρῷρου   And with a guard upon her lovely
> φυλακᾷ κατασχεῖν   mouth, the bit's strong and stifling
> φθόγγον ἀραῖον οἴκοις.   might, to stay a cry that had been
>   a curse on his house.

It is not meant that the sacrificed Iphigeneia is going to curse

Agamemnon. The danger is that her mere death-cry will act as a curse on the family.[2]

The point is that once the thing is uttered it must take its course. So Isaac having blessed Jacob in error cannot revoke the blessing. It stands. The prophetic word or oracle is a real force working itself out in history.

If this is the case with human words or prophetic oracles, how much more when the speaker is God:

By the word of the Lord the heavens were made;
And all their host by the breath of his mouth.
For he spoke, and it came to be;
He commanded, and it stood forth. Ps. 33:6, 9.

Hence one of the favorite periphrases for the divine name among the Rabbis is "He who spoke, and the world came into being". Note in the above passage that "word of the Lord" is parallel to "breath of his mouth". The word is not the Greek λόγος or Reason: it is the spoken utterance; and this spoken word is a creative force.

What applies to creation applies equally to history. God utters his word, and like the "winged words" of Homer it is launched on its errand in the world. And it is effective. It works as surely and inevitably as natural causes work. As rain produces vegetation, "so shall my word be that goes forth from my mouth: it shall not return to me empty, but it shall accomplish that which I purpose, and prosper in the thing for which I send it" (Is 55:11). Similarly in Wis 18:15 f. the 'all-powerful word' of God is conceived as leaping like a warrior from heaven into the Land of Egypt to execute the judgment of God there.

In such passages as these the word is in a way personified; but not necessarily thought of as a person. We have to remember that the idea of impersonal forces is one that comes very late in the history of human development; and that even

---

2. For a curse checked when half uttered, cf. Euripides, *Medea* 83, where the old nurse, speaking of Jason, says: "Curse him—I will not; for he is my master."

our ideas of impersonal forces are produced by abstraction. The kind of force that we know best is the muscular effort made in response to our own volitions by our own limbs; and it is only by a difficult bit of abstraction that we have learned to think of the force apart from the volition. In the intermediate stages between an animistic view of things and a mechanical view, it is not easy to say how much of the old still survives in the words used, how far terms that suggest personality in the causes at work really mean all that they seem to say, and how far we are dealing with survivals of what once was serious prose and is now more or less consciously poetry. We may perhaps use the distinction—the word of God is here personified, but not personalized, spoken of as if it were a person, but not actually thought of as a person.

There is still one more factor to be taken into account.

4. *The Memra of Jehovah*

This word was for a time believed to solve the problem of the Logos doctrine in John. It was observed that in the Targums it frequently happens that where in the original Hebrew we have God himself represented as speaking and acting, in the corresponding Aramaic version the place of the divine name is taken by the *memr' d'YHWH*, the word of the Lord. The presence of God (*sh^ekhinah*) and the glory of God (*y^eqara*) are similarly used though not to the same extent. It is obvious that if in the original we have a personal subject—God—acting in personal ways, then in the Targums it will appear that the new subject—the word of God—is also a person working in personal ways. Then the 'word of God' can be thought of as a hypostatized attribute of God: and we have on Palestinian soil an even better explanation of the Logos doctrine than that which might be got from Philo. The *Memra* becomes a personal intermediary between God and the world.

There are two important points to remember in connexion with the *Memra* theory.

(*a*) It is not to be confused with the Old Testament use of the 'word of God' discussed in the preceding section. The reason for this is that in the Targum the Hebrew word *dabar* in such phrases as *debar Yahweh* (*'Elohim*) is not rendered by *Memra* but by *Pitgama* (or occasionally by *Milla'*). That is to say just where the 'word of God' in the Hebrew Scriptures is the medium or instrumentality of revelation or of communication with men, it is not in the Targum his *Memra;* nor is the creative work of God his *Memra.* This is really the most important thing to be said about *Memra* in the Targums—it is *not* the equivalent of the 'word of God' in the Old Testament corresponding to λόγος or 'ῥῆμα in the Greek versions.

b) The researches of Moore and Billerbeck into the use of *Memra* in the Targums go to show that it is not used then as the name for a hypostatized attribute of God, but simply as one of the many ways of avoiding the utterance of the divine name that was too sacred for utterance. "In many . . . contexts *Memra* is introduced as a buffer-word . . . where the literal interpretation seemed to bring God into too close contact with his creatures. But nowhere in the Targums is *Memra* a 'being'. . . . It is to be observed . . . that *Memra* is purely a phenomenon of translation, not a figment of speculation; it never gets outside the Targums"[3]. The result of that *Memra*—if this is correct —ceases to be a possible line of explanation of the Prologue, and the Logos doctrine of John.

If we leave the *Memra* theory out of account we still have three possible lines of explanation of the Logos doctrine: the Greek λόγος possibly mediated through Philo's λόγος doctrine, the σοφιά of the Wisdom literature, and the Old Testament "word of God". All three have been put forward at one time or another as adequate explanations of the Johannine doctrine. In making our choice it is necessary to remember that the age in which the Prologue was composed was an age of eclecticism and syncretism. Men picked and chose among the floating ideas and fitted their pickings together into new forms of thought and explanation. We are therefore *not* bound to suppose that John adhered strictly to any one of the possible lines of explanation available when he wrote his Prologue. At the same time we want to know what is fundamental in his way of thinking.

---

3. Moore, *Judaism* I, p. 419.

My own view is that Loofs is right in regarding the Old
Testament "word of God" as the basis of John's Logos doctrine.[4]
That, I think, is sound. For John the 'word' is the creative and
revealing word of God. And Jesus Christ is the supreme revelation of God.

At the same time I think it possible that the idea of σοφιά
lies in the background. As we have seen, the "word" is thought
of as a kind of half-way house between a wish and its fulfillment. It is the expression of utterance of the wish. And I am
inclined to think that the λόγος of God is the expression of the
σοφία of God. But the wisdom of God is still within God, so
to speak. It does not become revelation, it does not become
effective in creation or history until it becomes λόγος. If it is
permissible to make the σοφία of God a little more concrete by
saying that it is God's plan or purpose, then it is possible to say
that the λόγος is the first step in the realization of that purpose.
That is to say Jesus Christ is the fulfillment of God's purpose,
or the necessary link between the purpose and its realization.
If the Jew could equate the Torah with this σοφία of God, so
John can make Jesus say "I am the way, the truth and the life."

With regard to Philo I do not think that John is dependent
on him at all. The similarities between them are not due to the
borrowing by John from Philo, but to the fact that both have
borrowed from the same source—the Old Testament. The points
of similarity are just those that both have in common with the
Old Testament notion of the "word of God". Philo's λόγος is
really Stoicism blended with the Old Testament 'word of God'.
John's λόγος is Jesus Christ understood in the light of the same
Old Testament "word of God".

Finally, while it is very improbable that the *Memra* of the
Targums has anything to do fundamentally with John's Logos
doctrine, I cannot help thinking that the linguistic usage of the
Targum may have influenced the language of the Prologue.
In this connexion I think specially of John 1:14 where some
scholars find the *sheʰkhinah* and the *yeqara* all together. While
these may not be hypostases, they may well be indications of
a Palestinian background, indications that the author of the Pro-

---

4. F. Loofs, *What is the Truth about Christ?* pp. 187-90.

logue was at home where these expressions were at home. It is in accordance with this way of interpreting the λόγος of John's Prologue, that what he has to say about the λόγος is very largely conceived in terms of creation and revelation.

Creation:

   1:3: All things were made through him; and without him was not anything made that was made.

   1:10: He was in the world, and the world was made through him, yet the world knew him not.

Revelation:

   1:10: . . . and the world knew him not.

   1:14: And the Word became flesh, and dwelt among us . . . we have beheld his glory . . .

   1:18: No one has ever seen God; the only Son, who is in the bosom of the Father, he has made him known.

With regard to this latter, there is one point specially to be noted. That is the sharp distinction between this revelation and all that had gone before. To the prophets of the Old Testament the word came πὸλυμερῶς καὶ πολυτρόπως (Heb 1:1), but in Christ ὁ λόγος σάρξ ἐγένετο. They *had* revelation; he *is* revelation. Further, the revelation that came to the prophets was partial in another sense—that the whole nature of God was not revealed to them, but only the purpose of God with reference to some particular contingency or the will of God with reference to some given aspect of human life. The revelation is always a particular revelation—what God is about to do in the field of history or what God requires man to do in the sphere of morality. But the whole nature of God cannot be completely revealed in a succession of historical events or in a code of moral demands. The perfect revelation of the divine nature must be for us revelation not in events or propositions but in a person. And the claim of the Prologue is that that revelation has been given in the person of Jesus Christ. The word became flesh—took human form—and dwelt among us and it was a

3

revelation of the divine glory, of the very godlikeness of God. John's claim is that in Jesus we have revelation of God not in the sense of correct information *about* God or even communication *from* God, but a real manifestation in Jesus of that which constitutes the very divinity of God: so that the Prologue can say "Nobody has ever seen God" and the Jesus of the Fourth Gospel can say "He that has seen me has seen the Father."

Now, this is not an entire novelty. Already the germ of this way of thinking about Christ is present in the Synoptics. When we read in Q "Many prophets and just men have desired to see the things that you see", etc., or when we look at the Marcan account of the Transfiguration, we can see the beginnings of what was to become a leading conception in the Fourth Gospel. It might, of course, be argued that the Transfiguration story is just the first working of the idea that subsequently comes to full fruition in the form of myth. But it is at least equally open to us to argue that the Transfiguration story enshrines a real experience of the first disciples, even if we cannot say for certain how far we are to treat the details of the story literally. It may be that the story records the kind of impression that Jesus did make on those who knew him best, when they were most responsive to him and most sensitive to the appeal that he made. I think that this is the proper way to regard the Transfiguration story. It was experiences of this kind—real experiences with a real person—that two generations later produced the kind of doctrine that you find in the Prologue, and not doctrine of the Johannine sort that manufactured the story of the Transfiguration. Further, we can see another connecting link between this Jesus of the Synoptics and the Incarnate Logos of John in the teaching of Paul. When Paul speaks of Christians seeing the light of the knowledge of the glory of God in the face of Jesus Christ, he makes the bridge between the experience of the first disciples and the developed theology of the Prologue.

The importance of these considerations is that they suggest what is, I think, the truth: that the so-called metaphysical sonship of the Fourth Gospel is not introduced for its own sake, but rather in the attempt to explain something that had touched men and opened their eyes to see the very nature of God manifested in Jesus. The difference between the Synoptics and John is that in the Synoptics this vision comes at the high point of the story. For many chapters Jesus is just "going about doing good" then one day the eyes of the intimate disciples are opened and they see that in "just going about doing good", in being "the friend of publicans and sinners", Jesus has been showing them the essence of the divine: they see the Jesus they know, the Jesus that so many other sick and sinful and sorrowful people know, and they realize in a flash that a life of this sort reveals the glory of God—full of grace and truth. In John the light that flashed out in one dazzling blaze of glory on the Mount of Transfiguration is diffused through the whole narrative. Everything that the Evangelist has to say is made to reflect the glory. In a sense the light that gilds the pages of John is artificial light; but it is kindled at the original flame in the first instance. We know that because the quality of its radiance is really the same as in the Synoptics—grace and truth. At bottom what John finds marvellous and divine in Christ is just what those who saw and heard him in the days of his flesh marvelled at—the words of grace that proceeded from his mouth. The difference is that whereas the congregation in the Synagogue at Nazareth brought their marvellings to a head by inquiring "Is not this Joseph's son?", John asserts "This is the Son of God."

And again it is important to remember that notwithstanding the "metaphysical" ways of John's thought the basis is not metaphysics but—to put it in one word—love. Full of grace and truth. Grace and truth are the content of this supreme revelation of the divine nature, the grace and truth that belonged to Jesus of Nazareth. What John is trying to say is not the bare theological proposition "God was in Christ", where 'God' may mean anything and 'Christ' may mean anything. He is trying to say that in Jesus of Nazareth there came into the world a new power of saving love, glorious in its faithfulness and tenderness—and that all this that sprang upon men's vision in Jesus was a revelation of God himself. It is possible to say "God was in Christ", because in seeing Christ men discovered for the first time what the word "God" in its fullness really meant.

If that is the right way of understanding the Prologue, it links it not only with the Old Testament but also with the experience that is recorded in the Synoptics. No doubt the Old Testament conception and the original experience of the first disciples have been modified in passing through the mind of John; but the fundamental things are retained. The Old Testament conception of revelation may be strained to the utmost, but it is still the Old Testament conception. The Synoptic portrait of Jesus may be altered enormously; but it is fundamentally the portrait of the Jesus of the Synoptics.

And these are not the only indications that John is working all the time on the basis of the Palestinian tradition and the Old Testament conception of revelation. We have, for example, the very important fact that John regards Jesus as the Messiah of the Jewish hope. The salient facts are

a) John the Baptist's denial that he himself is the Christ (1:34; 3:27-36).

b) John the Baptist's recognition of Jesus (1:15, 20, 29-34).

c) The first disciples recognize Jesus as Messiah (1:41, 45, 49). (Note the *immediate* recognition. This is part and parcel of John's method. The vital features of the story are made to run through it from beginning to end. Cf. his use of "Father".)

d) The Twelve recognize him as "the holy one of God" (6:69); so too Martha (11:27).

e) The Messiahship is disputed by opponents (10:24).

f) Jesus enters Jerusalem as Messiah and is greeted as King of Israel (12:12-16).

g) He is tried and crucified as King of the Jews (18:33-40; 19:3, 12-15, 19-22).

Yet even here the Jewish expectation is not just taken over. It is changed and charged with a new significance. Jesus before Pilate is at pains to say plainly "My kingdom is not of this world. If my kingdom were of this world, my retainers would fight to prevent my betrayal to the Jews"; i.e. the arrest by the Jewish authorities would have been prevented by force—"but in fact my kingdom belongs elsewhere" (18:36). Immediately afterwards Jesus speaks of his mission in the world as "to bear witness to the truth" (18:37). The only other reference to the Kingdom of God in the Gospel is in ch. 3. Here we read (v. 3), "Unless one is born anew he cannot see the kingdom of God." And again in vv. 5 f., "Unless one is born of water and the Spirit, he cannot enter the Kingdom of God. That which is born of the flesh is flesh and that which is born of the Spirit is spirit." This is all in line with such Pauline statements as 1 Cor 15:50: "Flesh and blood cannot inherit the kingdom of God," and Rm 14:17: "The kingdom of God does not mean food and drink, but righteousness and peace and joy in [the] Holy Spirit."

To say 'My Kingdom is not of this world' does not mean that it has nothing to do with this world. We must remember that κόσμος in John means mankind or human nature primarily and not the material world. When Jesus says "My kingdom is not of this world" he means that it is not, as all the other world Empires are, the product of human skill or courage or ingenuity or wickedness. It is not a human institution at all, but a divine gift. It is God's own act and deed, not man's creation. And being so it is not only of divine origin, but also of divine character. Its power is not the sort of power in which men naturally put their trust: its ends are not the ends which men naturally seek. As it comes from the sphere of spirit so also it reflects the spiritual order or the very nature of God. Its power and glory rest on the fact that it is a revelation of God: and the supreme Messianic function of Jesus is to bear witness to the truth. "What is truth?" says Pilate. The answer, which he did not wait to hear, is that truth is the strongest thing in the world—stronger even than the Roman Empire. One is reminded of the story of the three pages of King Darius in 1 Esdras 3 f. and the conclusion (4:41) μεγάλη ἡ ἀλήθεια καὶ ὑπερισχύει "Great is truth, and strongest of all!"). And the supreme truth about God is that God is love.

In rejecting a purely political notion of the Kingdom of God John is at one with the earlier sources for the Life of Jesus. In the Synoptic Gospels two things are as clear as daylight: 1. that the mass of the Jewish people in the days of Jesus, so far as they cherished any Messianic expectation at all, looked for the Kingdom of God as a political revolution in which they would be vindicated by God and delivered from the foreign oppressor. I know that since the rise of the Eschatological School it is the fashion to pour cold water on this and to suppose that the faith of the average Jew about the beginning of the Christian era was nourished on the *Similitudes of Enoch*. But the *Similitudes* are known to us only in a very late Ethiopic version and they can only be dated by conjecture. Further we have a much more reliable source of information in the so-called Psalter of Solomon, which can be attributed with practical certainty to the Pharisees of the latter half of the first century B.C. and one has only to read *Ps* 17 in that collection to see what the Messianic expectation was among the creative minds of Judaism in the two generations before the Christian era. Again the background of the Synoptic account tallies with the *Ps Sol.* 17 in a way in which it does *not* tally with the *Similitudes of Enoch*. And finally the history of the Jewish people during this whole period—up to the Hadrianic revolt—shows that they not only believed in this kind of thing, but also were ready to act upon their belief, as the numerous political revolts testify.

2. The Synoptic record makes it equally clear that there was a strong temptation throughout for Jesus himself to fall in with this sort of hope and allow himself to become the leader of an anti-Roman revolt and that he decisively—even fiercely—rejected it. The Temptation narrative in Q is first-rate evidence for this. As Karl Holl[5] says of it: "The story contains a feature which I could not credit to anyone else but Jesus himself: it is the force with which Jesus casts away the Jewish picture of the Messiah. He doesn't say it is unworthy or fleshly; he says it is of the *Devil*." In place of this Jewish Messianic expectation the Jesus of the Synoptic Gospels puts something else. That something else is understood by John to be not a new Davidic kingdom, but a new revelation of God—the very truth of God which is great and must prevail. That is one way of interpreting the Messiahship of Jesus. There are others. What is important is the realization by John that Jesus radically

---

5. *Ges. Aufsätze* II (1928), pp. 16 f.

transformed the current Messianic expectation. Here, it seems to me, we are reading history even if we are only allowed to see the facts through John's spectacles.

I venture a few theses—not as final or authoritative statements, but rather as bases for further investigations:

1. For John the Kingdom of God is revealed in and through the Messiah Jesus.

2. This kingdom is not a world-empire but a spiritual power: its weapons are truth and love.

3. Since the Kingdom is God's Kingdom and its weapons truth and love, the manner of its operation must be understood in terms of truth and love, i.e. in terms of revelation and creation or better creative revelation. It works by making new men—men born from above—and it does this by revealing to them God as creative love.

4. This creative love belongs to the nature of God from the beginning. It was manifested in part in the creation of the world, in part in the work of the prophets, and now in fullness in the Messiah Jesus. John does not say the Messiah is pre-existent; but rather the pre-existent is Messianic.

5. It is thus legitimate to regard Jesus as the culminating point of the whole prophetic succession in Israel. From an historical and evolutionary point of view he is the latest stage in a development that begins—say—with Moses and can be traced through the Old Testament.

6. But John does not look at it from an historical-evolutionary point of view. He regards it from a theological point of view. The end stage is there from the beginning. The prophetic succession is not a series of *discoveries* of which each prepares the way for the next—as in the progress of natural science—but a series of partial *revelations* by God who has now revealed himself completely in the Messiah Jesus, or at any rate as completely as it is possible for God to be revealed to men. The Logos comes to the prophets; but the Logos comes *in* Jesus.

7. The outcome of this is that a new life becomes immediately possible for those who receive what is given in Jesus; a life in fellowship with God, sustained by God and therefore eternal.

8. How does John regard the relation between the pre-exist-

ent Logos and "Jesus the son of Joseph from Nazareth" (1:45)?
When Jesus is made to say "Before Abraham was I am" is it
"Jesus the son of Joseph from Nazareth" who speaks or is it
the Logos? I do not think this question can be answered with
certainty at present. All that one can do is make suggestions.
For my own part I think that for John it is the Logos who
is speaking in the utterances of Jesus. But it is necessary to be
cautious in estimating what that means. The Logos is the word
of God, the word that creates and reveals. To say the Logos
is speaking in the speeches of Jesus may mean no more than the
view that in the case of Jesus we have a continuous prophetic
inspiration throughout the Ministry, that what happened partially and by fits and starts in the case of the Old Testament
prophets, here happens totally and all the time. If this is so
it means that we are free in John from one hard problem of
Christology as it is commonly understood. The orthodox doctrine of the two natures in one person is commonly understood—
perhaps misunderstood—as if it meant two personalities in one
person. I very much doubt whether John thought in this way;
because I doubt whether he thought of the Logos as a personality. The only personality on the scene is "Jesus the son
of Joseph from Nazareth". That personality embodies the Logos
so completely that Jesus becomes a complete revelation of God.
But in what sense are we using the word "embodies"? I think
in the old prophetic sense, but with the limitations that attached
to the prophets removed. The word that Isaiah speaks is the
word of the Lord, but it is also Isaiah's—it has become part
of him. Not every word of Isaiah is a word of the Lord. For
John every word of Jesus is a word of the Lord. There is
nothing in the activity of Jesus that belongs merely to his personal, local, temporary, selfish interests. All that side is over-
powered by the complete revelation of God. It is not that these
things are eliminated, but rather that they are all transformed
by the revelation. If we are to think of two natures at all
in this connexion we ought to think in terms of πνεῦμα and
σάρξ, of two sides of our experience—one on which we feel
ourselves to be akin to the animals, the other on which we
feel that we are in some sense children of God. And then we

may go on to consider whether the Logos in Christ does not mean that in the single personality of Jesus this divine element is continually on top, not in the sense that the other ceases to exist, but in the sense that it is completely subject to the divine. Then the question arises: Is that possible apart from some continual inflow of the divine? And that question carries with it another: When does this process begin?

Loofs in the work from which I have already quoted expressed the opinion that the theology of John does not assert an incarnation in the sense in which that word is ordinarily understood. That is, I presume, there is no idea of the Logos taking the place of the human personality of Jesus. Does John suppose that the Logos entered into Jesus in this complete way at the moment when Jesus as a separate person began to exist? I doubt it. What he does say is that John the Baptist testified: I saw the spirit descending on him like a dove from heaven, and it remained on him. And I did not know him, but he who sent me to baptize with water said to me: On whomsoever you see the spirit descending and remaining on him, this is he who baptizes with the holy spirit. And I have seen and testified that this is the elect Son of God (1:32 ff.).

Burkitt (*Church and Gnosis*, pp. 98 f.) argues that this implies an adoptionist Christology. If Burkitt is right then:

A second question arises—what becomes of the Prologue? For the Prologue is commonly regarded as a sort of metaphysical program or preface indicating the standpoint from which the rest of the work is composed. But if the Logos descends on Jesus at the Baptism and remains on him, then the whole of the Prologue is not a preface, but really chapter 1 of the story. In particular the fact that λόγος in this sense does not reappear after 1:14 is no longer significant, because the Logos is still there—only now acting and speaking *in persona Christi*.

Life:

    Cf. 1:4   That which has been made was life in him
               (RSV mg.)
    11:25 I am the resurrection and the life.
    14:6 I am the way, the truth, and the life.

Light also:

1:4, 9	... and the life was the light of men. The true light ... was coming into the world.
3:16, 19	... that he gave his only begotten Son ... light is come into the world.
8:12	I am the light of the world.
9:5	As long as I am in the world, I am the light of the world.
12:35 f., 46	Yet a little while is the light with you ... I am come a light unto the world.
1 John 2:8	The true light is already shining.

Pre-existence:

1:1 f.	In the beginning was the word.
8:58	Before Abraham was, I am.
17:5	And now, O Father, glorify me with thine own self with the glory which I had with thee before the world was.

One is tempted to think that the peculiarity of the discourse in the Fourth Gospel arises just from this: that it is the Logos that speaks in the person of Jesus. The Jewish interlocutors get at cross-purposes with the Johannine Christ because they think they are holding a debate with Jesus the son of Joseph from Nazareth, whereas they are really listening to the incarnate word of God. But if this is the case, then the Prologue is not just a prologue in the sense of a preface. It is really an introductory chapter, explaining all that follows. The Prologue is an explanation in a few words of the whole history of the world down to the beginning of the Ministry of Jesus. Everything from the commencement of the creation to this moment is the preparation for this culminating moment. The Logos was there in the creation. The Logos was the source of prophetic inspiration. Now comes the culminating point. The Logos dates completely into a human life and speaks to men not by occasional oracles or partial revelations, but totally and all the time. Here at last is a full and perfect revelation of God's nature made to man through man. In that sense the Prologue is just a statement in general terms of what is now to be shown in detail in the rest of the Gospel.

Now, that is not all. If that is the correct way to regard the Logos doctrine, there is not only a Prologue—Prelude would be the better word—there is also an Epilogue: and the Epilogue is connected with another characteristically Johannine word—παράκλητος. The Jesus of the Fourth Gospel is the middle term between the λόγος and the παράκλητος. The λόγος is the term that covers all divine revelation up to and including Jesus himself: παράκλητος is the term that covers all the Christian era from Jesus himself to the Church. The λόγος is the inspiration of the Old Testament and the λόγος is fully manifested in Christ. The παράκλητος is the inner life of the Church and in some sense is also to be identified with Christ.

Some Conclusions

1. The Johannine Theology is primarily a theology of Revelation. The essence of the Gospel is that it is a full and complete revelation of the truth.

2. By truth is meant the knowledge of God as he really is and to the full extent that his nature can be known to finite human beings.

3. Knowledge is not merely knowledge *about* God. It is knowledge *of* God. God in Jesus reveals not propositions but himself.

4. Since the revelation is a revelation of God it must be in terms of the highest category we know, which is personality. The revelation of God's nature takes place in the *person* of Jesus, not merely in certain theological statements, but in his whole life and death.

5. The content of the revelation is that God is love and this is revealed not by stating the proposition 'God is love', but in the fact that Jesus knows this love directly in his own person to the full, and manifests it through his person to the rest of the world. The supreme manifestation of this divine love is the laying down of his life for the world.

6. Man is saved by discovering the truth at the Cross. There he learns the meaning of sacrifice, sees the love of Christ,

and so discovers God who has manifested his nature there. This sacrificial love operates in two ways. It cleanses him from sin and it propagates itself in the believer. So that there is a break with the past and there is a new life marked by unselfish love. We know that we have passed from death to life because we love the brethren.

7. This saving revelation is the crown and fufillment of the long course of God's dealing with the world in Creation and Revelation. God made the world by his word. His word came also to mankind through the prophets. But these revelations are partial and occasional. From each you may learn a little about God. In the revelation in Jesus we have the complete and final manifestation of God. Here the λόγος is present *in toto* and all the time, i.e. in Jesus all that *we* can know of God is made known.

JOHN'S JESUS:
BIBLICAL WISDOM AND THE WORD EMBODIED

BASIL DE PINTO

The opening lines of John's gospel (1:1-18) are not only a solemn introduction, they are also a summary, an epitome of the whole history of salvation, the entire plan of God for man whom He has created and destined to share in the glory of His inner life. The very first words take us into that realm of inaccessible light where God has decreed that all things shall be, and in a few deft strokes the evangelist sets before us all that follows from this decree: the creation of all things, united in the harmony of the divine plan; filled with the light of life; the struggle of the powers of darkness to overcome this light, but their failure to restrain or overcome it; the triumph of the light in the hearts of those who willingly and lovingly accept it.

The idea of light is one of the key threads of the Prologue; strictly connected with it is the idea of life: there is even an identification between the two—"the life was the light of men".

But the most characteristic expression of the Prologue, the one which has always been indissolubly associated with it, and even sometimes unduly stressed, is the Word. It is here that John shows his dependence upon the Old Testament and this leaves the reader with no doubt that he is in strict continuity with the thought of the children of Israel and the sacred writings which had nourished their hopes throughout all the trials and vicissitudes of their existence. The first word of the fourth gospel is the same as the first word of Genesis: "In the beginning." One cannot stress too much the significance of this association. The first words of Holy Scripture have always had for the people of God a quality of sacredness, a sacramental value which raises them above all the other words in the Bible. The beginning (*rosh*, head in Hebrew) in some ways recapitulates and contains the whole thing. The rabbis conceived of the Torah as being itself eternal; the Torah was the word which was always in God, the wisdom by means of which in the beginning he made all things. All of this is present in the first lines of John's gospel. He is making a conscious reference to the beginning of Genesis where the word of God is seen as the power by which God brought all things into being: "And God said, Be light made. And light was made." By his word alone, God creates the entire order of living things in the universe. But for John, the word of God is not an impersonal attribute, nor even a poetic personification of one. The Word for John is the Son, the one who was in the beginning with God. Our English preposition *with* does little to communicate the sense of the Greek *pros*. As used in the first verse of John's gospel this term indicates a dynamic relationship between God and the Word; it even implies the idea of movement. Later theology would speak of this as the personal distinction between the Father and the Son. Such language is completely foreign to John, but the essential idea is there all the same. From all eternity God and the Word live in a dynamic exchange of love, and this living communication of being from one Person to the Other (for God *is* love, as John says in his epistle) is the source out of which all other being springs.

There was a current of thought in modern biblical study (it is already outmoded) which maintained that the doctrine found in John's writings and especially in the gospel was taken from the movement of religious and philosophical thought known as Gnosticism, that had been circulating for some time in the Mediterranean world. There can be no doubt that the gospel, in the final literary form in which it has come down to us, intentionally uses a mode of expression which will make it accessible to the minds of those for whom it was written. Hence it would be foolish to deny all Gnostic influence whatsoever. But it would be equally exaggerated to suppose that the fourth gospel is simply an attempt to reconcile the faith of the early Church with the ideas of salvation current in the Graeco-Roman world of the time. The truth is much simpler: the terminology in which John clothes his ideas are indeed borrowed from the

Gnostic vocabulary, but the ideas themselves represent the Christian transformation and fulfillment of the Hebrew Old Testament. John's supreme source book was the Bible itself.

The clearest evidence of this is in the use of the term *Word* in the prologue. Whatever may be the Hellenistic and other non-biblical references to the Logos of John, they are strictly secondary and subordinate to the important Old Testament idea of the Word of the Lord. This Word has a variety of forms in the Bible. It is first of all, as we have seen, the creative Word. This notion appears not only in the book of Genesis, but also in the sapiential literature of the Old Testament where the creative Word is poetically personified; it is the Wisdom of God, the one who was with him in his creative work, present beside him and aiding him "in the beginning" when he laid the foundations of the earth and stretched out the heavens above it and enclosed the oceans within their limits (Pr 8:22 f.). In the book of Ecclesiasticus the identification of the Wisdom of God with his creative Word is explicit: "Wisdom speaks in her own behalf. I came forth from the mouth of the Most High" (24:1-3). In this discourse of Wisdom about herself, she is seen living and acting among the people of God in some of the most important events of sacred history: present in all the acts of creation (5-6), manifesting the Lord's presence in the cloud that followed the Israelites through the desert (7) dwelling in the Holy Place of the Temple in Jerusalem (12-15).

In the gospel of John this Word of God who is also His wisdom, without whom was made nothing that has been made, appears among men and "pitches his tent" among them: the word in v. 14 of the Prologue usually translated "dwelt among us" has in Greek the same root letters as the word used in the Old Testament to indicate the presence of God dwelling among His people in the tent in the desert. Here John is very close to one of the important wisdom passages of the Bible, Baruch 3:29 f.: "Who has gone up to heaven to capture her (wisdom), and brought her down from the clouds? Who has crossed the sea to find her, and buy her at the price of purest gold? There is none who knows her ways, nor that can search out her paths. But he who knows all things knows her ... and has bestowed her on Jacob his servant, and upon Israel his well-beloved. *And thus wisdom appeared upon earth, and conversed with men."* Throughout his gospel John presents Jesus as the wisdom of God incarnate, living among his own and doing the works of God among them: "My Father works even until now, and I work. . . . For the Father loves the Son and shows ˙ him all that he himself does" (Jn 5:17-20). Like the wisdom of the Book of Proverbs (8:32-33; cf. 4:11) Jesus goes about teaching the way of truth which he has heard from God and comes to reveal to men: "My teaching is not my own, but his who sent me . . . I have not come of myself, but he is true who has sent me . . . I know him because I am from him, and he has sent me" (Jn 7:16 and 28-29). Jesus is the one who has come down from heaven (3:13), who belongs to the world beyond man's reach; because he comes from above, he is over all, (3:31), and when he has been exalted again to his heavenly glory, he will draw men after him that they too may live in that heavenly world with him (12:23 and 32). This was the reason he came into the world, to bear witness to the truth of God's glory and his will to save the world (18:37); he comes to bring to the world the Father's word of salvation; as wisdom incarnate he reveals what he alone has seen and heard in the bosom of the Father: "No one has ever seen God, (but) the only-begotten Son, who is in the bosom of the Father, he has revealed him" (1:18).

The Old Testament had spoken of the word of God in another way, the way of the prophets. They too had known the word of the Lord, but it was not always the glowing illumination of wisdom for them. The prophetic word was more often the word of the cross, the word of scandal that came to announce the judgment of God. The formula "Thus says the Lord" or "the word of the Lord that came to the prophet" or "the word of the Lord came to me" occurs repeatedly in the prophets; see the abundance of these expressions in the first lines of many of the chapters of Jeremiah, for example. The word comes to the prophet with great power and cannot be resisted: "The lion roars, and who is not afraid? The Lord God has spoken, and who shall not prophesy?" (Am 3:8).

Jesus is filled with this great prophetic word, the word that has been present among the people from the time of Moses:

"You search the Scriptures, because you think that in them is life everlasting. And it is they that bear witness of me . . . if you believed Moses you would believe me also, for he wrote of me. But if you do not believe his writings, how will you believe my words?" (5:39 and 46-47). The message that Jesus brings is the word that has been given him by God: "Amen, amen, I say to you, he who hears my word, and believes him who sent me, has life everlasting" (5:24). But like all the great prophets, Jesus is faced with the unbelief of men, their failure to accept the word of the Lord: "Now though he had worked so many signs in their presence, they did not believe in him; that the word which the prophet Isaiah spoke might be fulfilled, 'Lord, who has believed our report, and to whom has the arm of the Lord been revealed?' This is why they could not believe, because Isaiah said again, 'He has blinded their eyes and hardened their hearts, lest they see with their eyes and understand with their mind, and be converted and I heal them.' Isaiah said these things when he saw his glory and spoke of him" (12:37-41).

But the prophets also knew of the word of God which is the same as His power and His wisdom, and so is stronger than all the unbelief of men. The plan of God to save man is contained in this word, and when God sends his word on its mission of salvation, it is filled with His own strength, and so cannot in the end fail to do its work: "As the rain and the snow come down from heaven and return there no more, but soak the earth and water it and make it to spring, and give seed to the sower and bread to the hungry, so shall my Word be, that goes forth from my mouth: it shall not return to me void, but it shall do my will and prosper in the things for which I sent it" (Is 55:10-11). Jesus himself is this prophetic word, fulfilled on the day of his resurrection: "Go to my brethren and say to them, I ascend to my Father and your Father, to my God and your God." The Word that had dwelt with the Father, whom the Father had sent forth, had then indeed done his will, and prospered in the work of salvation for which he had been sent. Now he could return to the Father as the firstborn from the dead, the firstborn of many brethren.

But of all the manifestations of the word of God which the

Old Testament had known, none was so sacred as the word of
the Law, and this word too John predicates of Jesus. The idea
flows naturally out of the identification of the Word and the
wisdom of God, for nowhere is God's wisdom so plainly manifest as in the Torah. We have seen how the author of the book
of Ecclesiasticus shows the wisdom of God at work with him
throughout creation and in his blessings bestowed on the chosen
people. Immediately following this passage (Si 24:1-31), in
which wisdom personified speaks for herself, the author declares, "All this is nothing other than the book of the covenant
of the Most High God, the Law promulgated by Moses" (Si
24:32). The very same mode of expression appears in Baruch:
after the announcement that the wisdom of God has appeared
on earth and conversed with men (3:38), it is solemnly proclaimed that what has appeared is "the book of God's commandments, the Law that abides forever. All those who keep
it shall live, those who abandon it shall die. Return, O Jacob,
walk in the way of its brightness, in the presence of its light"
(4:1).

The relation of all this to the Word of John's gospel is transparent. Not that it is a question of his having written his
gospel with the Bible open before him so as to make a direct
and explicit reference in every case. John had simply assimilated
the Old Testament and the rabbinic teaching associated with
it to the point at which it is no exaggeration to speak of his
work as a mass of tacit allusions to the great traditions of Israel
through which he aims at persuading his readers that the
whole of Scripture has been fulfilled in Jesus. Where the Law
is concerned, it is clear that in the prologue John has simply
transferred its attributes to the Word: he was in the beginning
with God; he is life and the life is the light of men. Because
he is the wisdom of God, he is also the Torah. The repeated
references in the discourse after the last supper (ch 13-17)
to keeping the Lord's commandments is one of the elements
that gives structural unity to this scene; Jesus embodies in himself, in his own person, all that had previously made the Torah
the object of supreme veneration for the pious Israelite.

This is the point at which John goes beyond the mere identification of the Word and the Law; for to say that Jesus "em-

bodies the Law or Wisdom or the Word is to put oneself in the precise context which is the essential and all-embracing one in the fourth gospel. The climax of the Prologue indicates this: verses 14 and 16 through 18 (verse 15, the testimony of John the Baptist, can be regarded here as a parenthesis). "The Word was made flesh": In Christ the world of the divine is manifested in visible, palpable form. This had also taken place in some way when God revealed his eternal Torah to Moses. The Law given by God is the revelation of his inner being; and so in the thirty-fourth chapter of the Book of Exodus, the actual words of the Covenant of God with his people, given through Moses, the ten Words or Commandments, are preceded by the divine apparition in which God himself declares who he is, "the Lord, the Lord, God of tenderness and mercy, slow to anger, rich in grace and truth" (Ex 34:6). These attributes of grace and truth: the descending and compassionate love of God coupled with His unswerving fidelity, recur throughout the Bible, especially in the prophets and the Psalms, but they always refer back, in one way or another, to this revelation and self-definition which God makes known to Moses, the prophet who never had an equal in Israel: "And there arose no more a prophet in Israel like unto Moses, whom the Lord knew face to face" (Dt 34:10).

Yet the fullness of grace and truth had not been revealed to Moses. Wonderful as had been the revelation of Sinai, unique as had been the privilege of Moses, it had only been the preparation for the coming of him who was *full* of grace and truth, the one in whom the divine glory of the Father dwelt in its plenitude. Moses had caught a glimpse of God, he was chosen by God from among men to be the mediator through whom the Torah was given. But the grace and truth of which the Law was a revelation and embodiment merely passed by him in a fleeting mystical experience (cf. Ex 33:18-23). "For the Law was given through Moses; grace and truth came through Jesus Christ." Here (Jn 1:17) again the usual translation fails to convey the profound meaning contained in the original text, which says, not "came" but "was made": it is the same term as that used in v. 14 to describe the incarnation of the Logos: the Word was made flesh, and grace and truth, taken together

as embodied in the Word, was made flesh. Grace and truth
are taken together because they refer to the one person of the
Word in whom they are united; they evoke the divine reality
of Jesus Christ and his bringing that reality into the world of
men in his own human flesh. Grace and truth were seen in the
Old Testament as the chief distinguishing characteristic of
God, especially as he revealed himself in the Word of the Law;
now they appear in the Word made flesh, the one who brings
that grace and truth in all their fullness, the one who is not, like
Moses, only the mediator through whom the gifts of God are
given, but who is himself the fullness of the Father, and of
whose fullness we have all received.

Ultimately then, the Word of God is not an abstraction, not
a dead commandment, but a living Word, the person of Christ.
It is not surprising that John should make this personal identification between the Word of God and Jesus, since already behind him lay the primitive Christian tradition in which the Word
is synonymous with the Gospel, conceived of not as a lifeless
doctrinal system, but "the power of God to everyone who believes" (Rm 1:16). Christ himself, "the power and wisdom of
God" (1 Cor 1:24), is the content of this Word. What we find
therefore at the end of John's Prologue and throughout his
gospel, is the person of Christ, the eternal, divine Logos, the
wisdom of God, giving light and life to the world, but at the
same time the man Jesus, the Word made flesh: After this
passage the term "Word" is no longer applied to the Lord:
now he has a name, and it is by believing in this name, Jesus
Christ, that the life-giving light of divinity can shine in men's
hearts and make them what he is—sons of God. This was what
Jesus had promised to his disciples on the night before he died:
"I live and you shall live" (14:19), what he had promised to
all those who would come to him: "I am the bread of life.
He who comes to me shall not hunger" (6:35). It is because
he is the Son of God that Jesus is the living one, and it is because he makes those who believe in him become sons of God
that they live. But notice the condition: "to as many as received
him he gave the power of becoming sons of God, to those who
believed in his name" (1:12). It is by faith that we adhere
to Christ, become one with him in the fullness of his Sonship.

By faith we cling to him and are transformed in him in that act of total self-donation which we noted was the prime characteristic of it. It is as though the author of the fourth gospel wanted to infuse into his readers some of the reality of that all-absorbing contemplation into which his love of Christ had drawn him and in which he had found life. Indeed he explicitly states that this is his purpose in writing: "you may believe that Jesus is the Messiah, the Son of God, and that believing you may have life in his name" (20:31).

This more than anything else is what we should take away from our reading of John: a total dedication to the simple and humble reality of faith. The author of John was privileged to soar to great heights in his penetration of the mystery of the Word made flesh. This is such a great mystery that to tell of it in its entirety is beyond human power; to do this, "not even the world itself . . . could hold the books that would have to be written" (21:25). But John shows us that to reach the Word, to share in the life he came to give to the world, we need only reach out to Christ in faith, that faith whose obscurity diminishes none of its reality. In the faith of the risen Savior, the darkness of this world is already illumined with the dawn of eternal light, and in that light, shining in our hearts with an imperishable confidence, we, like the disciples whom Jesus loved, can recognize him and say, "It is the Lord" (21:7).

THE QUMRAN SCROLLS AND JOHN:
A Comparison in Thought and Expression

RAYMOND E. BROWN

The Qumran Scrolls are part of a large number of scrolls and fragments of manuscripts found since 1947 in the hills along the western shore of the Dead Sea. Found near the ruins of an ancient settlement called today Khirbet Qumrân, the Qumran literary material is what remains of the library of a community or sect of Jews who occupied the settlement between 130 B.C. and A.D. 68. While many of the scrolls and fragments are from copies of biblical books, others represent writings composed in the community. Since such literature comes from a period just before the New Testament, naturally much interest has been focused on comparing the Scrolls and the New Testament. We shall be particularly concerned with the relations between the Qumran literature and the Johannine writings.[1]

Such a discussion can follow varied lines. The method of "historical" identifications within the Scrolls has already been employed, but not with much success. Dupont-Sommer's first book[2] on the Scrolls painted a very provocative portrait of the Teacher of Righteousness (the great hero of Qumran)—a just man, nay "divine," who, having been persecuted and put to death by the wicked priest, came back to life and founded a church. The volatile French press immediately interpreted this as a proof that there was a Christ before our Jesus, and that the latter was nothing but a pale image of the former. While

---

1. We do not intend to treat the Apocalypse, not primarily because of the authorship problem but because this literary genre has so many stereotyped qualities that it offers great difficulties for establishing interrelationship.

2. *The Dead Sea Scrolls* (Eng. transl., 1952), pp. 33-44 and 98f.

recognizing the value of the many original observations of Dupont-Sommer, a good number of scholars have rejected the theory of the Teacher's death and resurrection (which are dependent on his interpretation of a very obscure text, 1 QpHab xi, 4-7); and under closer examination, many of the similarities between the Qumran Teacher and Jesus Christ have been found wanting.

Another example of "historical" identification is that of J. Teicher,[3] who claims that the community described in the Qumran Scrolls is that of the Ebionites, the second-century Jewish-Christian group, who were destroyed by Diocletian. For Teicher the wicked priest and the Teacher are Paul and Christ. Despite interesting similarities between the Scrolls and Ebionite literature (which may well indicate that some of the Qumran ideas were adopted by the Ebionites), the excavations at Khirbet Qumran eliminate Teicher's hypothesis by showing that the Qumran community was destroyed in A.D. 70. Today the majority of writers recognize the Qumran community to be Essene, although perhaps not in exactly the same stage of development as the Essenes described by Josephus and Philo. At any rate, in view of our very incomplete knowledge of the history of the Qumran community, an attempt to build a theory of Qumran-Christian relationship on identifications of characters within the Scrolls seems unwise.

However, if we establish relationships on the basis of terminology and ideology, which this article hopes to do, we are on much more solid ground. There is enough of Qumran literature to determine certain aspects of the sectarians' thought and its phrasing, aspects which we may compare to similar points in the Johannine literature. Similarities in thought and terminology between two such groups of documents could be expected because they are mutually dependent on the Old Testament and the Pseudepigrapha, and because they are dealing with roughly the same religious subject matter. Therefore, to

---

3. Teicher's articles constitute a long series, chiefly in the *Journal of Jewish Studies* from 1951 on. For a complete treatment see J. A. Fitzmyer, "The Qumran Scrolls, the Ebionites and Their Literature," *Theological Studies*, 16 (1955), pp. 335-372.

establish interdependence, we must concentrate on similarities which are *peculiar* to the two.

Modified Dualism

The outstanding resemblance between the Scrolls and the New Testament seems to be the modified dualism which is prevalent in both. By dualism we mean the doctrine that the universe is under the dominion of two opposing principles, one good and the other evil. Modified dualism adds the corrective that these principles are not uncreated, but are both dependent on God the Creator.

In the Old Testament there is really no predominant dualism. True, there are evil spirits, such as the tempter of Gn 3, and evil men whose ways are opposed to those of good men (Ps 1). But it does not emphasize any theory that the world is divided into two great camps locked in eternal struggle. In their very practical outlook, the Hebrew Scriptures are more interested in the individual man's struggle to follow the Law and live righteously. In the Qumran literature we find a new outlook. All men are aligned in two opposing forces, the one of light and truth, the other of darkness and perversion, with each faction ruled by a spirit or prince. While much of this ideology is phrased in a quasi-biblical language, the guiding inspiration of the dualism is clearly extrabiblical.

In a series of brilliant articles, K. G. Kuhn of Heidelberg seems to have successfully identified this source as Iranian Zoroastrianism. In its primitive form, the Zoroastrian religion taught a dualism where the forces of good and evil, led by Ahura Mazda and Angra Mainyu, respectively, are in combat. As Kuhn stresses, this dualism is not physical (i.e., an opposition between matter and spirit); it is an *ethical* struggle between truth and deceit, light and darkness. And it is *eschatological,* for the ultimate triumph of Ahura Mazda is definitely envisaged. In comparing the dualism of Qumran with early Zoroastrianism, Kuhn has found a great deal of similarity; for in the former the ethical, eschatological trend predominates too. In fact, there are interesting points of resemblance between passages of the Gathas and the Scrolls. One great dif-

ference separates them: in Zoroastrianism the good and evil
spirits are coexistent, independent, uncreated forces; in Qumran
thought, as will be seen, they are both created by God. The
imported dualism of Qumran has come into contact with the
Old Testament theology of God the Creator, and is subservient
to that great truth.

Zoroastrian influence on Qumran is not at all difficult to
postulate if we realize that many Jews remained in Mesopotamia
after the Captivity, and lived side by side with Iranians. Such
proximity may well have influenced Jewish thought, especially
in those elements which were compatible with the Hebrew
religion. From time to time Babylonian Jews returned to Palestine (witness Ezra in the late fifth century); and undoubtedly the formation of the Maccabean free state in the second
century drew many more. It seems to have been just at the
end of the Maccabean wars that the Qumran community came
into existence. If the founders of the community were of Babylonian Jewry, or in contact with it, the strain of Zoroastrian
influence need not astound us.

When we turn to the Johannine writings, we find there also
a modified dualism. Once again there is talk of forces of light
and truth struggling with forces of darkness and perversion.
There are hints of this elsewhere in the New Testament, especially in St. Paul; but nowhere does it reach the intensity of
St. John's works. To account for this, many suggestions have
been made. The fact that the Fourth Gospel was so popular
with the Gnostics gave rise among the critics to the hypothesis
of a Gnostic background. However, the discovery of the Gnostic
codices at Chenoboskion in Upper Egypt in 1945 has considerably enlightened us on the true nature of this heresy. As W. F.
Albright remarks, "We now know that the Church Fathers did
not appreciably exaggerate their accounts of Gnosticism, and
that the gap between Christianity and any form of second-
century Gnosticism was tremendous. The efforts of recent historians of religion to picture a Gnosticism which resembled
the Gospel of John more closely than anything known from
Patristic tradition have been nullified. . . ." The dualism of
Gnosticism is a physical one; the dualism of John is ethical and
eschatological, like that of Qumran. Both streams may have

had their very ancient sources in Zoroastrian dualism, but into Gnosticism have poured the muddy tributaries of pagan Greek philosophy and Judeo-Christian heresy; in the end Gnosticism flows far away indeed from the Evangelist's "living waters."

Now a new attempt has been made to identify the source of the modified dualism of John. Kuhn, Albright, Reicke, Brownlee, Braun, and Mowry see in the ideology and terminology of Qumran the Jewish background of Johannine thought and phrasing. A careful comparison of the two literatures on various points connected with this modified dualism will enable the reader to review some of the evidence for such a theory.

a) *Creation.* Qumran states unequivocally the biblical doctrine of creation: "From the God of knowledge exists all that is and will be" (1 QS iii, 15). "And by his knowledge everything has been brought into being. And everything that is, he established by his purpose; and apart from him, nothing is done" (xi, 11). We get a very similar statement in the Prologue of John, "All things were made through him, and apart from him nothing came to be."

The Qumran literature goes on to state specifically that the two spirits, or leaders, of the forces of good and evil were created: "He created the spirits of light and darkness. . . ." (1 QS iii, 25). For John, as we shall see, the problem does not arise; and so there is no similar statement. If the Zoroastrian background of Qumran dualism is correct, the specific statement of the creation of the two spirits may have been intended as a corrective. Mowry suggests the possibility of a similar apologetic motive in John. Perhaps the position of his universal statement of creation at the very beginning of his Gospel was directed against the idea of an uncreated evil spirit. Yet John is never specific on the creation of such a spirit, and he never returns with emphasis to the theme of the universality of creation.

b) *The Two Spirits.* The world, according to Qumran, is divided under two created leaders, one of whom God hates, while loving the other. The good spirit is called variously "the spirit of truth, the prince of lights, the angel of His truth, the holy spirit." The evil spirit is called "the spirit of perversion,

the angel of darkness, the angel of destruction." Most often
the name "Belial" is applied to him. This evil spirit seems to
have subordinate spirits in his forces too, for the spirits of Belial
are mentioned (CD 14:5).

In any case the names applied to the two principal spirits
are clearly of a personal nature. As personal entities outside of
man, they help or hinder man: "the God of Israel and his angel
of truth have helped all the sons of light" (1 QS iii, 24-25;
1 QM xiii, 10). "And it is because of the angel of darkness that
all the sons of righteousness go astray" (1 QS iii, 21-22). Yet
they also conduct their struggle within man: "Until now the
spirits of truth and perversion strive within man's heart" (iv,
23-24). Consequently, in many instances, one gets the definite
impression that the spirits are being spoken of impersonally
as ways of acting. The two aspects are not necessarily contradictory: it is natural to shift from speaking of two personal
spirits exercising a dominion over man to speaking of two spirits
of acting by which man shows his respective adherence to their
dominion.

In John we have both pairs of terms which Qumran uses
interchangeably: light and darkness, truth and perversion. However, in his theology there is a difference between the leader
of the forces of light and the Spirit of Truth; and so for the
present we shall concentrate on only the light and darkness
antinomy. For John, "God is light, and in him is no darkness"
(1 Jn 1:5). With the Son of God, Jesus Christ, light has come
into the world, so that Christ can call Himself "the light of
the world" (Jn 9:5). Thus in the Fourth Gospel there is no
created spirit of light such as we find in the Qumran literature
—the leader of the forces of light is the uncreated Word Himself.

John often speaks of the darkness, and he mentions an evil
spirit—the devil or Satan. Yet nowhere does he characterize
Satan in the exact terminology of Qumran as the leader, spirit,
or angel of the forces of darkness. (St. Luke with his mention
of the "power of darkness" and Paul's Belial are terminologi-
cally closer to Qumran on this point than John is.) Perhaps
we may see a similarity to the Qumran literature in the struggle
which John paints between Christ and "the prince of this world."

In summary we may say that there is a similar general outlook in John and in the Qumran literature on the forces of light and darkness, each with its personal leader. Yet in John, Christ as the light of the world is a significant development over Qumran's created angel of light. There is difference too in the terminology for the leader of darkness.

c) The Struggle. In the Qumran literature we are told that between the two spirits there is undying enmity and bitter conflict—a struggle which, until the last age, is waged on equal terms. Clearly, however, the evil spirit is equal only by the sufferance of God, and at the end God will intervene and crush him: "Now God through the mysteries of his understanding and through his glorious wisdom has appointed a period for the existence of wrongdoing; but at the season of visitation, he will destroy it forever; and then the truth of the world will appear forever" (1 QS iv, 18-19). Apparently, this divine intervention will be seen in a great battle where, thanks to God and His angels, the sons of light will be victorious. 1 QM gives a detailed plan for the organization of the forces, for standards, signals, and weapons of battle. The punishment of the wicked, after their defeat, will be severe, and their sufferings are graphically described in apocalyptic language: a multitude of plagues, eternal ruin, everlasting terror, destruction in the fire of the dark regions, calamities of darkness. The end result will be that "wickedness will disappear before justice as darkness before light."

In this whole picture of the struggle it is noteworthy that the writers always seem to be living in the period of trial, when Belial is still loose and waging war on equal terms. 1 QM, with all its minute details, is still a description of a future battle.

When we turn to John, we find there also a struggle between light and darkness, but a struggle which is passing through its climax and where victory is already decided. Christ has brought light into the world; darkness has tried to overcome this light, but "the light shines on in the darkness, for the darkness did not overcome it" (Jn 1:5). As a result, "the darkness is passing away and indeed the true light is now shining" (1 Jn 2:8). John also phrases the victorious aspect of the conflict in terms of Christ's casting out the prince of this world

(Jn 12:31), so that the Savior can cry out, "But take courage, I have overcome the world" (16:33). The victory, as we know, has not reached its culmination; only the second coming of Christ can establish the conclusive triumph of light. The Book of Revelation presents the ultimate battle between the forces of good and evil. However, it must be admitted that even in this work we have no real parallel to the detailed accounts of 1 QM.

Once again, in summary, we see a similarity of thought between the two groups of writings on the conflict, and both are sure of the ultimate success of light. Yet here, as before, Christ makes a tremendous difference in John's outlook. For Qumran victory is still in the future; for John light is already triumphant.

d) *Man's Role.* Coppens has said that the Qumran community gives no evidence of deep abstract religious speculations. This seems particularly true in the problem of predestination and free will—a problem at the root of the domination of man by the spirits of light and darkness. As is inevitable when two trends of thought meet and are harmonized, difficulties occur which did not exist before the union. From the Old Testament there came to Qumran the basically simple Hebrew notions of morality, involving the obviously free behavior of man and his consequent reward or punishment. From outside, presumably from Zoroastrianism, came the idea of two spirits dominating the human race, so that man acts according to one or the other: this is a concept which, when developed logically, would lead to a deterministic predestination. The sectarians never seem to have defined the conflict between these two notions, or to have attempted a speculative solution of it. Throughout their works are statements which favor one or the other view; but to me it does not seem accurate to classify them definitely on either side as if they had passed a reflex judgment on the problem. It was only later, when Jewish thought came into closer and closer contact with Hellenic and Hellenistic philosophies, that the full depth of the problem was realized and discussed; twenty centuries afterward it is still a mystery.

Grossouw says of man's role according to Qumran theology: "The so-baffling difference in the conduct of good people and bad people is reduced here to the influence of 'the spirit of truth' and 'the spirit of perversion or deceit.' " And of these spirits he says: "On the other hand, their mastery over man's moral actions seems to be absolute, the consequence of which would be that these actions are determined and no longer free." Certainly there are many statements in the Qumran literature which can be so interpreted. 1 QS iii, 15 ff., states: "From the God of knowledge exists all that is and will be. Before they existed, he established all the design of them. And after they exist, according to their ordinances (in accordance with his glorious purpose), they fulfill their task; and nothing can be changed.... Now, he created man for dominion over the world and assigned him two spirits by which to walk until the season of his visitation." Again in iv, 15, we find, "In these (two spirits) are the families of all mankind; and in their divisions do all their hosts receive an inheritance according to their societies and in their ways do they walk." And finally iv, 24, adds: "Until now the spirits of truth and perversion strive within man's heart; they walk in wisdom and folly; and according as man's inheritance is in truth and righteousness, so he hates evil; but in so far as his heritage is in the portion of perversity and wickedness in him, so he abominates truth."

Thus man would seem to be placed under one or the other spirit and to behave accordingly. In fact, the two spirits are so in control that they can be said to raise up men for their work: "For aforetime rose Moses and Aaron through the prince of the Lights. But Belial raised Jochanneh and his brother with his evil device...." (CD 7:19). In the case of the sons of light, there seems to be a special divine predilection whereby they are chosen by God almost independently of their works. "For God has chosen them for an eternal covenant" (1 QS iv, 22). In fact they may be called "the ones chosen according to God's good pleasure."

Such texts certainly seem to favor determinism. When we peruse some other statements, however, we find observations which appear to demand freedom of will. Throughout 1 QS the importance of virtuous works is emphasized, and even the men of the community are blamed for succumbing to temptation and committing bad deeds. In general, the evil are pun-

ished precisely because they have rejected the will of God
and have done *their own will*. "Because they did their own will
and kept not the commandment of their Maker" (CD 3:7 and
4:9-10). A heinous sin is the refusal to accept the sectarians'
interpretation of the Torah, and this refusal is spoken of as
deliberate. A very clear passage is 1 QS v, 11, where the
wicked are said to have committed both "unknown sins" and
"deliberate sins." And finally we might note the strong emphasis of the Qumran texts on repentance, and the possibilities of
reform offered to recalcitrant sectarians. All these ideas can
scarcely be harmonized with a hopeless determination.

In John no such conflict of ideas exists. Of course there is
a very orthodox statement of God's predilection: "You have
not chosen me, but I have chosen you" (Jn 15:16). There is
no hint, however, of anyone's being determined to evil without
choice. Rather the culpable deliberateness of man's adherence
to darkness is emphasized: "The light has come into the world,
yet men have loved the darkness rather than the light, for their
works were evil. For everyone who does evil hates the light,
and does not come to the light, that his deeds may not be exposed" (Jn 3:19-20). In view of this obstinate refusal, Christ
tries to persuade men to come to the light before it is too late.
"Yet a little while the light is among you. Walk while you have
the light, that darkness may not overtake you. He who walks
in darkness does not know where he goes" (Jn 12:35). This
idea of walking in light and darkness is very similar to the
two ways in which men are to walk according to the Qumran
texts.

Yet in spite of all Christ's pleading and that of His apostles,
some will always continue to walk in darkness. "If we say that
we have fellowship with him, and walk in darkness, we lie,
and are not practicing the truth" (1 Jn 1:6). The free and
deliberate choice of darkness is the basis for God's ultimate
judgment of man: "Now this is the judgment: The light has
come into the world, yet men have loved the darkness rather
than the light" (Jn 3:19).

In summary, we find that in the Qumran texts, men are
aligned under the banners of light and darkness, and this seem-
ingly without much choice on man's part. Yet other passages

suppose that man deliberately walks in either of the two ways. In John's terminology, too, man walks in the ranks of either light or darkness, but he does so freely inasmuch as he accepts or does not accept Christ, the light of the world.

e) The Sons of Light. What ultimately constitutes a man one of the sons of light (1 QS i, 9; iii, 24; and *passim*)? It is clear from the above that, for Qumran, refusal to do God's will makes one a son of darkness. Yet if we are to say that doing God's will makes one a son of light, we must understand "God's will" in a very restricted sense. Apparently the sectarians felt that no one could do what God wanted unless he was acquainted with the Torah as explained in the Qumran community. Nowhere is the question broached of those who do good works and are not members of the community. Thus, for all practical purposes, the sons of light are equated with the sectarians. Some citations from the Qumran literature make this quite clear.

In 1 QM we have a description of the forces of the sons of light in their ultimate struggle with the sons of darkness; the former consist of the sectarians. 1 QS i, 7-8 and 11, tells us: "All who dedicate themselves to do God's ordinances shall be brought into the covenant of friendship, to be united (or, to become a community) in God's counsel. ... All who dedicate themselves to his truth shall bring all their mind and their strength and their property into the Community of God." The short poetical citation of 1 QS viii, 5-8, describes the community as the "witnesses of truth" and "those chosen according to God's pleasure." They are the ones who have been set apart as a house of holiness in Israel (ix, 6). And so we see that the Qumran sons of light are marked by the exclusiveness typical of small sectarian movements whether in Israel or in Christianity.

The precise factor in the community which sanctifies its members is their acceptance of, and obedience to, the teaching of the sect. The early chapters of 1 QS give the Covenant of the community. They are told that they have "to walk before him perfectly (in) all things that are revealed according to their appointed seasons ..." (i, 8-9). The idea of submissiveness to revealed teaching comes up again in the instruction of

4

iii, 13: "For the wise man, that he may instruct and teach all the sons of light in the generations of all mankind with regard to all the varieties of their spirits. . . ." The hearts of the sectarians are illumined with the "wisdom of life"; and they can look upon the "light of life."

Historically, God seems to have raised up the Teacher of Righteousness to instruct men in this marvelous wisdom. CD 1:7 says: "And he raised them up a Teacher of Righteousness to lead them in the way of his heart." Since this revealed wisdom is a special interpretation of the Torah, throughout the history of the sect there has been a strong emphasis on studying the Law. The enigmatic figure called "the Star" is described in CD 9ª:8 as one who studied the Law. In the present circumstances the communication of such teaching is the function of the overseer (mebaqqer) of the camp; it is he who "shall instruct the many in the works of God, and shall make them understand his wondrous mighty acts, and shall narrate before them the things of the world . . ." (CD 16:1).

Acceptance of such teaching is not conceived of as purely passive; it implies that sectarians do good works in conformity with this instruction. 1 QS iv, 2, gives a list of the desirable virtues which are the way of the good spirit: truth, humility, patience, compassion, understanding, wisdom, zeal, purity— an interesting parallel to St. Paul's fruits of the Spirit (Gal 5:22 ff.). Periodically the neophyte is to be examined "with respect to his understanding and his deeds in Torah, in accordance with the views of the sons of Aaron." CD 10ff. gives a detailed series of laws for the community to follow. And, as we see from 1 QS vi, 24 ff., backsliding or misbehavior was seriously punished. And so in general the sons of light, the Qumran Community, can truly be said to be "the doers of the Law in the house of Judah whom God will deliver from the house of judgment for the sake of their labor and their 'faith' in the Teacher of Righteousness."

When we turn to the "sons of light" in St. John we find ourselves at a distance from Qumran. As we would expect, good men are attracted to the light of Christ. "But he who does the truth comes to the light that his deeds may be made manifest, for they have been performed in God" (Jn 3:21).

Yet it is not good deeds that constitute one a son of light—
it is *faith in Christ, the light of the world!* ". . . believe in the
light, that you may become sons of light."—"I have come a
light into the world, that whoever believes in me may not remain in the darkness" (Jn 12:36, 46). This same idea is expressed in Jn 8:12: "I am the light of the world. He who follows
me does not walk in the darkness, but will have the light of
life."

Nevertheless, if by faith in Christ we are constituted sons
of light, our obligations to perform good works have not ceased.
Rather we are now expected to walk as sons of light, and to
conduct ourselves virtuously. Naturally, this includes all the
virtues, but John stresses charity. "He who says that he is in
the light, and hates his brother, is in the darkness still. He
who loves his brother abides in the light, and for him there
is no stumbling" (1 Jn 2:9-10). And in this way, just as those
who walk in the darkness are judged, so those sons of light
who believe in Christ and keep His commandments are saved
from their sins: "But if we walk in the light as he also is in
the light, we have fellowship with one another, and the blood
of Jesus Christ, his Son, cleanses us from all sin" (1 Jn 1:7).

Summing up this point, we say that, while Qumran and John
characterize good men in much the same way, they differ greatly
in their notion of what brings one into the domain of light.
For Qumran it is acceptance of the community's interpretation
of the Law; for John it is faith in Jesus Christ. Both insist that
sons of light live up to their name in virtuous behavior.

These five points of comparison should enable us to form
an idea of the similarities and differences that exist between
the modified dualistic concept of light and darkness in the
Qumran and in the Johannine literature. In retrospect, it should
be evident that *the basic difference between the two theologies
is Christ.* Both believe in the creation of all things by God.
Both conceive of the world as divided into the two camps of
light and darkness, and see these camps arranged under personal leadership. For Qumran the leaders are the two created
spirits or angels of light and darkness (truth and perversion);
for St. John, however, the leader of light is the uncreated Word,
while the leader of evil is the prince of this world. For Qum-

ran the struggle between the forces is still on an equal plane, although light will shine victoriously at the end; for John light is already conquering darkness. Both the literatures maintain that all men are to be assigned to either of the two camps. Yet througout the Qumran literature there is a curious mixture of determinism and free will, while John is quite clear that men remain in darkness because they obstinately turn away from light. And, finally, Christ is also the point of difference between John and Qumran with respect to the ultimate constituent of the sons of light. If the terminology and ideology are often the same, St. John's whole outlook has been radically reoriented by the revelation that is Christ.

Granting this all-important difference, we may ask if the similarities are sufficient to posit dependence of St. John's outlook upon Qumran ideology. We have considered only one point: modified dualism; in succeeding pages we shall take up others, e.g., the spirits of truth and perversion, the emphasis on charity, the fountain of living waters. With this added evidence the reader will be in a better position to make a judgment. Yet this much may be said of the dualism already discussed: in no other literature do we have so close a terminological and ideological parallel to Johannine usage. Can such peculiar similarities between the two trains of thought (which were in existence in the small region of the world at the same period of time) be coincidental?

Other Similarities

a) *Truth and Perversity.* For Qumran the terms "truth and perversity" are interchangeable with "light and darkness" as expressions of modified dualism. In 1 QS iii, 19, the leaders of the forces of light and darkness are called the spirits of truth and perversion. The way of the spirit of truth (iv, 2 ff.) is contrasted in detail with the way of the spirit of perversion (iv, 9 ff.); and in one or the other way all men walk.

In the New Testament "the spirit of truth" is a term peculiar to St. John. In his theology we notice a difference between the leader of the forces of light (Christ) and the Spirit of truth (the Paraclete or the Holy Spirit). There are three places where the latter term is used with a personal meaning. In Jn 14:16-17, Christ says: "And I will ask the Father and he will give you another Paraclete to dwell with you forever, the Spirit of truth whom the world cannot receive, because it neither sees him nor knows him." This is continued in 15:26: "But when the Paraclete has come, whom I will send you from the Father, the Spirit of truth who proceeds from the Father, he will bear witness concerning me." And finally 16:13 says: "But when he, the Spirit of truth, has come, he will teach you all the truth." Thus, if St. John found "light" an ideal term for the revelation that is Jesus Christ, he seems to have discovered in the "Spirit of truth" an apt description for the Holy Spirit, the true witness of Christ.

Yet in 1 Jn 4:1-6 one finds a different use of "the spirit of truth" in opposition to "the spirit of error": "Beloved, do not believe every spirit, but test the spirits to see whether they are of God; because many false prophets have gone forth into the world. . . . We are of God. He who knows God listens to us; he who is not of God does not listen to us. By this we know the spirit of truth and the spirit of error." Here we certainly find a remarkable similarity to the two spirits of 1 QS.

The similarity grows even more striking when we compare sections of Qumran and Johannine phraseology. In 1 QS i, 5; v, 3; and viii, 2, the sectarians are urged "to practice" or "to do the truth." Jn 3:21 says: "But he who *does the truth* comes to the light that his deeds may be made manifest, for they have been performed in God." The same expression occurs in 1 Jn 1:6: "If we say that we have fellowship with him, and walk in darkness, we lie, and are not *practicing the truth.*"

The Qumran texts also share with John the idea of walking in truth. "I rejoiced greatly that I found some of your children walking in truth. . ." (2 Jn 4). An almost identical statement occurs in 3 Jn 3: "I rejoiced greatly when some brethren came and bore witness to your truth, even as you walk in the truth. I have no greater joy than to hear that my children are walking in the truth."

Because of their devotion to truth, the sectarians are called "witnesses of truth" (1 QS viii, 6). Only in the Fourth Gospel, where it is used both of John the Baptist and of Christ, does this phrase occur in the New Testament: "You have sent to John, and he has borne witness to the truth" (5:33); and "I am a king. This is why I was born, and why I have come into the world, to bear witness to the truth" (18:37).

In both the Qumran texts and John, truth is seen as a medium of purification and sanctification. 1 QS iv, 20-21, states "And then God will purge by his truth all the deeds of man ... to cleanse him through a holy spirit from all wicked practices, sprinkling upon him a spirit of truth as purifying water." This may be compared with Jn 17:17-19: "Sanctify them in truth. Your word is truth. Even as you have sent me into the world, so I also have sent them into the world. And for them I sanctify myself, that they also may be sanctified in truth."

Finally, we may compare two sentences which we have quoted in part before, but which are most effective when seen together: "According as man's inheritance is in truth and righteousness, so he hates evil; but in so far as his heritage is in the portion of perversity and wickedness in him, so he abominates truth" (1 QS iv, 24).—"For every one who does evil hates the light, and does not come to the light, so that his deeds may not be exposed. But he who does the truth comes to the light, that his deeds may be made manifest, for they have been performed in God" (Jn 3:20-21).

b) Brotherly Love. The Qumran literature (and, of course, the Bible itself) maintains the principle that one must hate evil and love good. 1 QS i, 3-4, urges those who seek God "to love everything that he has chosen, and to hate everything that he has rejected; to keep far from every evil and to cling to every good deed." (Also CD 3:1: "... to choose what he approves, and to reject what he hates.") As might be expected, however, we encounter difficulty when we pass from evil and good to persons who do evil and good.

The Qumran texts inculcate a hatred of those who are not sons of light, i.e., are not members of the community. 1 QS i, 10, requires one "to hate all the sons of darkness each according to his guilt in provoking God's vengeance!" The Levites of Qumran curse the sons of Belial: "May you be cursed without compassion, according to the darkness of your deeds, and damned in the gloom of eternal fire! May God not favor you when you call; and may he not be forgiving to pardon your iniquities" (ii, 7-8). The sectarian is admonished to separate himself from perverse men, and to conceal from them the community's special interpretation of the Law (v, 11, and ix, 17-18).

Yet within the Qumran texts, as Grossouw remarks, "several passages struggle as it were to break through their narrow boundaries (or hatred)." The hymn of 1 QS x, 18, is magnificent in its spirituality: "I will repay no man with evil's due; (only) with good will I pursue a man; for with God is the judgment of every living thing." Continuing in xi, 1, the author speaks of the duty "to teach the straying of spirit understanding, and to make murmurers wise through instruction; and to respond humbly before the haughty of spirit, and with broken spirit to men of injustice."

These two trends are puzzling. Certainly Qumran never reached the heights of Mt 5:44: "But I say to you, love your enemies, do good to those who hate you, and pray for those who persecute and calumniate you, so that you may be children of your Father in heaven, who makes his sun to rise on the good and the evil." Christianity represents both a doctrinal and a moral development over all that went before. Yet, and we shall see this especially in the question of brotherly love, "One gets a strong impression that in these [Qumran] writings man's mind is preparing for the Christian precept of love."[4] The formulae of hate are found in the initiation ceremonies and formalized instructions of 1 QS: they may be ancient, stylized renunciations of evil as personified in the sons of Belial. The hymns are, perhaps, more representative of the ideal of personal piety at Qumran.

Whatever may be the moral defects in the sectarians' dealing with outsiders, the fraternal affection is truly edifying. Over and over again 1 QS insists that there be a spirit of loving devotion in the community. The instruction of i, 10, says that all who join the group have "to love all the sons of light, each according to his lot in God's counsel." This is made more practi-

---

4. Grossouw, "The Dead Sea Scrolls and the New Testament," *Studia Catholica*, 26 (1951), p. 292.

cal in v, 26: "One shall not speak to his brother in anger, or
in complaint, or with a (stiff) neck or a callous heart, or a
wicked spirit; nor shall he hate him. . . ." If there are to be re-
bukes, they must be administered in the manner least calcu-
lated to offend. Punishments for sins against one's brother
are quite severe (vii, 4-8).

In the New Testament, while the Synoptics transmit Christ's
command of universal charity, it is John who stresses love of
one's brother within the Christian community. Christ's great
commandment for John is that of mutual love within the Church:
"A new commandment I give you, that you love one another:
that as I have loved you, you also love one another. By this
will all men know that you are my disciples, if you have love
for one another" (13:34-35; also 15:12). This theme runs all
through the Johannine epistles, e.g., "He who loves his brother
abides in the light, and for him there is no stumbling" (1 Jn
2:10). It reaches breathtaking heights in 1 Jn 4:7-8: "Beloved,
let us love one another, for love is from God. . . . He who does
not love does not know God, for God is love."

The prevalence of the theme of brotherly love in both the
Qumran and the Johannine literature is not a conclusive proof
of interrelationship. But it is certainly remarkable that the New
Testament writer who shares so many other ideological and
terminological peculiarities with Qumran should also stress the
particular aspect of charity which is emphasized more at Qumran than anywhere else in Jewish literature before Christ.

c) *Fountain of Living Waters.* The metaphorical use of
this term occurs several times in the Old Testament. In Jer
2:13 it refers to God: "For my people have committed two
evils: they have forsaken me, the fountain of living waters,
and hewed out cisterns for themselves, broken cisterns, that
can hold no water." And again, in Ps 36:9: "For with you is the
fountain of life; in your light do we see light." Prv 13:14 gives
another application: "The teaching of the wise is a fountain
of life."

CD has its own use for the metaphor: the community's interpretation of the Law is the well of living waters. 9ᵇ:28 warns:
"So are all the men who entered into the New Covenant in

the land of Damascus and yet turned backward and acted treacherously and departed from the spring of living waters." On the other hand, of those who stay in the community it may be said: "They dug a well of many waters: and he that despises them shall not live" (5:3). The most specific identification occurs in a commentary on Nm 21:18 (CD 8:6): "The well is the Law, and they who dug it are the penitents of Israel who went forth out of the land of Judah and sojourned in the land of Damascus."

In the New Testament this terminology occurs in only two books, the Fourth Gospel and Apocalypse. In his conversation with the Samaritan woman, Christ says, "He, however, who drinks of the water that I will give him shall never thirst; but the water that I will give him shall become in him a fountain of water, springing up unto eternal life" (Jn 4:14). And again in 7:38 he cries out, "As the Scripture says, 'From within him [Jesus or the believer?] there shall flow rivers of living water.'" Ap 7:17 speaks of the Lamb guiding those who have suffered for Christ "to the fountain of the water of life." And toward the end of Ap (21:6), Christ, the Alpha and Omega, promises, "To him who thirsts I will give of the fountain of the water of life freely."

Because of the occurrence of the term in the Old Testament, this usage is not a conclusive proof of interrelationship between the Qumran and the Johannine literature. But it is interesting to notice that the metaphor betrays the characteristic interests of Qumran and of St. John. For Qumran the water of life comes from the community's discipline and lore; for John it is given by Christ to those who believe in him—the same difference we found in the discussion of "the sons of light."

Conclusions

There remains a tremendous chasm between Qumran thought and Christianity. No matter how impressive the terminology and ideological similarities, the difference that Jesus Christ makes between the two cannot be minimized. We would do well to avoid any policy of hunting for Christian parallels to every line of the Qumran texts. The Essene sectarians were not Christians, and the recognition of this will prevent many misinterpretations. On the other hand, it is even more incorrect to turn the early Christians into Essenes. In his second volume on the Scrolls, Dupont-Sommer rejects some of the wild conclusions that were based on his first work. Yet he still states, "Christianity, I repeat, is not Essenism, it is 'an Essenism' as Renan said." We do not think that the adaptation of Essene terminology and ideology to Christianity in the New Testament makes Christianity *an* Essenism any more than the use of Platonic terminology and ideology by the Fathers makes it a Platonism. Christianity is too unique to be classified as any earlier "ism."

Having made these very important reservations, we can turn to evaluate the evidence. If we add the similarities we have just discussed to what we saw about the modified dualism, the argument for interrelation between the Johannine writings and the Qumran literature is indeed strong. The resemblances do not seem to indicate immediate relationship, however, as if St. John were himself a sectarian or were personally familiar with the Qumran literature. Rather they indicate a more general acquaintance with the thought and style of expression which we have found at Qumran. The ideas of Qumran must have been fairly widespread in certain Jewish circles in the early first century A.D.[5] Probably it is only through such sources that Qumran had its indirect effect on the Johannine literature.

W. F. Albright has pointed out how important this interrelationship is for dating the Fourth Gospel. We now realize that John's peculiar terminology (which was often the reason for a late dating of the Gospel) has parallels in a Palestinian tradition which flourished before the Christian Era. Therefore, even if we allow time for the oral transmission of the Gospel in the Diaspora, we may still date its final writing within the first century A.D.—a far cry from the very late dating of some critics. As for authorship, the knowledge that the tradition of the Fourth Gospel is local Palestinian weakens the position of those who deny utterly that it could contain tradition from John the Apostle.

---

5. Josephus, *Bell.*, 2, 8, speaks of the Essenes: "They have no certain city, but many of them dwell in every city."

The reader may wonder how the Qumran parallels in John compare with those of other books of the New Testament. After the Johannine literature, the Pauline corpus shows the greatest affinities to Qumran. Certainly the parallels throw an interesting light on St. Paul's "mysteries" and on his theology of faith. The Epistle to the Hebrews has also some interesting points of contact with the Qumran literature. The remaining New Testament books show scattered Qumran affinities, but less frequently than the Johannine or Pauline works.

These facts may cause us to wonder why similarities to Qumran thought are more frequent in some portions of the New Testament than in others. At the present there are only indications toward a solution. For St. John the answer may lie in a verse of the Fourth Gospel: "Again the next day John (the Baptist) was standing there and two of his disciples" (1:35). One of these disciples was Andrew; his anonymous confrère has traditionally been identified as John, son of Zebedee. Now virtually everyone who has studied the Qumran texts in the light of the New Testament has recognized the startling Qumran parallels in the narratives concerning John the Baptist; almost every detail of his life and preaching has a *possible* Qumran affinity. From this it would seem likely that the Baptist, before his contact with Christ, was in relationship with Qumran or other Essenes (perhaps he was raised by the community, or in contact with the community, or the head of a quasi-Essene group). If this is true, and if John, son of Zebedee, was his disciple, we can explain very well the Qumran impact on the Fourth Gospel.

External evidence adds an interesting note. Tradition is almost unanimous that this Gospel was written at Ephesus. Acts 18:24 ff. speaks of the presence at Ephesus of disciples of John the Baptist who were not yet fully Christian. An hypothesis might be constructed that John the Baptist was familiar with the Qumran Essenes and their thought, and that through him certain of these ideas passed on to his disciples, including John, son of Zebedee. The latter formed his ideas of Jesus in the light of this background, and, of course, remembered and stressed those *logia* of Jesus which were in close harmony with his own feelings. Later at Ephesus, disciples of the Baptist

who had not accepted Christ became part of the audience to
whom the Johannine preaching was directed, and Christ was
interpreted to them in familiar terms. Christ is the light they
speak of; true sons of the light are those who believe in him;
the "spirit of truth" is the Holy Spirit, etc. Yet such an hypothesis, while it fulfills the tradition of the origin of the Gospel, is
based on so many surmises that it can remain only an interesting possibility for the present.

THE JOHANNINE "SIGNS" OF JESUS

W. D. DAVIES

Some years ago there appeared on the front page of *The New York Times* a photograph of Pope Paul VI giving away his papal tiara as a sign of concern of the Pontiff and of the Roman Catholic Church for the poor. This act is reminiscent of the signs which frequently occur in the Fourth Gospel.

In fact many claim that, for John, everything Jesus did pointed, beyond itself, to a truth about Jesus and his significance. The acts of Jesus were "signs," (*sêmeia*). To understand the meaning of the term "sign" is essential.

The meaning of signs in the Old Testament

In the Old Testament, two kinds of events are distinguishable, although they are not always sharply differentiated. There are events which are *merely* strange or odd; these are usually referred to as wonders (*môphêthôth*). The action of a man jumping from the top of the Empire State Building in New York City to the street below and then walking away unhurt would constitute a "wonder." Such an act would be odd, but not significant. Consider, however, the following passage from Exodus 4:1-9.

Then Moses answered, "But behold, they will not believe me or listen to my voice, for they will say, 'The Lord did not appear to you.'" The Lord said to him, "What is that in your hand?" He said, "A rod." And he said, "Cast it on the ground." So he cast it on the ground, and it became a serpent; and Moses fled from it. But the Lord said to Moses, "Put out your hand, and take it by the tail"—so he put out his hand and caught it, and it became a rod in his hand—"that they may believe that the Lord, the God of their fathers, the God of Abraham, the God of Isaac, and the God of Jacob, has appeared to you." Again, the Lord said to him, "Put your hand into your bosom." And he put his hand into his bosom; and when he took it out, behold, his hand was leprous, as white as snow. Then God said, "Put your hand back into your bosom." So he put his hand back into his bosom; and when he took it out, behold, it was restored like the rest of his flesh. "If they will not believe you," God said, "or heed the first sign, they may believe the latter sign. If they will not believe even these two signs or heed your voice, you shall take some water from the Nile and pour it upon the dry ground; and the water which you shall take from the Nile will become blood upon the dry ground."

In this passage, the turning of a rod into a serpent is an odd event; but it is not only called a wonder, but a sign (*ôth*), because it points beyond itself to the power of Moses' God. The same applies to the other events recorded; they, too, are wonders but also signs.

But an event, which is not in itself odd, can be a sign. The prophets sometimes performed acts which, in themselves, were ordinary, but which are designed to point to a truth. The accounts of such signs are too long to be quoted in full. Examples can be found in Isaiah 20:1 ff.; Jeremiah 27:1 ff.; Ezekiel 4:1 ff. In the second passage referred to, the prophet Jeremiah walked about Jerusalem carrying a yoke about his neck to indicate the coming of foreign domination. The act of carrying the yoke was both a sign of domination and something more. This something more can again be illustrated by the gesture of Pope Paul VI. In dedicating his tiara to the poor, the Pope was making a sign—pointing to the concern of the Church. But his action was not merely a sign in this sense. In some measure it was also effective; it helped to bring about more care for the poor. Not only would the actual price of the tiara be given to the poor, but many would undoubtedly be spurred to greater charity by this act. The Pope's sign helped to bring about what it signified. This analogy is not to be pressed, but it is not irrelevant, because in the Old Testament a sign is regarded as something more than a mere symbol; it actually helps to bring about what it signifies.

Signs in the Fourth Gospel

The transition from signs in the Old Testament to signs in the New, and especially in *The Fourth Gospel,* is easy. In the latter, the acts of Jesus are treated as signs, and understood as were the signs which the Old Testament prophets performed. John takes the first half of his Gospel, that is, chapters 2 to 12 to present the signs of Jesus. Many scholars are convinced that he drew upon a special source, a Book of Signs, for these chapters. Traditionally, seven signs have been recognized:

1. The miracle at Cana of Galilee, 2:1-12.
2. The healing of the nobleman's son, 4:47-54.
3. The healing of the sick man at the pool of Bethesda, 5:1-16.
4. The feeding of the five thousand, 6:1-14.
5. The walking on the water, 6:15-21.
6. The healing of the man blind from birth at Siloam, 9:1-17.
7. The raising of Lazarus from the dead, 11:1-44.

As they stand in John, these signs have been combined with other narratives which may be derived from the same source. Often the evangelist takes episodes or signs which he needs and then makes these a point of departure for dialogues or discourses in which he sets forth the truth of the Gospel. But he follows no fixed pattern. The long allegory of The Good Shepherd in chapter 10 stands alone, attached to no episode or sign; the discourse material in chapter 3, discussing rebirth, is much longer than the narrative, which is very brief. On the other hand, the sign at Cana of Galilee (2:1-12) stands alone without a corresponding discourse and ends merely with an editorial comment. After the cleansing of the Temple (2: 13-16) there is only a short dialogue. But the most striking arrangement is that in which John makes the sign or episode the occasion for a long dialogue or discourse. The following examples occur:

1. *Episode* (3:23-26): John the Baptist at Aenon near to Salim, is questioned about Jesus.
   Discourse (3:27-36): Jesus must increase and John decrease.
2. *Episode* (4:1-8): The woman of Samaria and Jesus at the well.
   Dialogue (4:9-38): On the water of life (vv. 9-15)
   On worship (vv. 20-26)
   On mission (vv. 35-38)
3. *Episode* (5:1-16): The healing of the impotent man at at the pool of Bethesda.
   Discourse (5:17-47): On the authority of Jesus.
4. *Episode* (6:1-31): The feeding of the five thousand.
   Discourse-dialogue (6:32-65): On the bread of life.
5. *Episode* (7:1-16): The appearance of Jesus at the Feast of Tabernacles.
   Discourse (7:16-52: 8:12-59): On Messiahship: Christ the Light of the world.
6. *Episode* (9:1-7): The healing of the blind man at the pool of Siloam.
   Dialogue (9:8-41): On judgment.
7. *Episode and Dialogue intermingled* (11:1-53): The raising of Lazarus and the discussion of the resurrection of the dead.
8. *Episode* (12:20-23): The Greeks inquire after Jesus.
   Discourse (12:23-36): The Passion.

As the Gospel now stands, episodes and dialogues or discourses have been combined to form seven major divisions, and the whole of chapters 2-12 can be regarded as a Book of Signs, in which John sets forth the meaning of Jesus Christ in terms of his acts. Some have found a development in ideas from one sign to the other; others have claimed that the whole truth of the Gospel is brought out in each sign. To enter into this debate is not possible here. What must be insisted upon is that each part of the Fourth Gospel belongs to the other; the Gospel is to be understood as a whole. No attempt will be made in these pages to trace a logical development from one section to another in John, at all points, but each section does gain in depth if set over against the whole of the Gospel. The following are the divisions of chapters 2-12 suggested by Professor C. H. Dodd in his great work, *The Interpretation of the Fourth Gospel.*

SIGNS THAT JESUS BRINGS A NEW ORDER: 2:1-4:42

1. The Wedding at Cana: Water is Turned into Wine

The section begins with a wedding at Cana in Galilee. The wine fails, but water is turned into wine at the word of Jesus. The purpose of John is not to relate a marvel, but to set forth a sign of the fact that, with the coming of Jesus, the religion of the Law, symbolized by water (see especially 2:6: "Now six stone jars were standing there, for the Jewish rites of purification each holding twenty or thirty gallons"), was transformed into the religion of the Gospel, symbolized by the wine (for the use of wine as a symbol for the new order of the Gospel, see also Mt 9:17; Mk 2:22; Lk 5:37), which is better than any wine previously available. Later on, in chapter 15, Jesus declares: "I am the true vine"—the giver of the true wine.

2. The Cleansing of The Temple: A New Temple is to Arise

The theme of "newness" is carried further in the story of the cleansing of the Temple in 2:13-22. The meaning of the cleansing is given in 2:18 f.:

The Jews challenged Jesus: "What sign," they asked, "can you show as authority for your action [cleansing the temple]?" "Destroy this temple," Jesus replied, "and in three days I will raise it again."

The Jews, naturally, take these words to refer to the actual Temple in Jerusalem. But John, as so often, is playing with words to set forth his message. In 2:21, the explanation is

given that the "temple" referred to by Jesus is "his body."
The raising of the temple points, therefore, to the resurrection
of Jesus.

But the term "body" (especially at Ephesus) was familiar
as a term for "the Church." When Jesus spoke of the raising up
of the temple, his body, he was suggesting also the coming
into being of the Church, through his resurrection. Like the
story of the wedding at Cana, the cleansing of the Temple is
a sign that in the coming of Jesus a new order has begun;
Judaism has given place to the Gospel; the Old Israel to the
New Israel, the Church; the old order of purification to a new.

3. Jesus and Nicodemus: New Birth

Two further sections are devoted to the illumination of this
theme of newness in terms of a new birth and new worship.
In chapter 3, Nicodemus, a leading Jew, recognizes that Jesus
is from God but is puzzled by him. (This last may be the
reason why he comes to Jesus by night; his attachment to
Jesus is uncertain.) Jesus informs him that the new order, here
called the kingdom of God, can only be appreciated by those
born anew or from above. But Jesus' statement is misunderstood. Nicodemus asks:

> "But how is it possible," said Nicodemus, "for a man to be
> born when he is old? Can he enter his mother's womb a
> second time and be born?"

Then the explanation is given as follows:

> Jesus answered, "In truth I tell you, no one can enter the
> kingdom of God without being born from water and spirit.
> Flesh can give birth only to flesh; it is spirit that gives birth
> to spirit. You ought not to be astonished, then, when I tell
> you that you must be born over again. The wind blows
> where it wills; you hear the sound of it, but you do not
> know where it comes from, or where it is going. So with
> everyone who is born from spirit." (Jn 3:5-8)

The force of the explanation is that entry into the kingdom of

God, or the new order, is only possible by the invasive, dynamic energy of God himself, the Spirit, which cannot be humanly controlled at all. Human effort alone will not avail to gain entrance into the kingdom, but a radical activity of God, symbolized by the water of baptism (this is probably the force of the phrase "from water and spirit"). To recognize in the ministry of Jesus the presence of the kingdom of God is not easy for mundane men; it is only made possible by God himself.

All this puzzles Nicodemus still further. Jesus then goes on to explain that this truth is only accessible to himself, the Son of Man, who, out of God's love for the world, came down from above and, therefore, can reveal the things above, that is, the nature of God's reality or of his kingdom. Jesus, as the light, enters the dark world to offer eternal life to those who believe in him. In this he is the Savior.

But he is also judge. The object of Jesus' coming into the world was to reveal the truth and to draw men to himself. But, because he came as the light, he judged. As light, by its very nature, reveals darkness, so the coming of Jesus reveals the depth of human darkness in a new way. Many a television artist has learned, to his cost, that the light which pours upon him when he faces the cameras is relentless in its honesty, merciless in its truth; every feature of the face—light and dark —is exposed to view. The cameras are candid. So, too, the light of Jesus is merciless, even though its purpose is mercy. In his light, men saw their own evil with a new clarity. For some, the intensity of this light was too much; they turned away from it to the gentler, more comfortable darkness to which they were accustomed. The light pained their eyes. Like Byron's prisoner of Chillon, who was so long in the dungeon that at last he almost lost the desire to be free, men preferred darkness to the light; they would

> ... have done with this new day,
> Which now is painful to these eyes.

In thus turning away from the light of Jesus, men passed judgment, and even condemnation, on themselves. The supreme test of existence was the encounter with Jesus. To turn away from him was to be judged and condemned, not by Jesus, but by themselves. The following verses give the heart of the matter:

God loved the world so much that he gave his only Son, that everyone who has faith in him may not die but have eternal life. It was not to judge the world that God sent his Son into the world, but that through him the world might be saved.

The man who puts his faith in him does not come under judgment; but the unbeliever has already been judged in that he has not given his allegiance to God's only Son. Here lies the test: the light has come into the world, but men preferred darkness to light because their deeds were evil. Bad men all hate the light and avoid it, for fear their practices should be shown up. The honest man comes to the light so that it may be clearly seen that God is in all he does. (Jn 3:16-21)

The closing verses in the above quotation are important. Not anything in human nature or existence, as such, is evil; not life in the flesh, as such. The enemy of man is not any state or condition in which he may find himself, not "in his stars"— as Shakespeare might put it—but in his perverse will, which disobeys and rejects the good when it is revealed. It is this that brings condemnation and death:

This is death and the sole death
When a man's loss
Comes to him from his gain;
From knowledge ignorance,
And lack of love
From love made manifest.[1]

4. Jesus and the Woman of Samaria: A New Worship

In the chapter in John which follows chapter 3, the emphasis on the newness of the order brought by Jesus is continued

---

1. Robert Browning, *Poems of Robert Browning* (Boston, 1896, pp. 406ff.), "A Death in the Desert," lines 482ff.

still further. Consider the following dialogue between Jesus
and the Samaritan woman:

"Sir," she replied, "I can see that you are a prophet. Our
fathers worshipped on this mountain, but you Jews say
that the temple where God should be worshipped is in
Jerusalem." "Believe me," said Jesus, "the time is coming
when you will worship the Father neither on this mountain,
nor in Jerusalem. You Samaritans worship without knowing what you worship, while we worship what we know.
It is from the Jews that salvation comes. But the time approaches, indeed it is already here, when those who are
real worshippers will worship the Father in spirit and in
truth. Such are the worshippers whom the Father wants.
God is spirit, and those who worship him must worship
in spirit and in truth." The woman answered, "I know that
Messiah (that is, Christ) is coming. When he comes he will
tell us everything." Jesus said, "I am he, I who am speaking
to you now." (Jn 4:19-26)

Jesus himself has replaced both Gerizim and Jerusalem, the
supreme holy places of Samaritans and Jews respectively, as
the place of worship; he himself has become the "place" where
God and man meet in spirit and in truth. This new order of
worship in and through him is already a present fact. "But
the time approaches, indeed it is already here." The phrase
"it is already here" is emphatic.

In the first section, 2:1-4:42, we note, then, three ways in
which Jesus has introduced a new order. He has replaced the
cultic center of Judaism, the Old Temple; he has brought into
the very present what Judaism expected at the end of the
days: the ultimate judgment takes place here and now in the
confrontation of men with Jesus. And, lastly, he has transcended
the practice of Samaritan religion and that of Judaism. In Jesus:

The old order changeth giving place to new
And God fulfills himself in many ways.

Cultic and Apocalyptic Judaism, and Samaritan and Jewish
forms of worship are all transcended in Christ. The whole

section closes with the confirmation of Christ as the Savior of the World by many Samaritans.

SIGNS THAT JESUS GIVES LIFE: 4:46-5:1-47

1. The Healing of the Nobleman's Son and of the Sick Man at the Pool of Bethesda

Two signs occur in this section, but only one discourse. The story in 4:46-54 is described in 4:54 as the second sign. A nobleman's son who was at the brink of death is given a new lease on life by the word of Jesus. Jesus' word has life-giving power:

> "Return home; your son will live." The man believed what Jesus said and started for home. (Jn 4:50)

This theme is then carried over into the second story—that of the man who had been sick for forty-two years at the pool of Bethesda (5:1 ff.). For forty-two years he had waited to be cast, at the opportune moment, into the healing waters of the pool, but he had waited in vain. At the word of Jesus, however, he was healed. The sick man had been outside the reach of healing until Jesus came. The two healings in this section, then, illustrate the power of the word of Jesus to give new life.

2. Discourse

The discourse material, which follows both signs, at first sight is not closely connected with them; but at certain points it does revert explicitly to the theme of the signs. Thus, in 5:21 and again in 5:26 the life-giving power of the Son is that of the Father:

> As the Father raises the dead and gives them life, so the Son gives life to men, as he determines. For as the Father has life-giving power in himself, so has the Son, by the Father's gift. (Jn 5:21, 26)

And again, in 5:39-40, Jesus is the fountain of life:

> You study the scriptures diligently, supposing that in having them you have eternal life; yet, although their testimony points to me, you refuse to come to me for that life.

The intricacies of the whole discourse material in 5:17-47 cannot be traced here. Its main thrust is that the Father, out of love for his Son, has given his own power of giving life to Jesus. The power of God is present in Jesus.

A SIGN THAT JESUS IS THE BREAD OF LIFE: 6:1-58

The Feeding of the Five Thousand

The sixth chapter records the feeding of five thousand people who were following Jesus. Jesus provides physical bread for the hungry multitudes. The meaning of this sign is then expounded in three parts:

(1) 6:26-34. The food of Eternal Life is understood in terms of the manna given to the people of Israel in the wilderness. The claim is made that it is not through Moses but in Jesus that God gives eternal life—the true bread.

> Jesus answered, "I tell you this: the truth is, not that Moses gave you the bread from heaven, but that my Father gives you the real bread from heaven. The bread that God gives comes down from heaven and brings life to the world." (Jn 6:32-33)

(2) 6:34-51. Christ is and gives the bread of life.

> I am the bread of life. Your forefathers ate the manna in the desert and they are dead. I am speaking of the bread that comes down from heaven, which a man may eat, and never die. (Jn 6:48-51)

(3) 6:52-59. Jesus gives the bread of life in the Eucharist and through his indwelling in the life of the Christian.

Jesus replied, "In truth, in very truth I tell you, unless you eat the flesh of the Son of Man and drink his blood you can have no life in you. Whoever eats my flesh and drinks my blood possesses eternal life, and I will raise him up on the last day. My flesh is real food; my blood is real drink. Whoever eats my flesh and drinks my blood dwells continually in me and I dwell in him." (Jn 6:53-56)

A SIGN THAT JESUS IS THE LIGHT OF THE WORLD:
CONFLICT WITH THE JEWS: 7:1-8:59

Jesus at the Feast of Tabernacles

The best commentary on this section are the words:

I came not to send peace but a sword.

There is here no act of Jesus which can be called a sign; instead, the appearance of Jesus in the Temple at Jerusalem, on the Feast of Tabernacles, gives rise to six dialogues which reveal both commitment to and hatred of him. The very presence of Jesus stirs controversy, and in itself is a sign that a time of conflict has begun. Jesus' very appearance inspired loyalty and murderous opposition. Why?

The only action which lies behind this section, as we stated, is the visit of Jesus to Jerusalem to attend the Feast of Tabernacles. But in Judaism, this feast was associated with the Day of Judgment, the Day of the Lord, when God would establish his universal kingdom.

Then every one that survives of all the nations that have come against Jerusalem shall go up year after year to worship the King, the Lord of hosts, and to keep the feast of booths [that is, The Feast of Tabernacles]. (Zc 14:16)

The Ritual of the Feast: Water and Light: The Unutterable Name

Associated with this Feast were certain rituals. First, water from the pool of Siloam was poured over the altar in the Temple at Jerusalem in order that the rains for the coming year might be blessed, rain being the means to life. Secondly, gigantic candelabra were brightly lit in the Temple so that they would illumine every court in Jerusalem. These two aspects of the Feast probably lie behind words which Jesus uttered:

On the last and greatest day of the festival Jesus stood and cried aloud, "If anyone is thirsty let him come to me; whoever believes in me, let him drink." As Scripture says, "Streams of living water shall flow out from within him." (7:37-38)

Later Jesus uttered the words:

I am the light of the world. No follower of mine shall wander in the dark; he shall have the light of life. (8:12)

Water and light—terms used of the Law, the ultimate revelation in Judaism—are found in Jesus. He is the living water of revelation, the light of revelation to the whole world. Even more, in 8:21-30 Jesus is given the very name of God, *"I am He"* —the term used for the hidden name of God in Judaism and associated with the Feast of Tabernacles.

That is why I told you that you would die in your sins. If you do not believe *that I am what I am,* you will die in your sins.

Criticisms of Jesus

This section, therefore, brings together claims that the Johannine Christ makes. But these claims are set over against and partly called forth by criticisms made of him. John has here gathered the Jewish objections to the Messianic claims of Jesus. These are:

1. Jesus was an ignorant man. (7:14-24)

How is it that this man has learning, when he has never studied? (7:16-17)

The answer is that Jesus' teaching is that of God.

Jesus replied, "The teaching that I give is not my own; it

is the teaching of him who sent me. Whoever has the will
to do the will of God shall know whether my teaching comes
from him or is merely my own" (Jn 7:16-17)

This answer raises the question of the relation of Jesus' teaching
to that of Moses. The claim is made that Jesus' conduct on the
Sabbath does not differ fundamentally from that of his opponents; but the theme is not developed. (7:19-24)

2. Jewish tradition claimed that when the Messiah came the
place of his origin would be unknown. But the origin of Jesus
of Nazareth was known, so that he could not be the Messiah.
The answer given to this was that the Jews only thought that
they knew Jesus' origin; in fact, he was from God.

Thereupon Jesus cried aloud as he taught in the temple,
"No doubt you know me; no doubt you know where I come
from. Yet I have not come of my own accord. I was sent
by the One who truly is, and him you do not know. I know
him because I come from him and he it is who sent me."
(Jn 7:28-29)

3. Witness borne by a person to himself was not valid. Self-
praise is no recommendation. In 8:12-19, it is objected that
Jesus bears witness to himself. But Jesus asserts that God is
his witness.

I pass judgment on no man, but if I do judge, my judgment is valid because it is not I alone who judge, but
I and he who sent me. In your own law it is written that
the testimony of two witnesses is valid. Here am I, a witness in my own cause, and my other witness is the Father
who sent me. (Jn 8:16-18)

The above accusations and their rebuttal take place between
Jesus and the people, but in the background are the chief
priests and the Pharisees, who sent the Temple police to arrest
Jesus. As he more and more divides the people, the opposition
to Jesus mounts. Aware then of the situation, Jesus speaks
of his death, "of the lifting up [that is, crucifixion] of the Son

of Man" (8:28) and of the Jews' intent to kill him. This leads to the amazing claim of Jesus in 8:58:

Truly, truly, I say to you, before Abraham was, I am.

And the last words of the section are:

They picked up stones to throw at him, but Jesus was not to be seen; and he left the temple. (8:59)

Jesus and the World

The whole section 7:1-8:59 may, therefore, be taken as a commentary on the verse in the Prologue 1:11: "He came to his own realm and his own would not receive him." The light and life (8:12) and the very presence of God (*I am he*) has appeared to Israel and to the world (7:4, 36; 8:12) only to be rejected. The presence of Jesus in itself is a sign of the Divine Presence, and it is accompanied by three things:

First, *the judgment of this world.* Jesus exposes the wickedness of the world's ways (7:7). He does this, not because he judges men (7:16), but because men in rejecting him judge themselves. Jesus judges although he is no judge.

Secondly, *the sifting of this world.* In the presence of Jesus, men are compelled to take sides, to be for him or against him. Even before he goes to the Feast, men are divided by him:

. . . and there was much whispering about him in the crowds. "He is a good man," said some. "No," said others, "he is leading the people astray." However, no one talked about him openly, for fear of the Jews. (7:12-13)

This division runs through the dialogue. Those who accept and those who reject Jesus join opposite camps. Jesus is a two-edged sword cleaving the hearts of men and, thereby, sifting them. Neutrality in his presence is impossible.

Thirdly, *the opposition of the world.* In this section, the death of Jesus, which in previous chapters had only been hinted at, becomes inescapable; he will be "lifted up" on the cross. The confrontation of Jesus and the world can have only one end. From this section onward, it is the death of Jesus that more and more comes to the fore.

A SIGN THAT JESUS BRINGS JUDGMENT: 9:1-10:21, 10:22-39

A connection between the different parts of this section is not obvious, but it does exist. The stream of thought probably runs as follows.

The Man Born Blind

In 9:1-41, a man born blind is given his sight by Jesus. This healing of the blind man is a sign of the fact that Jesus is the light of the world (9:5). But John is primarily concerned here, not with Jesus as the light, but as the judge of those who encounter his light.

The Pharisees and Jesus

Jesus had healed the blind man on a Sabbath day. But, ask the Pharisees, would a man from God so desecrate the Sabbath? The blind man's condition was not urgent; he had been blind from birth; another day would make little difference to him; would not a man of God have waited to heal him on a weekday? In this way the Pharisees call good evil and evil good; they refuse to rejoice generously in the healing activity of Jesus. They consider him a commonplace fellow of unknown origin. Confronted with his mercy, they cavil at him. Despite all protests, they condemn both him and the one whom he has healed. The healed man is expelled from the synagogue. Both Jesus and he have been judged and found wanting. But this is not the last word. At the end, the tables are turned:

> Jesus heard that they had expelled him. When he found him he asked, "Have you faith in the Son of Man?" The man answered, "Tell me who he is, sir, that I should put my faith in him." "You have seen him," said Jesus; "indeed, it is he who is speaking to you." "Lord, I believe," he said, and bowed before him.
> Jesus said, "It is for judgment that I have come into this

world—to give sight to the sightless and to make blind those
who see." Some Pharisees in his company asked, "Do you
mean that we are blind?" "If you were blind," said Jesus,
"you would not be guilty, but because you say 'We see,'
your guilt remains." (9:35-41)

In fact, it is not Jesus and the healed man who have been
judged and found wanting, but their judges, the Pharisees.
The blind have gained sight; those supposed to see have become blind. True judgment has not been exercised by, but
upon, the Pharisees. The leaders of Judaism have been found
wanting.

The Good Shepherd

The full force of this judgment against the Pharisees must
be noted. John was writing at a time when the Christian Church
was increasingly being estranged from the Synagogue. After
the fall of Jerusalem in A.D. 70, the Pharisaic leaders of Judaism
had gathered at a place called Jamnia in order to reorganize
the life of the Jewish people. They became convinced that
Christianity was a menace to Judaism and so, somewhere around
A.D. 80-85, the Pharisaic leaders inserted in the chief prayer of
the Synagogue a prayer called *The Birkath ha-Minim* (Blessing—
a euphemism for curse—on Heretics) which was designed to
exclude Christians from the Synagogue. The Pharisees were
putting out of Israel those who had accepted Jesus. The leaders
of Israel were rejecting the Messiah and his followers, who
had been blind but had been given their sight by Jesus.

It is over against this background that the next section,
chapter 10, the allegory of The Good Shepherd, is to be understood. Its imagery is drawn from Ezekiel 34, where Israel is
represented as God's flock, and her rulers as false shepherds
who prey upon the flock. For this reason, the rulers are cast
out and God himself cares for his flock and saves them. Over
his flock he will set one shepherd, the Messiah. This imagery
is applied by John, in chapter 10, to the Israel of his own day.
The Pharisaic leaders have been like thieves and robbers; they
have expelled from the flock of Israel a man enlightened by

Christ; Christians are cast out of Israel. But Jesus himself is the Good Shepherd set over Israel by God. This Good Shepherd lays his life down for the sheep; Jesus chose to die. But his death is a means of bringing life to his flock, which is no longer confined to the fold of Israel, but draws upon all the world. In 10:16, we read:

> But there are other sheep of mine, not belonging to this fold, whom I must bring in; and they too will listen to my voice. There will be one flock, one shepherd.

Such a claim for Jesus—that he is the Messiah, the shepherd of Israel—inevitably raises conflict. The conflict is given expression in 10:22-39 where it is declared that Jesus is Messiah, but in a far deeper sense than Judaism had anticipated; he is the Son of God (10:36), one with the Father (10:30). No greater claim could be made for him.

A SIGN THAT JESUS IS THE RESURRECTION AND THE LIFE: 11:1-53

Up to this point all the signs presented, except one, where the sign is embedded in the midst of the narrative in chapters 7 and 8, have stood out clearly as independent stories followed by interpretative discourses. But in this section, the sign is inseparably interwoven with dialogue. The dialogue comments on the narrative, and the narrative interpenetrates the dialogue.

1. The Raising of Lazarus from the Dead

The story, which serves as a sign, is that Lazarus, a friend of Jesus, is ill at his home at Bethany in Judaea. But, on the ground that his friend's sickness is designed to reveal his own glory as the Son of God, Jesus delays going immediately to his help. It is only after two days, by which time Lazarus is already dead and thus beyond human help, that Jesus returns to Judaea. But notice that he does so at the risk of death at the hands of the Jews. And four days after the entombment, that is, when it is quite certain that Lazarus is really dead and not merely asleep, Jesus raises him from the dead.

2. What It Signifies

Such is the narrative which can be reconstructed. The sheer inhumanity of Jesus' conduct in refusing to go immediately to the help of Lazarus alone makes it clear that the mere recital of such a story is not the evangelist's intention. As he relates it, each step of the story becomes the occasion for discussion; the story is for the thought.

On Jesus' arrival, Martha, the sister of Lazarus, converses with him.

Martha said to Jesus, "If you had been here, sir, my brother would not have died. Even now I know that whatever you ask of God, God will grant you." Jesus said, "Your brother will rise again." "I know that he will rise again," said Martha, "at the resurrection on the last day." Jesus said, "I am the resurrection and I am life. If a man has faith in me, even though he die, he shall come to life; and no one who is alive and has faith shall ever die. Do you believe this?" "Lord, I do," she answered; "I now believe that you are the Messiah, the Son of God who was to come into the world." (Jn 11:21-27)

Jesus assures Martha that her brother will rise again. She understands him to refer to a physical resurrection of the body expected at the last day. But, as so often in John, a physical phenomenon suggests a spiritual reality. Jesus now claims that what was expected in the future—resurrection at the last day— is already present in him; he has the life-giving power which Judaism associated with the end of all things.

I *am* the resurrection and I *am* the life. (11:25; N.E.B., our italics)

The future powers of Jewish expectation are already at work in Jesus. At the same time, in 11:25-26, we also read:

Jesus said, "I am the resurrection and I am life. If a man has faith in me, even though he die, he shall come to life; and no one who is alive and has faith shall ever die."

To believe in Jesus, here and now, is to pass beyond death into true life which is present in him. Whether life is thought of as a present reality or as a future endowment given in a resurrection at the end of all things or at the Day of the Lord, it is Jesus who possesses it. It is as if John were saying: whether you consider life at its best here and now or life as it will be in an ideal "world to come" to be established in the future, the standard of measurement for it is Jesus Christ; his is the ultimate life, present and to come. True life "now" and "then" means the life of Jesus Christ, who is the giver of life and the conqueror of death.

3. The Shadow of the Cross

John asserts this last because, in going up to Judaea, Jesus faced death at the hands of the Jews. But, as his readers know, although Jesus did die, he was alive in their midst; he had conquered death. He had conquered death by dying. Life came through his death. This truth that Jesus could only raise Lazarus by facing the perils of Judaea, that is, through dying to himself, explains why before the story of Lazarus in 11:5-8, and after it in 11:45-57, John has placed references to the threat to his life. The life-giving power of Jesus is connected with his self-sacrifice even unto death. .

SIGNS THAT JESUS BRINGS LIFE THROUGH DEATH: 11:55—12:36

1. The Anointing of Jesus at Bethany by Mary

Two stories occur in this section, the anointing of Jesus by Mary at Bethany in 12:2-8, and the triumphal entry of Jesus into Jerusalem (12:12-15). The former is interpreted as pointing forward to the burial of Jesus. Jesus refuses to agree that the act of Mary in anointing him with very costly perfume was wasteful. To Judas, the treasurer of the company of the disciples, who had objected that the money would have been better given to the poor, he says:

Leave her alone. Let her keep it till the day when she prepares for my burial; for you have the poor among you always, but you will not always have me. (12:7)

The act of Mary is a sign that Jesus is to be buried.

2. The Triumphal Entry of Jesus to Jerusalem on an Ass

The other story, the triumphal entry, describing Jesus entering Jerusalem riding on an ass, ends with the words of the Pharisees in 12:19:

The Pharisees then said to one another, "You see that you can do nothing, the world has gone after him."

This event, then, is a sign that the Lordship of Jesus would be universally recognized. But before the final verse is given, John has made it clear that the one riding on an ass is followed by the crowds because he had raised Lazarus from the dead. It is as conqueror of death, through his readiness to risk his life, that Jesus is to be universally acknowledged.

3. Life Through Death

It is this thought, that Jesus' power comes through his death, which conquers death, that governs the rest of this section. First, as a seed of grain dies to reproduce itself, so it is the death of Jesus that creates or gathers together a world-wide community.

Among those who went up to worship at the festival were some Greeks. They came to Philip, who was from Bethsaida in Galilee, and said to him, "Sir, we should like to see Jesus." So Philip went and told Andrew, and the two of them went to tell Jesus. Then Jesus replied: "The hour has come for the Son of Man to be glorified. In truth, in very truth I tell you, a grain of wheat remains a solitary grain unless it falls into the ground and dies; but if it dies, it bears a rich harvest. The man who loves himself is lost, but he who hates himself in this world will be kept safe for eternal life. If anyone

serves me, he must follow me; where I am, my servant will be.
Whoever serves me will be honored by my Father."

The Greeks can only see Jesus because he died. And in the
following section, which in part corresponds to the scene at
Gethsemane in the Synoptics, it is made clear that the lifting
up of Jesus on the cross—that is, the hour of his shame—is the
hour of his glory; the cross is his crown. And through the
death on the cross—his lifting up, as John, using a play on
words, calls it—a power is at work which will eventually draw
all things to God in reconciliation. At last, the real meaning
of Christ's glory, or glorification—terms which have haunted
the Gospel right up to this point—is made clear; it is not what
men mean by glory—power, worldly success, fame; but the
exact opposite—self-giving to the bitter end of the cross. The
hour of his death is the hour of Christ. And this hour, in which
Jesus' glory appears, is the hour of the judgment of this world.

Now is the hour of judgment for this world. (12:31)

Judaism had placed the judgment of the world in the future.
Its accompaniments were clear—the victory of Israel over its
enemies; the condemnation of the Gentiles:

They all were looking for a King
To slay their foes and lift them high.

But the judgment, John declares, begins at the death of Jesus,
which, viewed from one side is the work of sinful men, but
viewed from another is God's act of glorification. The ultimate
"lifting up" is that of self-sacrifice. "The mark of the true glory,"
writes C. H. Dodd, "is precisely renunciation of personal security."

REVIEW OF THE SIGNS: THE DEATH OF JESUS THE REAL SIGN

The life of Jesus, as John has presented it in chapters 2-12,
consists, then, of a series of signs that he is the true life and
light of men, their judge and their Savior, the true expression
of the glory of God. The presentation of the signs culminates

in the death of Jesus as his glorification. To bring forth the significance of the culmination of the signs of Jesus in his death, it is necessary to ask what the relation is between the death and the signs.

Is the death to be understood as a sign like the signs that precede it? For example, is there any essential difference between the act of feeding the multitudes, as a sign that Jesus is the bread of life, and the act of dying on the cross? There is. The signs are pointers to what Jesus is. They refer beyond themselves to a truth about Jesus. What they signify exists in a reality outside them. The turning of water into wine illustrates the truth that with Jesus the old order of Judaism has passed into the new order of the Gospel. But the same truth could be illustrated in another way. The sign is not essential to the truth to which it points, but only illustrative. But the death of Jesus is not simply an illustration or a sign; it is an actual death. It illustrates the love of Christ, yes. But it also *is* the love of Christ in action; it is what it illustrates. In no other way than by actually dying—not illustrating death—could the love of Christ be finally demonstrated as *real*. Let us return to the Pope's tiara. The giving of the tiara to the poor as a sign is understandable. But—with all due reverence—it must be asserted that this "sign" does not carry the conviction of the self-imposed, actual, poverty of St. Francis of Assisi, in which sign and deed were one. So is it with the signs of Jesus as compared with his death. The signs point to the intent and potentiality of Jesus to be the bread of life and the light of the world, to the truth that he is these. But in the cross, the intent of Jesus has become deed; the reality signified in the signs is there made actual. The death of Jesus *is* that to which it points. It not only indicates the principle of self-giving; it is not only a symbol of self-sacrifice: it *is* self-giving. Consider the life of a home. The mother wears a golden ring as a sign of her marriage and of her status as mother in her home. But the ring in itself avails nothing. What draws a family to a mother is a life of self-giving, in which the meaning of the ring is lived out and a mother *is* what her ring signifies her to be. Where sign and life are one, the mother has potency to draw her children to herself. So is it with the death of Jesus; it *is* what the signs had pointed to. As *actual self-giving,* the death of Jesus possesses a reality that the signs do not possess. In it, the idea has become deed; the sign is *really* lived; and so "if I be lifted up, I will draw all men unto myself." Life and power come through the *actual* self-giving. Claims to Messiahship of all kinds are cheap; signs are cheap. But death is not cheap. And, because it costs, it is in the death that the glory is finally revealed. The cross—not as a symbol or an idea—but as an actual act of self-giving is, for John, the point where God's glory is actually seen. Not the sign, not the intent, but the deed is the manifestation of the glory. Drinkwater was right: men have need of the deed.

> We know the paths our feet
>   should press,
> Across our hearts are written
>   Thy decrees
> Yet now, O Lord, be merciful to
>   bless
> With more than these.
>
> Knowledge we ask not—knowledge
>   Thou hast lent,
> But, Lord, the will,—there lies
>   our bitter need,
> Give us to build above
>   the deep intent
> The deed, the deed.[2]

Or recall the yearning expressed by Byron for a world where there is no hypocrisy, no separation between word and act. His experience has taught him that "words are not things," or as John would put it, that not all "signs" are real or effective. These are his poignant lines at the end of the third Canto of *Childe Harold's Pilgrimage* (cxiv):

I have not loved the World, nor the World me—

---

2. John Drinkwater, "A Prayer" from *Collected Poems,* Vol. I (London: Sidgwick & Jackson, Ltd., 1923).

But let us part fair foes, I do believe,
Though I have found them not, that there may be
Words which are things—hopes which will not deceive,
And Virtues which are merciful, nor weave
Snares for the failing: I would also deem
O'er others' grief that some sincerely grieve;
That two, or one, are almost what they seem—
That goodness is no name, and happiness no dream.

For John, in Jesus of Nazareth, the Word is "a thing": Jesus not only gave signs of his intent; he actually died and so became the Lord of Glory. The instinct of Goethe was right when, in seeking to translate the first verse of the Gospel, ". . . In the beginning was the Word," he came to render it by: "In the beginning was the Act." The Word is Jesus as "act," and nowhere is he more "act" than in his death. The symbolism of the cross is bound up with the actuality of the cross; without the actuality the symbolism is trifling.

The Book of Signs is now complete. It is followed by a brief epilogue which sums up its main motifs in 12:37-50. And after this, John turns to a new, though of course intimately related, portion of his work. He has first made it clear that in all his acts Jesus has shown to the world the glory of God.

THE *EGŌ EIMI* ("I AM") PASSAGES
IN THE FOURTH GOSPEL

Raymond E. Brown

Johannine Usage

The Gr. *egō eimi*, "I am," can be simply a phrase of common speech, equivalent to "It is I" or "I am the one." However, it also has had a solemn and sacral use in the Old Testament, the New Testament, Gnosticism, and pagan Greek religious writings. Bultmann has classified four different uses of the formula: (a) *Präsentationsformel*, or an introduction, answering the question, "Who are you?" Thus, "I am Socrates"; or in Gen 17:1, "I am El Shaddai." (b) *Qualifikationsformel*, or as a description of the subject, answering the question, "What are you?" Thus, "I am a philosopher"; or in Ezek 28:2, the king of Tyre says, "I am a god." (c) *Identifikationsformel*, where the speaker identifies himself with another person or thing. Bultmann cites a saying of Isis, "I am all that has been, that is, and that will be." The predicate sums up the identity of the subject. (d) *Rekognitionsformel*, or a formula that separates the subject from others. It answers the question, "Who is the one who...?" with the response, "It is I." This is an instance in which the "I" is really a predicate.

Now keeping in mind this spectrum of usage, extending from the banal to the sacral, let us consider the use of *egō eimi* in John. Grammatically we may distinguish three types of use:

(1) The absolute use with no predicate:
   8:24: "Unless you come to believe that I AM, you will surely die in your sins."
   8:28: "When you lift up the Son of Man, then you will realize that I AM."
   8:58: "Before Abraham even came into existence, I AM."
   13:19: "When it does happen, you may believe that I AM."

There is a natural tendency to feel that these statements are incomplete; for instance, in 8:25 the Jews respond by asking, "Well, then, who are you?" Since this usage goes far beyond ordinary parlance, all recognize that the absolute *egō eimi* has a special revelatory function in John. According to Daube, T. W. Manson has proposed that the formula really means, "The Messiah is here." The meaning is suggested for Mark 13:6, Lk 21:8: "Many will come in my name, saying, I am"—here Mt 24:5 supplies a predicate, "I am the Messiah." However, there is not much in the context of the Johannine passages that would incline us to think that Jesus is speaking of messiahship. A more common explanation, as we shall see below, is to associate the Johannine use with *egō eimi* employed as a divine name in the Old Testament and rabbinic Judaism.

(2) The use where a predicate may be understood even though it is not expressed. 6:20: The disciples in the boat are frightened because they see someone coming to them in the water. Jesus assures them, "*Egō eimi;* do not be afraid." Here the expression may simply mean, "It is I, i.e., someone whom you know, and not a supernatural being or a ghost." We shall point out, however, that divine theophanies in the Old Testament often have this formula: Do not be afraid; I am the God of your ancestors. In 6:20 John may be giving an epiphany scene, playing on both the ordinary and sacral use of *egō eimi*. 18:5: The soldiers and police who have come to the garden across the Kidron to arrest Jesus announce that they are seeking Jesus, and Jesus answers, "*Egō eimi.*" This means, "I am he"; but the fact that those who hear it fall to the ground when he answers, suggests a form of theophany which leaves men prostrate in fear before God. Once again John seems to be playing on a twofold use of *egō eimi*.

(3) The use with a predicate nominative. In seven instances Jesus speaks of himself figuratively:

6:35, 51:	"I am the bread of life [living bread]."
8:12; 9:5:	"I am the light of the world."
10:7, 9:	"I am the [sheep]gate."
10:11, 14:	"I am the model shepherd."
11:25:	"I am the resurrection and the life."

14:6:   "I am the way, the truth, and the life."
15:1, 5:   "I am the [real] vine."

(On the borderline of this group of "I am" statements would be two others: 8:18, "I am one who gives testimony on my behalf"; and 8:23, "I am of what is above.") In discussing these "I am" statements in the light of the four possible formulas that are given above, Bultmann thinks that, as they now stand in the Gospel, five of the seven belong to his group (d). Accordingly, this means that Jesus is saying, "*I am* the bread, the shepherd, etc.," and this predicate is not true of some other person or thing. Zimmermann agrees that the use is exclusive; the accent is on the "I" and the predicate is only a development —thus, this type of "I am" sentence is related to the absolute use in (1). Those who think that the "I am" sentence with a predicate came from proto-Mandean sources hold that in the Gospel Jesus is contrasting his claim to be the bread, the shepherd, etc., with that of the claimants put forward by the proto-Mandeans.

A more obvious contrast is suggested by the Gospel context. "I am the bread" is found in a context where the crowd suggests that manna given by Moses was the bread from heaven (6:31). The statement at the feast of Tabernacles, "I am the light," was probably by way of contrast with the festal lights burning brightly in the court of the women at the Temple. The double claim, "I am the gate" and "I am the shepherd," was probably by way of contrast with the Pharisees mentioned at the end of chapter 9.

Bultmann thinks that two of the "I am" statements, 11:25 and 14:6, belong to group (c) of the "I am" formulas where the predicate identifies the subject. Thus, these statements are not primarily a contrast with another's claim to be the resurrection, the life, the way, and the truth. In our opinion, not only is this correct, but it is also probable that the five statements that Bultmann attributes to (d) have features that belong to (c) as well. The stress in all of these "I am" statements is not exclusively on the "I," for Jesus also wishes to give emphasis to the predicate which tells something of his role. The predicate is not an essential definition or description of Jesus in himself;

it is more a description of what he is in relation to man. In his mission Jesus is the source of eternal life for men ("vine," "life," "resurrection"); he is the means through whom men find life ("way," "gate"); he leads men to life ("shepherd"); he reveals to men the truth ("truth") which nourishes their life ("bread"). Thus, these predicates are not static titles of autodoxology but a revelation of the divine commitment involved in the Father's sending of the Son. Jesus is these things to men because he and the Father are one (10:30) and he possesses the life-giving power of the Father (5:21). Jesus' statement, "I am the truth, the light, . . ." must be related to similar statements about the Father's relation to men: "God is Spirit" (4:24); "God is light" (1 John 1:5); "God is love" (1 John 4:8, 16).

There are other indications that the predicate cannot be neglected in these statements. The discourses associated with the "I am" statements explain the predicate; this is clear in the explanations of the bread, the gate, the shepherd, and the vine. Moreover, there is much to be said for the parallelism that some scholars would establish between this class of "I am" statements and the Synoptic parables that begin with "The kingdom of heaven [God] is like. . . ."

Finally, it should be noted that there are "I am" statements with a nominal predicate in Revelation as well as in John. But, while in John the predicates are adaptations of Old Testament symbolism (bread, light, shepherd, and vine are all used symbolically in describing the relations of God to Israel), the predicates in Revelation are frequently taken directly from Old Testament passages. Note the following examples: Rv 1:8: "I am the Alpha and the Omega"; 1:17: "I am the first and the last, and the living one" (cf. Is 41:4, 44:6, 48:12); 2:23: "I am the one who searches mind and heart" (cf. Jr 11:20).

The Background of Johannine Usage

There are many pagan examples of a sacral use of "I am," e.g., in the Isis magical formulas, the Hermetic corpus, and the Mithraic liturgy. We have already mentioned the existence of Mandean parallels. Many scholars, like Norden and Wetter, have suggested that the background of the Johannine formula is found in such pagan religious usage—a usage which passed from the Oriental world into the Greek world. However, as Zimmermann has pointed out, it remains difficult to find pagan parallels to John's absolute use of *egō eimi*, a use which is the most important for understanding this formula in John. The magic texts that read simply "I am" are not examples of an absolute use, for a name is to be supplied by the user of the text. Of course, the question of the background of the Johannine *egō eimi* is but a small facet of the larger question of influences on the religious thought of the Fourth Gospel. The Gnostic and Hellenistic parallels for the "I am" formula are not so convincing as to change the general position that the most likely place to look for Johannine background is in Palestinian Judaism.

The Old Testament offers excellent examples of the use of "I am," including the only good examples of the absolute use. Zimmermann begins his study of the Old Testament formulas with a treatment of the passages containing the statement, "I am Yahweh," or "I am God," for the absolute use of "I am" is a variant of this statement. In Hebrew the statement contains simply the pronoun "I" (*'anī*) and the predicate "Yahweh" or "God" (*'ēl; 'elōhīm*), without a connecting verb LXX uses *egō kyrios, egō theos,* but sometimes supplies the connecting verb *eimi.* The statement has various uses. It may be used as God tells who and what He is, much in the manner of Bultmann's group (*a*) of the "I am" formulas (Gn 28:13; Ezk 20:5). These instances where God presents Himself to man are often designed to reassure man, and so may be accompanied with a directive not to fear (Gn 26:24). Another use of "I am Yahweh" occurs when God wishes to give a foundation for accepting His statement (Ex 6:6, 20:1, 5; Lv 18:6). The formula assures the hearer that what is stated has divine authority and comes from God. Thus, this use is revelatory in a limited way.

A use that is more closely associated with revelation is where God promises, "You shall know that I am Yahweh." This knowledge of Yahweh will be gained through what He does (Ex 6:7, 7:5). Many times what God does will help or save; other times it is God's punishing judgment that will cause men to know that He is the Lord. This Old Testament use offers interesting parallels for class (1) of the Johannine "I AM" statements.

There Jesus says men will come to know or believe that "I AM." In John 8:24 this is related to God's punishing judgment; in 8:28 it is related to the great salvific action of death, resurrection, and ascension.

The most important use of the Old Testament formula "I am Yahweh" stresses the unicity of God: I am Yahweh and there is no other. This use occurs six times in Deutero-Isaiah, as well as in Ho 13:4 and Joel 2:27. The Heb *'anī YHWH* in Is 45:18 is translated in LXX simply as *egō eimi*. In this use which stresses unicity a Hebrew alternate for *'anī YHWH hū* ("I [am] He"), and the latter expression is always translated in LXX as *egō eimi*. As the formula stands in the Hebrew text of Isaiah, it is clearly meant to stress that Yahweh is the only God. We pointed out in discussing the banal use of *egō eimi* that it normally means "I am he" or "I am the one," and so it is quite appropriate as a translation for *'anī hū*. Nevertheless, since the predicate "He" is not expressed in the Greek, there was a tendency in LXX for the formula to stress not only the unicity of God but also His existence. We see this same tendency at work in LXX translation of Ex 3:14, the all-important text for the meaning of "Yahweh." If we understand "Yahweh" as derived from a causative form, the Hebrew reads, "I am who cause to be," or perhaps more originally in the third person, "I am 'He who causes to be.'" But LXX reads, "I am the Existing One," using a participle of the verb "to be," and thus stressing divine existence.

There is even evidence that the use of *egō eimi* in LXX of Deutero-Isaiah came to be understood not only as a statement of divine unicity and existence, but also as a divine name. The Hebrew of Is 43:25 reads, "I, I am He who blots out transgressions." LXX translates the first part of this statement by using *egō eimi* twice. This can mean, "I am He, I am He who blots out transgressions"; it can also be interpreted, "I am 'I AM' who blots out transgressions," a translation making *egō eimi* a name. We have the same phenomenon in LXX of Is 51:12, "I am 'I AM' who comforts you." In Is 52:6 the parallelism suggests a similar interpretation: "My people shall know *my name;* in that day (they shall know) that I am He who speaks." LXX can be read, "that *egō eimi* is the one who speaks"; and thus *egō eimi* becomes the divine name to be known in the day of the Lord. Dodd, *Interpretation*, p. 94, cites rabbinic evidence from the 2nd century A.D. where the passage is taken to mean, "In that day they shall know that 'I AM' is speaking to them." Dodd gives other passages to show that not only the Greek form *egō eimi*, but also the Hebrew form *'anī hū* served as a divine name in the liturgy. A variant form *'anī wᵉhū*, "I and he," was also used, and Dodd thinks that it indicated the close association or quasi-identification of God and His people. Daube points out the stress on the formula "I am" in the Passover *Haggadah* where God is emphasizing that He and no other delivered Israel: "I and not an angel ... I and not a messenger; I Yahweh—this means, I AM and no other."

Against this background the absolute Johannine use of *egō eimi* becomes quite intelligible. Jesus is presented as speaking in the same manner in which Yahweh speaks in Deutero-Isaiah. In 8:28 Jesus promises that when the Son of Man is lifted up (in return to the Father), "then you will know that *egō eimi*." In Is 43:10 Yahweh says that He has chosen His servant Israel, "that you may know and believe me and understand that *egō eimi*." John draws attention to the implications of divinity in the use of *egō eimi* by Jesus. After the use in 8:58, the Jews try to stone Jesus; after the use in 18:5, those who hear it fall to the ground.

The use of "I AM" as a divine name in late Judaism may explain the many Johannine references to the divine name that Jesus bears. In his ministry Jesus made known and revealed the Father's name to his disciples (17:6, 26). He came in the Father's name (5:43) and did his works in the Father's name (10:25); indeed, he says that the Father has given him His name (17:11, 12). The hour that brings the glorification of Jesus means glorification of the Father's name (12:23, 28). After this hour has come, believers can ask for things in Jesus' name (14:13, 15:16, 16:23). In the name of the glorified Jesus the Father sends the Paraclete (14:26). The great sin is to refuse to believe in the name of God's only Son (3:18). What is this divine name that has been given to Jesus and that he glorifies through his death, resurrection, and ascension? In Acts and Paul (e.g., Ph 2:9) the name given to Jesus at which every knee should bend is the

name *kyrios* or "Lord"—the term used in LXX to translate "Yahweh" or "Adonai." While John too uses the title *kyrios* for
Jesus (20:28), it is quite possible that John thinks of *egō eimi*
as the divine name given to Jesus. If this name is to be glorified
through the hour of the death and resurrection, John 8:28 says,
"When you lift up the Son of Man, then you will know that
'I AM.'"

We have seen that the absolute use of "I am" in John is the
basis for other uses, in particular for the use in class (3) with
a nominal predicate. If the background of the use in class (1)
is the Old Testament and Palestinian Judaism, we may well
suspect the same for class (3). We have already mentioned
that most of the nominal predicates used in John are adaptations
of Old Testament symbolism. The Old Testament offers examples
where God uses the formula "I am" with a nominal predicate
descriptive of God's action on behalf of men, e.g., "I am your
salvation" (Ps 35:3); "I am the Lord, your healer" (Ex 15:26).
See also Old Testament parallels cited above for "I am" statements found in Revelation. Occasionally a verbal formula offers
a semantic parallel to a Johannine "I am" statement, e.g., "I kill
and make alive" (Dt 32:39) compared with John's "I am the
life." As further Old Testament background for Johannine usage
we may mention the first person discourses of Wisdom in
Proverbs and Sirach. Although Wisdom does not speak in the
"I am" formula, the habit of having Wisdom speak in an "I style"
(Pr 8:; Si 14:) may in part explain John's preference for having
Jesus say, "I am the vine," instead of "The kingdom of God is
like a vineyard."

The Synoptic Usage

Is the phrase "I am" on the lips of Jesus a Johannine creation,
or are there examples of this use in the Synoptic tradition as
well? We are interested primarily in the "I am" sayings without
a predicate.

There are three Synoptic passages where "I am" is used in
a way very similar to the examples we saw under class (2) of
Johannine usage, i.e., no predicate is expressed, although it may

be understood; and the evangelist seems to play on both a banal and a deeper use of *egō eimi.*

Mk 14:62; Lk 22:70: When Jesus is asked by the high priest if he is the Messiah, the son of the Blessed One, he answers, *"Egō eimi."* This may be simply an affirmative, "I am." Yet, his answer provokes the charge of blasphemy—a charge that would be more understandable if Jesus were claiming a divine name rather than simply affirming messiahship.

Mt 14:27 (Mk 6:50): As Jesus comes walking across the water, he says to the disciples in the boat, *"Egō eimi;* do not be afraid." This is the same use we saw in John 6:20. That Matthew intends more than a simple "It is I" is suggested by the profession of faith elicited from the disciples (Mt 14:33), "Truly, you are God's Son!"

Luke 24: 36 (some witnesses): After the resurrection Jesus appears to his disciples and says, *"Egō eimi;* do not be afraid." Once again this may simply mean, "It is I" (see 24:39); but the post-resurrectional context suggests a revelation of the Lordship of Jesus.

There is one example of an "I am" statement in the Synoptic Gospels which approaches close to the absolute Johannine usage of class (1). When speaking of the signs of the last days, Jesus warns, "Many will come in *my name,* saying *egō eimi"* (Mk 13:6; Lk 21:8). Some would supply a predicate, e.g., "I am he, i.e., Jesus or the Messiah." Mt 24:5 does supply a predicate, "I am the Messiah." However, the context does not clearly suggest the predicate; and the juxtaposition of *egō eimi* and "my name" does bring us very close to Johannine usage.

Thus, John's absolute use of "I am" in classes (1) and (2) may be an elaboration of a use of "I am" attributed to Jesus in the Synoptic tradition as well. Once again, rather than creating from nothing, Johannine theology may have capitalized on a valid theme of the early tradition. There are no explicit Synoptic parallels to class (3) of John's "I am" sayings, but this class is, as we have seen, a possible variation on the Synoptic parabolic theme.

References

Daube, D., "The 'I Am' of the Messianic Presence," *The New Testament and Rabbinic Judaism* (London: Athlone, 1956), pp. 325-29.

Zimmermann, H., "Das absolute *'Egō eimi'* als die neutestament-liche Offenbarungsformel," BZ 4 (1960), 54-69, 266-76.

JOHN'S THEOLOGY OF MAN AND THE WORLD

KARL SCHELKLE

In the Gospel of John and in the Epistles of John there are numerous declarations concerning the world (the *kosmos*), in which *world* signifies the *world of men*. The chief interest in such passages centers not so much on the world around man, but on man himself. Man is both central point and objective in the stylized and theologically concentrated history of creation as found in the prologue. The Creator Logos was and is the life and light of men (Jn 1:4, 9). The incarnate Word of God is full of grace and truth (Jn 1:14).

a) The excellences of the world (life, light, truth).

The Gospel of John speaks of life, light, and truth as the greatest goods of men. Since they are ever the object of man's yearnings, it is evident that man inclines to them and is concerned about them. The Gospel recognizes these longings and promises their fulfillment.

A first and very comprehensive good is life. It is for man a thing of great value always and everywhere; indeed, under normal conditions, the highest value of all. The men of the Bible, too, treasure life greatly. To the primitive man of the Old Testament life is the greatest good, plainly and simply. Occasionally the reward for keeping the commandments of God is long life; nor is anything more than long life promised: "Honor father and mother, so that you may live long and that it may be well with you in the land which God will give you as your own" (Dt 5:16; 16:20; 30:19). Life has reached its perfection and fullness, if it has been a long and successful one. And in any case, at death man but awaits a joyless and shadowy existence in the realm of the dead (Is 38:18).

In Scripture God is the source and Lord of life. He gave

man the breath of life (Gn 2:7). He is ever the fountain of life: "With you is the fountain of life. In your light we behold the light" (Ps 36:10). As the one who gave and does yet give life to all, God is plainly and simply "the living God" (Dt 5:26). The difference between God and man is that God possesses life in imperishable fullness and power, while man is mortal. Faith presumes to a hesitant hopefulness that God will even in death preserve the life of the pious; and this hope is stabilized through some centuries until it becomes the belief in the resurrection of the dead.

The New Testament continues the Old Testament theology of life. It pertains to God alone as a substantial possession. That is why he is called, as in the Old Testament, "the living God" (Mt 16:16; 2 Cor 6:16; 1 P 1:23). It were foolish and deceptive for a man to believe that he could do anything to secure his own life (Lk 12:5). The only real life is the future life in association with God. Man can obtain such life only as a gift from God. Man hopes that he will "inherit eternal life" (Mk 10:17). An inheritance is always an unearned gift. The New Testament has its message to tell, that the new life is promised and guaranteed to the faith in the raising up of Christ from the dead and in the now existing life of the one raised. Christ is the "ruler of life" (Ac 3:15). "May you live to God in Christ" (Rm 6:11; 14:9).

The Gospel of John also says this, and with even greater forcefulness. As Son of God, Christ is life. "In him was life, and the life was the light of men" (1:4). He has life not only as his own proper abundance of life which is his essence, but as the creative force which brings forth the life of all things. "All things were made by his Word" (1:3). He came "to give life to the world" (6:33). Christ himself says: "I am the resurrection and the life" (11:25). "I am the way, the truth, and the life" (14:6). Whoever is bound in faith to the dispenser of life receives this life: "Whoever believes in me shall have eternal life" (3:15). John's own is the emphatic assurance that possession of such life does not belong still to the future, to the beyond, but is a gift already in the present time. Whoever believes has "already passed over from death to life" (5:24). "Whoever believes will not die in eternity" (11:25 f.).

The promise of life is not a realization of a primitive avidity for life; for this life is a spiritual good. This life is knowledge of God and of his Son. "This is life, that they may know you, and him that you have sent" (17:3). To live is to abide in the love of God and of brother (15:9-17; 1 Jn 3:14 f.). This life shows itself in the confidence which overcomes every fear (1 Jn 4:18) and in the joy which banishes every sorrow (Jn 16: 20-22).

The promise of life is quite clear in the Gospel of John. The lengthy and detailed conversation with the Samaritan woman reveals Jesus as the one who is and who bestows the water of life (Jn 4:7-30). The long address after the multiplication of the loaves says of Jesus that he is the bread of heaven and the bread of life (Jn 6:26-59). The declaration is supplemented by the figure of Jesus as the true vine (Jn 15:1-9).

These declarations, in their basic mentality, are understandable to anyone. They play upon man's will to live. They proceed from the experience that life is sustained by nourishment, and that earthly nourishment has no lasting value. It is perishable, just as the life sustained by it is perishable. If man hungers and thirsts, he does not want ordinary bread and water; rather, he wants that which will give him life and will rescue him in the face of death. He wants living water and living bread. Man wants such nourishment as will produce eternal life. The report of such nourishment and the longing for it are ancient and widely disseminated. Man's musings on the fulfillment of his desire leads him to the conclusion that perhaps this wonderful nourishment is to be found on earth and in the present age; or that an eschatological meal first obtains for men and guarantees them that, philosophically considered, the spirit of man is itself, in the present time, nourished by the true and eternal, thus becoming immortal.

The Gospel of John responds to this longing, announcing Christ as its fulfillment. Whoever comes to him and believes in him will no longer hunger and thirst; and whoever believes in the Son has everlasting life (6:35, 40). Christ does not simply give the bread as a gift apart from himself, but the bread is himself (6:51).

The longing of man for life as such is not expressed in the

Bible alone. The New Testament promises especially the fulfillment of the Old Testament hope in respect to life. In the Gospel
of John the term *life* and the concept thereof are given an
emphatic urgency. In John the term occupies the place of such
concepts, central to the synoptic accounts, as the *kingdom of
God* and *salvation.* The Old Testament alone, however, is hardly
sufficient to account for this terminology. In the milieu of the
New Testament there is gnosticism, which seems to have used
a similar terminology. Here the divinity is often designated as
light and *life,* just as *light* and *life* can designate salvation.
Perhaps in this instance as also in others, the Gospel of John
has come to an understanding with the gnosis. This would
mean, then, that the Gospel recognizes in the gnosis an an-
imated concern for the question of life, and that it intends to
proclaim Christ as the genuine answer thereto.

Just as Christ is the life, so too he is the light of God
in the world. In the Old Testament the heavenly world is
God's light. He created the light and separated light and darkness (Gn 1:3 f.). The light is his gift. The light is his place.
"Glory and majesty is your raiment, you that clothe yourself in light
as with a garment" (Ps 104:1 f.). The light given by God is
the salvation of men. "God is my light and my salvation" (Ps
27:1). Absence of salvation is darkness. "The land is full of
dark places, the dwelling places of violent deeds" (Ps 74:20).

The Gospel of John says that the darkness in the world is
universal and deep, and that men are in danger of perishing
in it (Jn 1:5; 3:19). Still, there is no life without light. Light
so operates as to make things visible. The genuine light is first
of all the possibility of recognizing God, and with it, the possibility of man's recognizing himself. This light is, for each life,
the quality of being illuminated. Without light, life is dullness
and fear, indeed, the darkness of death. Light signifies also
the perception of other men, and thus it makes love possible.
Without light, life is calamity and fear, indeed, the darkness
of death.

Nevertheless, light is not plainly and simply among the natural capabilities of man; rather, it is a gift, and can only be
bestowed as divine light. The world was not only established

in the beginning of creation by the Logos (Jn 1:4), but this Logos remains always the light in the world. "He enlightens every man who comes into the world" (Jn 1:9). Everyone who believes comes out of the darkness into the light. With a mighty voice Christ says: "I am the light of the world. Whoever follows me does not wander in the darkness; rather, he will have the light of life" (Jn 12:46). The departure or loss of Christ were night for the world and darkness for men (Jn 8:12; 9:5). "He that walks in the darkness knows not whither he goes" (Jn 12:35). The darkness here spoken of has the same significance as death.

In view of the Johannine concept of light, exegesis asks also whether in employing the term the Gospel is perhaps influenced by the spiritual movements of its milieu. Here too reference to the Old Testament as the influencing agent is insufficient of explanation. The linguistic usage of John seems to be related to the religious linguistic usage of his period. For the ancient Greeks the light of the sun and of the day was a precious and divine gift which brightens the world and life. This original joy and confidence in the presence of the natural light later comes to a halt. Now the earthly light is reckoned as insufficient; indeed, it is no more than darkness. Man is moved by a longing for the true light, the light beyond.

This is especially emphasized in the gnosis. It teaches that the soul originates in the heavenly region of light and is banished to the darkness of earth. For the soul, earthly light is "dark light." Man seeks illumination, which will immediately procure life for him. In the *Corpus Hermeticum*, a collection of gnostic texts, the one sent from God says of himself: "I am the light." God's revelation is called "word of God," and "life and light." In other texts the revealer says: "I am the one sent from the light." And again: "The wicked are blind and see not. I call them to the light. And still they bury themselves in darkness." The Qumran texts employ a similar terminology; thus, in 1 QS 3:18-21, "In the region of light are the fountains of truth; but out of the wellspring of darkness come the generations of perversity. The children of righteousness walk in the way of light. ... The children of perversity walk in the way of darkness." Perhaps, then, the Gospel of John is intended to inform its own generation, whose language it speaks, of the advent of the true Light.

The Son of God and the Word of God are the truth which the world needs. The term *truth* is, in the New Testament, a word rich in signification. In the Greek version of the Old Testament the Greek term for *truth* usually stands as a translation of the Hebrew *'emeth*, a substantive related to *'amen* = *firm, valid*. *'Emeth* means the truth, in the sense of that which occurs and endures. It is often translated straightforward by *fidelity*. This is the truth which is an attribute of God. Thus, Ps 25:10 says: "all the ways of the Lord are mercy and truth (= mercy and fidelity)." Christ is "full of grace and truth" (John 1:14). The Christ of St. John's Gospel says of himself: "I am the way, the truth, and the life" (14:6).

Christ teaches not only the truth and imparts not only a right knowledge about God, but in him is revealed the reality of God himself. In him the reality of God is encountered as God's grace. The truth of which the Gospel of John speaks is not true knowledge and insight, such as man might have discovered on his own; rather, it is the revelation of God in Christ. Truth is not philosophy, but always theology.

Thus, the Gospel enjoins that God be worshipped "in spirit and in truth" (4:23). The saying is not to be interpreted according to that which philosophy and theology respectively understand by *spirit* and *truth*, but in accord with the meaning of the words in the New Testament and especially in the Gospel of John. Accordingly, then, spirit does not signify some internal, spiritual worship of God, in opposition, as it were, to the worship of God with material sacrificial gifts or with visible cult. Truth is not worship of God refined by philosophy. In the Gospel of John, spirit is the Holy Spirit of God. Truth is the reality of God revealed in Christ. Worship in Spirit and in Truth, then, is the service of God in union with Christ, who is Truth, and through the Spirit, whom God gives.

The biblical concept of truth becomes still more intelligible in contrast with the Greek concept. With the latter, truth = ἀλήθεια, means, in accord with its etymology, that which is not hidden, that which is known. For the Greek, truth is substantially the object of understanding; for the Bible, it is a thing of lasting existence. According to the Greek concept, a correct judgment is true. Things can be designated as true, insofar as they conform to a correct norm. Afterwards in the later Greek world of Hellenism, that which is always more readily perceived as truth is that which truly exists—therefore, the divine essence. Truth, then, pertains to the superterrestrial, divine region.

Contrariwise, the world of man is seen as a world which is the mere appearance of things waxing and waning, or, more sharply expressed, a deception and a lie. This viewpoint influences the Gospel of John. And again it seems that the gnostic literature is in a comparable position. In the latter it is said of the redeemer: "You showed us the way of life and allowed us to walk the paths of truth and faith. . . . You are the way of the perfect, the path which mounts up to the place of light. . . . You are truth without error."

Even in the texts from Qumran truth is found to be an important term. Man cannot by himself find the truth; it must be revealed by God. The elect are called "sons of truth" (1 QS 4:5 f.). God wants to purify the pious, "that all their ways may be in his truth" (1 QH 6:8 f,). This truth is not a truth of the intellect, but of performance: "Unjust conduct is an abomination to truth, and to injustice all the ways of truth are abomination" (1 QS 4:17). Exegesis, however, must reckon also with the possibility that the Gospel of John makes use of the terminology of its own time in order to be understood. If this be the case, the Gospel is seeking to announce that what its contemporaries search for is already there, as gift of God.

b) The perversion of the world to the wicked world.

Salvation is already present, even if it be hidden. In the future time of consummation its revelation and its fulfillment will take place. Nevertheless, it must ultimately be said of the present time, that it is a world of sin, of calamity, and of death. Just as John says of the world that it is wicked, he says the same still again about man, in whom this world is present.

The world had already rejected the Word of God, seeing that, as creator, he was always in the world (Jn 1:5); and now it has rejected him once more and conclusively, since he has become flesh. "He came unto his own. But his own received him not" (Jn 1:11). Thus does it become evident that the world is wicked. In its wickedness it refuses admittance to God's revelation (Jn 3:19). The word and concept *world* finally comes to have frequently for John the meaning *wicked world*, a meaning which is occasionally conveyed—just as with Paul (1 Cor 3:19; 5:10; 7:31; Ep 2:2)—simply by *this world* (Jn 8:23; 9:39; 12:25; 13:1).

Since the world did not accept the Son of God, it is deprived of the great benefits which are in Christ and which would have been given to it. Indeed, instead of benefits it has received the opposing world of death. The perversion is disastrous in every respect.

According to John (1:14; 14:6) Christ is the truth. If this truth is the reality of God, then the denial of God and of his reality is a lie. They who know not the Father are liars (Jn 8:55). The denial of the Father and of the Son is a lie (1 Jn 2:22). Whoever opposes this truth is found in a lie and consummates a lie.

If truth is light, then the oppositional factor to truth is darkness. The world of the lie is a world in darkness. "The light shines in the darkness, but the darkness has not comprehended it" (Jn 1:5). Darkness is not a primitive substance of the world, but a decision and sin peculiar thereto. "The light came into the world. But men loved the darkness more than the light. For their works were wicked" (Jn 3:19). Since men do not want to desist from their wicked works, they choose darkness for themselves, so that they will not have to recognize the wickedness of their deeds in the light. Man continues to make each new decision in accord with his wicked past, thereby gradually making his past conduct a perduring and definitively wicked nature. In everyone's case, John says, a critical decision is made.

The term must be twofold in meaning. A decisive separation does take place among men, but at the time of God's judgment. The present critical decision is certainly an anticipa-

tion of the coming judgment. Men would like to decide for
themselves by their own strength. Nevertheless, it is divine judgment that is carried out upon them. Living in darkness, men
are blind without even being aware of it. This becomes apparent
in the Johannine history of the man born blind (Jn 9:39-41;
1 Jn 2:11). To everyone, however, the call and the way out
of darkness into light remains always open, as the way of faith
(Jn 12:36). "I have come as light unto the world, so that whoever believes in me may not remain in darkness" (Jn 12:46).

The world lives in sin because it rejects the revelation of
God—indeed, because it hates Father and Son. Nor has the world
any excuse. "If I had not come and had not spoken to them,
they would have no sins. But now they have no pretext for
their sins" (Jn 15:22 f.). The primary sin of the world is disbelief. "The Spirit will convict the world of sin, because they
do not believe in me" (Jn 16:9). The present tense *because they
do not believe* expresses the continuing present. The disbelief
of the present generation is the form of the permanent disbelief of the world. The world stands accused in a great court
trial. The world's sin becomes evident in the face of the Spirit
who is in constant operation in the Church and therefore in
the world. Its disbelief is discovered.

With the knowledge of truth, freedom is promised. "The
truth shall make you free" (Jn 8:32). The rejection of truth for
the sake of disbelief thereupon becomes the reverse of freedom,
that is, servitude, viz., the servitude of sin. "Everyone who
commits sin is the slave of sin" (Jn 8:34).

Since it rejects Jesus, who is life, the world must fall victim
to death. If faith has gone over from death to life, then disbelief remains in death. To the Jews, as representatives of the
disbelieving world, it is stated that they will "die in their sins"
(Jn 8:21, 24).

The wicked world is evident, personified in Satan as the
"ruler of this world" (Jn 12:31; 14:30; 16:11; 1 Jn 4:4). On
the stage of the world, he is the great adversary of Christ.
The salvation work of Jesus is a struggle with Satan. Though
the struggle still continues, however, Satan is already conquered.
"*Now* is judgment pronounced on this world. *Now* is the prince

of this world cast out" (Jn 12:31). The wicked world is already overcome. "Take courage! I have overcome the world!" (Jn 16:33).

Of Christ himself the Gospel says that, unlike the rest of men, he is not of this world. "You are from below; I am from above. You are of this world, I am not of this world" (8:23). From up there, he says he has come into the world (3:19). Moreover, his kingdom is not of this world (18:36). It has its origin not in this world, nor is its manner that of this world.

As the Lord, so too are the disciples separated from the world. Certainly they take their origins in the world (Jn 17: 11 f.), and they must remain in the world (Jn 13:1; 15:18 f.). Nevertheless, Christ has chosen them "out of the world" (Jn 15:19). The Father gave them to him out of the world (Jn 17:6). By Christ were they sent into the world (Jn 17:8). In the world they must bear witness to the Son and to the Father (Jn 17:21, 23). Just as it was against Christ, so too will the world's hatred be directed against the disciples (Jn 15:18-20; 17:14; 1 Jn 3:13). In the world the disciples are lonely and alien. The world always takes offence at the congregation of the disciples; for the congregation calls into question the security of a world which is in submission to sin. For this reason the lot of the disciples in the world is affliction (Jn 16:33) and grief (Jn 16:20).

Nevertheless, in all this affliction the disciples make welcome the Spirit of Truth, whom the world cannot receive (Jn 14:17). The world cannot receive this Spirit, because he is contrary to its nature. It must challenge its own nature, in order to receive him. But then it would no longer be the world. The disciples receive peace, and indeed, the true peace, which the world cannot give (Jn 14:27). Nor is this merely the subjective voice of peace of heart; rather, this peace is really present there, where the world is safe in God's keep. This peace is the true existence, as the existence that is in the truth and love of God. The disciples must lay hold of this grace of God in order to have existence therein. Judgment on the world and the overcoming of the world took place previously in the salvational work of Christ. And thus will the disciples also conquer the world (Jn 17:18). Indeed, this victory is already won (1 Jn 5:4 f.).

The Gospel of John, in its own manner of conception, says that man is utterly lost; for, in and along with the wicked world (8:23; 14:17; 16:8), he is flesh; and flesh is in opposition to the Spirit (3:6). By natural human birth, man is born into a lost world. Only by a new birth can man enter into the kingdom of God (3:3). Also according to the Gospel of John, man is in constant confrontation with sin.

In John 8:44 the devil is called a "liar and murderer of men even from the very beginning." The Gospel is alluding thereby to the history of the fall, as in Gn 3. Sin and death reign in the world, factors which, as it appears, John refers back to the machinations of the devil, the "prince of this world" (Jn 12:31; 14:30; 16:11). Since, in the Johannine mentality, truth and life are the existence proper to man, if the devil is liar and murderer it means that the devil destroys man's capacity for existence. This is the condition of being, prior to every existence concretely present. The basic assertion is along the lines of what Paul says in Rm 5:12-19. Only the basis is not to be explained as the primitive sin of Adam, but as the work of the devil, so that John can yet be in accord with the apocalyptic expositions of the satanic forces as seducers to sin.

According to John, creation has been perverted into the wicked world. The world, however, is not wicked by its original nature. On the contrary, it first became such through the guilt of man, since, contrary to the Word of God, he refused and does yet refuse to have anything to do with light and life. Certainly John knows a deepseated dualism of God and world. But his dualism is not a dualism from the beginning onwards of two wicked principles, an essential dualism such as is accepted by so many religions; rather, the Johannine dualism is one which comes about historically through man's decision. It is an ethical dualism.

c) The salvation of the world

Lost though the world be, this saying remains ever valid:

"God loved the world so much that he gave up his only Son, so that each one who believes in him may not perish but may have eternal life. For God did not send his Son into the world in order to judge the world, but that the world might be saved through him" (Jn 3:16 f.). Ever valid is the word of Christ himself: "I have not come to judge the world but to save it" (Jn 12:47). The world has always the possibility of believing (Jn 17:21). Whoever believes in Christ as the Son of God will have life. For he believes in the love of God, which has sent the Son. Love always implies life. "God sent his Son into the world so that we may live through him" (1 Jn 4:9). "He has loved the world" (Jn 3:16); and therewith is portrayed the solitary event which is attestation of love.

Nevertheless, the surrendering of the Son is not merely a solitary and passing event; it is ever present. As the true light, Christ enlightens "every man who comes into the world" (Jn 1:9). Whoever believes in the revelation of God in the Son, believes in the love which God has for us (1 Jn 3:16; 4:9). The love of God is a lasting presence in Christ. The confession of faith, placed in the mouth of the Samaritan woman, is ever valid: "This is truly the savior of the world" (Jn 4:42; *likewise,* 1 Jn 4:14). This is valid for the present and for every period, since the title will be fully realized only in the future, and since universal salvation is conceivable only as definitive redemption at the end of time.

"Whoever believes in him is not judged" (Jn 3:18). Unbelief, closing itself off from the love of God, turns that love into judgment. "He that does not believe is already judged, because he has not believed in the name of the only Son of God" (Jn 3:18). Albeit God is love, still, the announcement of judgment is always part of the gospel. The "God who can do naught but love" is the God of the Enlightenment, not the God of the biblical message. As man's current and proper decision, the judgment is self-judgment. The future judgment is only the climactic ratification of the decision already precipitated by man himself. With that, the idea of judgment acquires utmost seriousness. The judgment is changed from a future event to a present one, and is changed from an external ordeal into an internal decision of personal responsibility. Nevertheless, the offer of salvation always remains.

John describes the realization of salvation in man with a conceptualization which harmonizes with that of the synoptics as well as with that of Paul. Just as with Paul and the synoptics, John describes man in the conflict of flesh and spirit. The existence which is worldly and world bound, is corporal; that, however, which is separated from the world, existence in faith, is spiritual. Flesh and spirit are man's two capacities.

However, man cannot seize upon these two possibilities and choose arbitrarily between them. The new, true, spiritual life can only come from God as a new creation. "Whoever is not born again of the water and the spirit cannot enter into the kingdom of God" (Jn 3:5). The Gospel speaks of the sacrament of baptism. The sacrament imparts the Spirit; but also it must be received in the spirit, i.e., in faith. Otherwise it is only an external rite, only "flesh." This is true not only for the sacrament of baptism but also for the Eucharistic banquet. Certainly in the banquet the Bread of Life is offered and given to the world (Jn 6:33). But in the course of the discourse on the Bread, Christ says: "It is the Spirit that gives life; the flesh is of no avail" (Jn 6:63).

Along with Paul, the Synoptics too speak of the restoration of men to their status as children of God, with apparent reference to the declaration of creation history in regard to man's being in the image of God. John says much the same thing: that the Logos "gave to them who received him the power of becoming children of God" (Jn 1:12). "We are now the children of God, and it has not yet become apparent what we shall be" (1 Jn 3:2).

Like Paul, John too says that justification by faith must not be misunderstood in such wise that man were liberated by his own doing. God's gift frees man, giving him a capability of moral behavior and obliging him thereto. According to Paul, faith is genuine only when it is operative in charity (Gal 5:6). Faith in Christ as the light is genuine only if it is accompanied by conduct which can stand being tested in the light. "If we say that we have fellowship with him, and walk in the darkness, we lie and are not practicing the truth" (1 Jn 1:6). "He that says he is in the light, and hates his brother, is in the darkness still" (1 Jn 2:9). The new Spirit confirms the disciples. He is not a Spirit of extraordinary and miraculous events, but of the everyday occurrences of Christian living. "The fruit of the Spirit is love, joy, peace, patience, kindness, goodness, fidelity, gentleness and sobriety" (Gal 5:22 f.). The Gospel of John says similarly: "Whoever has received my commandments and keeps them, he it is that loves me" (Jn 15:10; 1 Jn 3:24).

When the Gospel of John speaks of the world lost in sin, it says that man is of himself unable to be justified in the sight of God, and therefore unable to bridge the gap between himself and God. Left to his own natural abilities, man remains ever in disbelief and in death. The statement, therefore, is applicable to every man: "If we say that we have no sin, we deceive ourselves, and the truth is not in us. If we acknowledge our sins, then he is faithful and just to forgive us our sins" (1 Jn 1:8 f.). Paul says the same thing when, in Rm 1: 18–3:20, he points out, in respect to both parts of mankind, Jew as well as Gentile, that "none is just, not a single one." By his own works no man is justified before God, but only "by his grace, given as a gift" (Rm 3:24).

MAN'S PARTICIPATION IN GOD'S LIFE:
A KEY CONCEPT IN JOHN

ANDRE FEUILLET

Origin and Meaning of the Concept

We need hardly emphasize here our conviction that the author of the fourth Gospel teaches that Christians enjoy a share in the very life of God. Some exegetes, however, have refused to acknowledge any mystical meaning whatever in Johannine thought. Bultmann, for example, would have in John no more than a "radicalizing" of traditional eschatology, whereby the fourth Gospel gives a "radical value" to the truth that the coming of Christ as Revealer is the decisive eschatological event, the *Krisis*. However, the text itself belies such impoverishment of Johannine theology. As a matter of fact, the text is so clear that most authors see it as distinctively mystical.[1]

The problems which we propose to treat here, however briefly, is how we should understand this lofty teaching, and what is its source. Both questions, that of the source and that of interpretation, are, obviously, inseparable.

1. Johannine Mysticism and Hellenistic Mysticism

Some authors see in this Johannine idea of the sharing by Christians of the very life of God, a more or less exact reflection of hellenistic mysticism. Fewer, however, would accept completely the views developed by A. Schweitzer in his famous book on the mysticism of St. Paul; more popular is the idea that John's doctrine has been influenced by the Greek world.

---

1. Although there are many definitions of mysticism, we prefer the following: the believer's present enjoyment of blessings which are properly divine, and which are to be the lot of the elect in the happiness of heaven.

We will propose two examples. The first is the already long-established thesis of J. Lindblom on eternal life, which holds that life, which in the Synoptics, the Acts and the Apocalypse, is essentially eschatological, is in John's Gospel rather close to the physico-metaphysical concepts of the Greeks, without, however, sacrificing the essence of Jesus' message. The second example is in C. H. Dodd's excellent work on the interpretation of the fourth Gospel. Dodd's erudition and prudence, as well as his deep religious sense, have won the admiration of many. The eminent professor of Cambridge recognizes that Johannine thought owes much to the Bible itself, and to the rabbinical tradition. He sees in it, furthermore, no little influence of the hellenistic milieu in which it was produced. Unlike Bultmann, he discounts any influence of the Mandean texts upon John's Gospel, but he does recognize traces of a relationship to Philo and to the hermetic literature.

When Jesus says, "He who believes in me, even if he die, shall live" (11:25), he treats of an atemporal concept, eternal life, having neither past nor future, lived in the endless present, apart from the action of death, an idea which recalls the thoughts of Plato and of Philo. John unites closely eternal life and knowledge (e.g., "Now this is everlasting life, that they may know thee" 17:3). The mysticism of such hellenists as Philo or the hermetics also holds that knowledge deifies man, making him a child of God, and God himself. Dodd concludes that John's thought combines elements of both Hebrew and hellenistic traditions, making of them an entirely new and original synthesis.

We are of the opinion that there is merit in the idea that the author of the fourth Gospel tried to adapt the Christian message somehow to the Greeks, showing them in this message the fulfillment of their own legitimate religious aspirations. For example, John stresses forcefully that Jesus is the only Revealer, because He alone has seen the Father. One might be inclined to think that he says this thinking of hellenism, in which mysteries, gnosis, and also philosophy, pretend to lead men to the knowledge and even the vision of God. Bultmann says that John deliberately uses these terms, which he knows to be current among the Greeks, and gives them an entirely new meaning.

Still, the deeply Semitic and biblical foundations of Johannine thought recommend caution in making such an affirmation. Furthermore, as Mollat says, even within Judaism itself there was a school of thought, recently brought to light by the Dead Sea scrolls, which attributed great importance to knowledge (*gnōsis*), and which used a gnostic vocabulary. It is not impossible that this may be the only way, however indirect, in which John was subject to Greek influence. Further research may lead to considerable enlightenment on these questions.

In any case, we must maintain that John's mysticism, like that of Paul, cannot at all be reduced to that of the hellenists, and that in speaking of hellenistic mysticism, we have in mind the contemplation of God in ecstasy, as in the hermetic texts, or the vision of God which comes from the celebration of the mysteries. In either case the result is a substantial union with God, the deification of man, and all this without any need of moral effort! The salvation thus given and obtained is merely a liberation from matter, and sometimes from fate.

John's mysticism is obviously different from this outlook—even opposite to it. It is not man who decides to go to God, by the practice of certain rites or intellectual exercises; but it is God, whom no man has seen, who, at a determined time of human history, introduces Himself to the Greek world, through Jesus, His incarnate Son. Everything comes back to God's free love for men. The Greeks had no knowledge of such a love.

Furthermore, the great obstacle to man's union with God, which Jesus wishes to remove, is not matter, or fate, but sin. Nor is this union with God a divinization. John's mysticism differs from the hellenistic concept of man's being identified with God ("Thou art I; I am thou"); John is always most careful to maintain the measureless abyss which separates man from God, even in the passages which teach the mutual indwelling of Christ and Christians. The same Christ who says, "He who eats my flesh and drinks my blood abides in me and I in him," distinguishes Himself clearly from his own disciples, saying, "I will raise him up on the last day" (Jn 6:55-56). Although man may have some experience of the divine, he can never enjoy on earth the perfect vision of God; he is always

144 A COMPANION TO JOHN

oriented toward the Parousia, which the coming of the Paraclete to men's souls can prepare, but never replace. It is interesting that the words *athanasia* and *aphtharsia*, which are rather common in St. Paul, are entirely absent from the Johannine writings. John never substitutes the Greek notion of immortality for the radically biblical notion of eschatology.

Bultmann himself admits that John has not suppressed Christian eschatology, but he holds that John had "radicalized" it, making of its various manifestations (death, judgment, resurrection, entry into eternal life) so many actual events, occurring at the moment in which Jesus speaks, or at the moment in which men take a position by faith or unbelief, for or against Jesus.

It seems that, in a way, there may be some merit in this interpretation of John's Gospel; the writer is fully aware of the drama which unfolds continually in the history of men's hearts. However, to recognize what has been called the "actuality" of the fourth Gospel is not at all to suppress its properly eschatological dimension, as Bultmann does. The Master of Marburg can sustain his thesis only by eliminating a number of texts from the fourth Gospel and from 1 John on the second coming of Christ and on the resurrection of the last day,[2] a dissection hardly justified.

John maintains the traditional eschatological perspective, which can be harmonized with the mystical perspective. The Christian now shares really, although imperfectly, in the life of God, but he will share it fully only at the Parousia. Already in the Old Testament, especially in the psalms, there is a real mysticism united to some eschatological and apocalyptic aspirations. Those who keep such Old Testament texts in mind will find little difficulty in reconciling these two tendencies of the fourth Gospel. They would, it is true, be contradictory, if Johannine mysticism were essentially Greek, but, as we have seen, it is fundamentally biblical, notwithstanding some possible borrowings from hellenism.

---

2. These texts are: 5:28-29; 6:51b-56; 6:39, 40, 44; 12:48; and 1 John 2:28; 3:2; 4:17.

2. Johannine Mysticism and the Synoptic Gospels

We have yet to face what seems to us to be the most important question, i.e., if it is true that the Christ of the fourth Gospel teaches that His disciples share (now) in the life of God (which we consider beyond question), how do we explain the apparent absence of such a lofty doctrine from the Synoptics? Is it really a teaching of the historical Jesus? Or would it not be better to admit rather that the doctrine thus attributed to Jesus in the fourth Gospel is pure fiction, unrelated to the real doctrine which Jesus gave to men? The answers to these questions are obviously beyond the scope of this limited treatment. We shall limit ourselves therefore to the essential points.

Certainly the idea of life has a greater place in John than in the Synoptics. Also, in the Synoptics it is almost always eschatological, referring to the new manner of being which will come about either at the Parousia and general judgment, or, in some texts, at the death of the individual. There are only a few rare passages (e.g., Lk 15:32; perhaps also Mt 4:4; Lk 4:4) in which the words "life" and "live" might be said to refer to a spiritual life on earth. Yet, how different it is in John! Whereas in the Synoptics the proclamation of the Kingdom is the basic theme of Jesus' preaching, in John it occurs only once or twice, (3:3-5 and perhaps 18:36), being replaced by that of life. We think that the first element of a solution to this problem is to be found precisely in the relationship which exists between these two themes.

In the Synoptics the Kingdom is a purely eschatological thing; Jesus' thought, however, is not as simple as some partisans of consequent eschatology would have it. Although in some passages, the Kingdom is a thing of the future, still, many of these texts, especially the parables of the Kingdom, presuppose that Jesus has already laid the foundation of this Kingdom. If this Kingdom is to be first of all a dynamic reality, the decisive intervention of God in human history, of which the prophets spoke, then, thanks to the coming of Jesus to earth, to His teaching, His healings and to His driving out of devils, this supreme intervention has already begun. When Jesus forgives sins, heals the sick, raises the dead, sin is conquered as are death and sickness, which entered the world together. Jesus establishes a close link between His miracles and the establishment of the kingdom. Still more profoundly, Jesus brings us the Kingdom of God; because He is uniquely the Son of God, perfectly subject to the Father. He is Himself the Kingdom of God (*autobasileia*), according to the beautiful expression of Origen. This explains why the choice which Jesus offers for or against the kingdom is a choice for or against His person; those who become His followers, enter the kingdom thereby.

Thus, the idea of (present) access to divine life is not as removed from the Synoptics as may seem at first glance. The Synoptics themselves equate "enter into the Kingdom" and "enter into eternal life" (Mk 9:43; 10:17; Mt 18:3; 19:17; Lk 18:29-30). Doubtless they mean here only the final kingdom, but since there is a certain anticipation of the entry into the kingdom, beginning with the moment in which one makes himself a follower of Jesus, a parallel anticipation of entry into life can be presumed to be part of the logic of the Christ of the Synoptics.

We think we could go further and say that, in fact, the Christ of the Synoptics promises, as does the Christ of John, access to the eschatological blessings from the moment in which one consents to follow Him. After all, the Kingdom of God is linked to the salvific blessings (pardon of sin, divine worship) which men enjoy on earth. The chief reason for our affirmative opinion here is the so-called Johannine logion, as it appears in Mt 11:25-30 and Lk 10:21-22. Although some have arbitrarily thrown doubt on the authenticity of this passage, because of its apparent relationship to hellenistic mysticism, Jesus presents Himself as the great Messiah of Daniel, possessed of sovereignty over the future. Far from expressing a secret teaching such as a manifestation of divine blessings in a *gnōsis*, the phrase *panta moi paredothē* has the very same meaning as the *edothē autō exousia* of Daniel, referring to the Son of Man who has been given power over all the nations of the earth. However, this dependence on Daniel is not the most essential characteristic of this declaration. The more important thing, and which has not been sufficiently emphasized, is that the structure of Mt 11:25-30 is based on that of the great sapiential texts of the Old Testament, in which the invitation to join the ranks of the followers of divine Wisdom ("Come to me"; "Listen to me") appears as the direct result of her prerogatives. Just as divine Wisdom foregoes, in a way, titles of nobility, in order to draw more to follow her teachings, so too Jesus emphasizes His special ineffable intimacy with the Father in order to draw His hearers to become disciples. This is no mere servile literary imitation devised by Christian writers, placing in Jesus' mouth words taken from the Old Testament. Rather, we are well within the realm of inspiration; Jesus knows that He is the Son, and to express His relationship with the Father, and His mission of teaching humanity, He invokes quite naturally the Old Testament passages which describe Wisdom's intimate relationship to God and her role among men.

Thus, when Jesus invites those who labor and are heavily burdened to come to Him and find their rest, the rest of which He speaks is that of the eschatological oracles of the Old Testament.[3] Still, He promises it to them as a good to be enjoyed now, provided only that they attach themselves to His person. He can give rest and He can give life, as can Wisdom; He uses the same phraseology as Wisdom; He is the supreme source of these blessings. In the Old Testament, divine Wisdom, which is not the Messiah but which has the role of the Messiah, has as an essential characteristic the actualizing of the eschatological blessings, because these blessings, and especially life, come forth in some way from its very being. By the same token, Jesus, by the simple fact of His presence among men, actualizes the blessings inherent in the final Kingdom of God.

Although the Johannine logion does not mention the gift of life explicitly, the rest which it promises would be illusory without it. This logion is related to many passages of the fourth

---

3. The phrase "you will find rest for your souls" is taken from Jr 6:16.

Gospel in which Jesus gives to those who cling to His Word a hope of finding in Him light and life. K. Kundsin[4] has shown that the revelation discourses of John's Christ are structurally distinct from all the suggested parallels found in the oriental religions. Rather than seeking only the glory of the Revealer by heaping Him with titles of honor, the phrases, and other similar texts of the fourth gospel, are essentially designed to serve as a basis for the promises of salvation. This is why they are usually followed by a secondary proposition indicating the condition on which the believer may have access to salvation, light and life (cf. 6:35, 51; 8:12; 10:9; 11:25; 15:5; 18:37 ...). This is precisely the structure, not only of the great Old Testament texts on Wisdom, but also of many declarations by the Christ of the Synoptics relative to His person (Mk 6:50; 14:62 and parallel texts), especially of the famous Johannine logion, particularly as it is reproduced in Mt 11:25-30. These are all so many reasons why the language which John attributes to Jesus, and the mysticism which He expresses, are more than a pure creation of the evangelist.

All in all, the Synoptics make a different arrangement of Jesus' teachings from that of the fourth Gospel. John has much from the eschatological point of view; he has none of the apocalyptic genre found in the Synoptics, none of the coming of the Son of Man on the clouds of heaven, no scene of the tribunal of the last judgment. We might speak of a partial actualization of eternal life, as of the manifestation of Jesus' glory, of salvation and of judgment.

Some explain this difference in doctrine between John and the Synoptics by saying that in the Synoptics Jesus speaks to the mass of the people, whereas in John He moves among the more cultured element of the Sanhedrin, and the Doctors. This is partly true. At the end of his fine discourse on "The gospel tradition and its beginnings", H. Riesenfeld shows in John's Gospel a tradition which, like that of the Synoptics, begins in the life and activity of Jesus; but here, he adds, (in John) is a treatment especially of discourses and meditations which

---

4. *Charakter und Ursprung der johanneischen Reden*, in *Acta Universitatis Lativiensis*, Theologijas Fakultates, Serija, I, 4, Riga, 1939, pp. 185-303.

Jesus made within the limited circle of His disciples. Some have said also that the Synoptics and John present two different aspects of the teaching which the Christian community offered about Jesus. E. Levesque[5] speaks of a basic catechesis, showing that Jesus is the Envoy of God, without insisting on His divine nature, and which the Synoptics follow. The fourth Gospel, on the other hand, reflects a loftier teaching about Christ, concerned principally with His person, a teaching which has some traces in the Synoptics (cf., e. gr., Mk 12:35-37 and parallels; 11:25 ff. and parallels; Mt 16: 13-20 and parallels). The actualization of divine life is thus linked, as we have seen, to this placing in relief of the real divinity of Jesus.

We feel that this comparison is deceiving. The fourth Gospel also has long discourses addressed to simple people: the conversation with the Samaritan woman (4:7-26), the Discourse on the Bread of Life (6), or on Christ's saving death (12:23-36). These teachings are just as profound as those addressed to the more polished audiences. What is more, the Baptist speaks like Jesus (cf. 1:29-31; 3:27-30); so does the evangelist in the prologue and in those passages which seem to be his own personal reflections (3:14-21; 31-36). It is significant that there is a direct transition here from the words of Jesus to those of the Evangelist. The first Epistle of St. John has the same literary and theological characteristics as Jesus' discourses in the fourth Gospel. From these observations we conclude that, at least with regard to the teaching on the gift of eternal life, John has given to Jesus his own manner of expression, whereas the Synoptics have preserved Jesus' words more literally, in their original form.

This does not mean, however, that John became so absorbed in metaphysics as to be indifferent to the facts of his account, or to attribute to Jesus his own personal speculations. Rather, he attached such great importance to the historical period of the activity of the Son of God on earth that he meditated continually on His words and deeds, thereby understanding their real meaning better than the Synoptics who had written before him. He proposed to present not so much the material form of

---

5. *Nos quatre évangiles*, Paris, 1917, pp. 206-212.

Jesus' words as their profound meaning. Profiting from the light which he received from the life of the Church over a period of several decades, and from his own mystical experience, he determined to be a faithful translator of the most intimate thoughts of Jesus, inaugurator on earth of the Kingdom of God by the sole fact of His presence among men, who, precisely because He is the Son, is also for His disciples the source of divine blessings.

St. Paul had shown the Christians the importance of their being associated with the risen Christ, thus being themselves sons of God, dependent upon the Son, *filii in Filio*. He had taught them their right to address God as Jesus did, as *Abba, Father* (Gal 4:6; Rm 8:15; cf. Mk 14:36, and parallel texts; Mt 11:25-26 and parallels; Lk 23:34, 46; Jn 11:11; 12:27-28; 17:1, 5, 11, 21, 24, 25). Such a formula had been unknown to the Jews as prayer, being used only by children referring to their earthly father. The fourth Gospel presents a similar phenomenon, equally moving and even more significant as regards the sharing of God's life. The statements of John's Christ, about His relationship to the Father, are far distant from the deductions of theologians on the mutual relations of the Persons of the Trinity. Given always the historical fact of the Incarnation, they are full of deep humility. For example, when Jesus says, "The son can do nothing of himself, but only what he sees the Father doing", and "of myself I can do nothing. As I hear, I judge", this impossibility is obviously on the human moral level. Jesus is constantly aware of what the Father has done; His whole human intelligence and will serve only to render the most perfect homage to the Father. But, as the context shows, this moral limitation, whereby Jesus cannot act without the Father, is merely a continuation of the Son's absolute inability to act outside the Father in the Trinity.

We see this dependence in equality of the Son upon the Father, shown in a human way in Jesus, so that His disciples may take Him as their model, receiving divine life from Him and living themselves as true Sons of God. "He gave them the power to become Sons of God" (1:12).

Thus the fourth Gospel does more than affirm that Christians now share in God's own life. Following St. Paul, and in an even better manner than he, John shows us in Jesus dwelling on earth, a sort of existential definition of the condition of those who are Sons of God. Living the life of God, they must also have their eyes always on the Father, with no concern for the glory that comes from men (5:44; 12:43), thinking only of the Father's glory, as Jesus did (cf. 5:41; 7:18; 8:50). The ideal would be never to do anything of themselves which would be outside the limit of this filial dependence.

Exegetes find in the fourth Gospel problems which are both exciting and difficult. It seems more oriented toward the Greek world than any other New Testament writing, yet its doctrine is authentically biblical. The author marks out his own path, different from that of the Synoptics, with no apparent desire to make his account match theirs. What is more, he attributes to Christ a new kind of language. Yet, the basic trends of the fourth Gospel are closely allied to those of the Synoptics, as we have tried to show, using the idea of life as an example.

THE JOHANNINE RELATIONSHIP OF LOVE TO FAITH

THOMAS BARROSSE

To attempt a synthesis of Johannine teaching is to undertake a formidable task. The fourth evangelist does not develop his thoughts by direct univocal statements, but through a series of repetitions gradually reveals the spiritual depths of now one, now another of his ideas, at times altering the meaning of terms in the process.[1] It is a difficult task to organize thoughts developed in this way into a completely satisfactory synthesis.

If this holds true for John's teaching on many points, it is especially true of his teaching on love, to the development of which he devotes a large part of his writings. Already in his account of the public ministry (Jn 1-12) he points out the all-important role love plays in the relations between the Father and Son and between God and man. In his account of the last discourse (Jn 13-17) he sets about explaining this role. Finally, in his first epistle, in which in four short chapters the verb *agapaō* and its derivatives *agapē* and *agapētos* recur more frequently than in any other book of the New Testament, he completes his explanation by revealing the full depths of love's meaning.[2]

---

1. A good example of this gradual exposition of a notion is John's presentation of Christ as the life. Men have life through Christ: Jn 3:15 (cf. 1 Jn 4:9); Christ has life within Himself to give to men: Jn 5:25 f.; 6:33 ff.; He gives it to those who unite themselves vitally to Him by eating His flesh: Jn 6:47-59; He *is* the life which He gives: Jn 11:25 f.; 14:6 (cf. 17:3; 1 Jn 1:2; 5:11 f., 20). For Christ as the truth see Jn 1:17 (the truth comes through Him); 14:6 (He is the truth). Perhaps the best example of all is John's presentation of Christ as the bread of life in Jn 6.

2. Whatever may be said about the inferiority of 1 John as compared with the fourth Gospel, the epistle certainly presents a more evolved and explicit doctrine on love (at least on fraternal love) than the Gospel does— a definite advance, therefore, over the Gospel. The majority of scholars,

Since the three sections of John's writings just named form more or less distinct units with distinct dominant ideas, probably the simplest and most satisfactory way to study the Johannine notion of love is to examine the pertinent texts of each section in connection with the important idea of that section. In fact, John himself links the gradual unfolding of his notion of love to the development of these great ideas. In the first twelve chapters of his Gospel he discusses faith in great detail and love especially in its relation to faith. In his account of the last discourse he speaks in particular of the union of Christ's disciples with their Master and with God. In his first epistle he stresses the relations of Christians with one another. The present study will be restricted to the first of these problems: the relation of love to faith.

The very first passage in which the fourth Gospel mentions love treats of it in relation to faith. In fact, faith is nothing more than a response to love—man's response to God's love. Besides, a certain type of love accompanies faith, and another type of love stands in opposition to it. In order to understand these various types of love, we must understand the faith with which they are so intimately related.

Johannine Faith

John's account of the public ministry (Jn 1-12) and a few verses of his first epistle give the entire doctrine of the Beloved Disciple on faith. The texts are abundant and clear. As for the abundance of the texts, in the first twelve chapters of his Gospel John uses the verb *pisteuō* more often than any other New Testament writer, Paul included (though the noun *pistis,* Paul's preference, does not occur).[3] As for the clarity of the texts, a glance at only a few of them shows the meaning of Johannine faith.

We find first of all, of course, the ordinary, untechnical sense

---

especially those that deny that the two writings have the same author, consider the epistle posterior to the Gospel and note that it recalls and develops ideas already presented in the earlier document.

3. The Johannine writings (excluding the Book of Revelation) contain the noun only once: 1 Jn 5:4.

of the verb "to believe" in John's writings: to accept on another's authority a statement which he makes. Thus, the Jews would not "believe" the man healed by Christ when he told them that he had been born blind and had been cured: they would not accept the man's word but called for his parents (Jn 9:18 f.; cf. v. 15).

The usual formula for Christian faith (the disciples' faith) is "to believe *in*" (Gk. *eis*) Christ. By believing in Christ a man becomes His disciple. Only by believing in Him can a man have the eternal life that goes to His disciples (Jn 6:29, 40). The various passages in which the expression occurs reveal the full meaning of this faith in Christ.

They show that it is, like ordinary faith, the acceptance of truth—but a truth about Christ: His identity. In Jn 6:69 Peter declares faith the reason why the Twelve have become followers of Christ and explains their faith as faith in His identity: "We have believed . . . that you are the Holy One of God." In Jn 11:27 Martha points out that she is ready to accept whatever Christ may demand—in other words, that she is completely at His disposal—because of her faith in His identity: "I have believed that you are the Christ, the Son of God come into the world." In the same passage (42 ff.) Christ tells His Father that He raises Lazarus in order to lead the Jews to faith—the saving faith that would make them disciples—and this is faith in His identity as God's envoy: "That they may believe that you have sent me." In Jn 17 Christ prays for His actual disciples (those who have already believed; v. 8) and for future disciples (those who will later believe; v.20), expressing His desire that the world itself may be converted and believe (21, 23). Throughout the passage the object of this faith which makes disciples is everywhere the truth of Christ's claim to be God's envoy: "That you [Father] have sent me." Christian faith, then, means accepting Jesus for what He is, i.e., as the Christ, and this means the Son of God sent or come into the world.

Now the Son of God is God's own image. By entering into the world of men in human form, He automatically becomes God's revelation of Himself to men, the revelation of the transcendent God whom no one has at any time seen (Jn 1:18). "He who has seen me has seen the Father," He says to His

apostles. "How can you say, 'Show us the Father'?" (Jn 14:9).
To accept or to reject God's revelation of Himself means to
accept or to reject God: "He who denies the Son does not
have the Father either; he who confesses the Son has the Father
too" (1 Jn 2:23; cf. 5:10-12). Christian faith, therefore, means
accepting Jesus as God's revelation of Himself to men.

Christ, of course, does not come simply to reveal God to
men's minds, i.e., to impart mere speculative knowledge about
God through His teachings or to give men through His own
behavior some idea of what God must be like. He comes to
reveal God's inner life to men by offering them an experience
of it or a share in it. Men are to come to know the mysteries
of God's life through a practical, first-hand experiencing of
them. If faith means fully accepting Christ for what He is,
it obviously cannot consist in mere intellectual recognition of
Him as Savior, i.e., in mere intellectual assent to the truth
that Jesus of Nazareth is the Son of God come into the world
or the Word made flesh. It must also mean practically accepting
Him as God's offer of Himself to mankind. Only when we
take faith in this full sense can we understand how John can
consider the consequence of faith in Christ to be intimacy
with God (koinōnia in 1 Jn 1:3; knowledge, in the Semitic
sense of intimacy or experience, in Jn 17:3), sharing in God's
life, or becoming God's child. "These things are written that
you may believe that Jesus is the Christ, the Son of God, and
that through faith (pisteuontes) you may have life in His name"
(Jn 20:31). "To as many as accepted Him He gave power to
become children of God, [i.e.,] to those who believed in His
name" (Jn 1:12). In short, Christ's salvific mission aims at
revealing God's inner life to men by making it a reality they
experience: "The Son of God has come and given us understanding that we may *know* the True One and *be in* the True
One through (en) His Son, Jesus Christ" (1 Jn 5:20).[4] Faith
is man's full practical acceptance of that salvific mission.[5]

---

4. 1 Jn 5:20 may also be translated: He "has given us understanding
that we may know the True One, and we are [in fact] in the True One."
The sense remains substantially the same. This alternate rendering takes
to "be in the True One" as synonymous with knowing Him ("knowing" in

Needless to say for John as for Paul it is not man who through his act of faith makes himself a child of God. By faith man submits to or accepts God revealing Himself in Christ; it is God who makes man His child: to as many as accept Him by faith the Word gives power to become children of God (Jn 1:12). Unlike Paul, John does not repeatedly emphasize this point by insisting, e.g., that faith removes all grounds for boasting. He does not need to stress the gratuity of justification, since he is not like Paul writing against those who vaunt the value and merit of man's works. An evident truth needs emphasizing only when someone denies it.

Johannine faith, like Pauline faith, is evidently man's initial step towards salvation, initial full acceptance of Christ which a man must never retract. But Paul very definitely conceives of faith as a dynamic reality which grows and develops.[6] In fact, faith seems to mean for Paul the whole of the Christian's attitude towards God from the moment of his conversion till his entrance into heaven. John appears to have a more static concept. Certainly he considers the Christian's life dynamic. But he does not speak of growth of the Christian's faith.[7] He usually uses the verb *pisteuō* in the aorist or the perfect when speaking of the disciples' faith.[8] To believe, for John, means to perform the initial but definitive act of totally (speculatively and practically) accepting Christ.

---

the Semitic sense of experience or intimacy, as in Jn 10:14 f.; 14:17; 17:3; 1 Jn 2:3 f., 13 f., 3:6; 4:7 f.); the version given in the text distinguishes the two terms and considers to "be in" God as adding the idea of effective union with Him to that of knowing Him (speculatively) through Christ's revelation.

5. Christ Himself explains faith as acceptance of Himself in Jn 5:43 f.: "You do not accept me [as having come in my Father's name]," is equivalent to not believing in Him.

6. For Paul faith is the initial act by which a man is justified, transferred from the state of sin to that of justice, and made a child of God (Rm 3:30; 5:1; Gal 2:16; 3:8, 26). But the Christian also lives by (*ek*) or in (*en*) faith (Rm 1:17; Gal 2:20; 3:11), stands firm by faith (Rm 11: 20; 2 Cor 1:24), has Christ dwelling in his heart by (*dia*) faith (Ep 3:17). Paul hears of his converts' faith (Phm 5)—obviously not their initial acceptance of Christ which he witnessed personally. He notes that their faith grows greatly (2 Th 1:3). Throughout the Christian's life his faith must continually express itself in works of charity (Gal 5:6).

The reason for this more static conception of faith lies in the great preoccupation—we might even say, the theme—of so much of the fourth Gospel, an idea expressed succinctly in the prologue and repeated and evolved in the following chapters. Christ the light, God's salvific manifestation of Himself to men, has come into the world. Men must choose between accepting and rejecting Him. Many choose to reject Him. Some accept Him by faith and are saved. The first twelve chapters of the Gospel tell the story of this momentous choice as made by Christ's contemporaries. They describe in great detail the incessant efforts of Christ to offer Himself to men, the acceptance of some, and the enormity of the refusal of the many. Throughout this twelve-chapter account of the public ministry John is wholly intent upon this all-important initial response of Christ's offer: the choice for Him by faith or against Him by refusal to believe. In other parts of his writings, where he gives more attention to other points, the thought of the far-reaching consequences for the world of that initial choice which men make never slips from his mind. Thus, the last discourse, though concerned principally with the disciples and their relations with Christ, does not merely present the rest of men as a group which stands in more or less active opposition to Christ's followers, but quite clearly indicates what has divided men into these

---

7. Obviously the imperfect faith of those who are not fully convinced of Christ's identity progresses. But once a man has performed the act of full and perfect acceptance of Christ, then John usually says that he *has* believed (see the following note).

8. The passages in which John employs the present tense in Jn 1-12 can all be understood of the act of initial acceptance of Christ; and they certainly should be taken in this sense, since these chapters treat precisely of that initial choice as made or refused by those to whom Christ presented Himself during His public ministry. The *future* faith of the apostles mentioned in Jn 13-17 (e.g., 13:19; 14:29) must also be understood of their initial acceptance of Christ; the context and many other passages (e.g., Jn 2:22; 12:16; 20:8 f., 25-29) make it clear that their faith or initial acceptance of Christ remained very imperfect. They did not accept Him perfectly and fully, until after the resurrection; see, e.g., Jn 14:10ff. on imperfection of their faith. Only in 1 Jn 5 do we find the present tense (the participle) used of the faith of Christians and referring not to the initial act of believing but, apparently, to the habitual attitude resulting from that act (in v. 13 and perhaps also v. 10).

two opposed camps: their choice to accept or to reject Christ. The first epistle too presents this view of mankind divided over Christ. John's vivid realization of the consequences of man's initial response to Christ's offer focuses his attention on faith as that first act which makes a man a disciple. Johannine faith, then, is more properly man's initial but total and definitive acceptance of Jesus for what He is: the Christ, the Son of God come into the world as God's salvific manifestation of Himself to men.

Faith is Man's Response to God's Love

Jn 3:14-21 is the first detailed text which explicitly discusses faith in the fourth Gospel after the prologue. And in this very first detailed text faith stands in a context of love: it is man's response to the advances of God's love; it is opposed by love of the darkness; it is accompanied (so the implication seems to be) by love of the light.

(14) And as Moses lifted up the serpent in the desert, even so must the Son of Man be lifted up, (15) that everyone who believes in Him may have life everlasting. (16) For God so loved the world that He gave His only-begotten Son, that everyone who believes in Him may not perish, but may have life everlasting. (17) For God did not send His Son into the world in order to judge the world, but that the world might be saved through Him. (18) He who believes in Him is not judged; but he who does not believe has already been judged, because he has not believed in the name of the only-begotten Son of God. (19) Now this is the judgment: the light has come into the world, yet men have loved the darkness rather than the light, for their works were wicked. (20) For everyone who does evil hates the light and does not come to the light, that his deeds may not be accused, (21) but he who does the truth comes to the light that his deeds may be made manifest, for they have been performed in God.

Verse 16 is clear: God's sending His Son into the world on His salvific mission is an act of love for the world. The verb standing in the aorist presents the divine love as something past. John certainly does not mean to imply that God's salvific love has ceased or that His love no longer offers salvation to all through Christ (Jn 12:44-50; 17:20, 23). But the act of love as expressed in the Son's coming into the world (the Father "gave" Him) is past.

"God loved the world." The universality of God's love expressed in Christ's coming is undeniable. Christ comes not "to judge the world" but only "that the world might be saved through Him" (17). If anyone fails to receive the salvation offered by the Son, all responsibility lies with him and none with Christ: condemnation does not come from the Son, but those who reject Him condemn themselves by rejecting their only hope of salvation (18). The universality of Christ's mission implies the universality of the divine love which inspires it.

The text just considered is the sole passage in the Johannine writings which speaks of God's *love* for all men. John refers frequently to divine benevolence for men but avoids using the word "love." He reserves the term to describe God's relations with Christ's disciples.[9] Even in the present text he does not leave divine love for "the world" unqualified: the advances of God's love call for correspondence on man's part. Without that response divine love will not, or cannot, realize its designs. By corresponding, man allows God's love to bestow upon him eternal life (16) or salvation (17). By refusing, man rejects the concrete expression of God's love, Christ. John says nothing about God's continued love for those who have spurned His love's advances. In not speaking of God's love for the wicked, he differs from the Synoptics, who hold up God's persistently kind treatment for the wicked, the unjust, and the ungrateful as the model of the Christian's love of enemies (Mt 5:44 f.; Lk

---

9. 1 Jn presents Christ as Savior of "the world" (4:14), expiation for the sins not only of His followers but for those of the whole world (2:2; cf. Jn 1:29). Since the Father's love has sent the Son into the world on this salvific mission (1 Jn 4:9), there seems to be no reason why John should not say that God "loved" the world. Yet he does not. Why not, if not to reserve the term to designate God's benevolence for those who have accepted the advances of His love (note especially 1 Jn 3:1—God has "given" love to those who have accepted)?

6:35).[10] John's limiting his usage of the term "love" in this way has important implications, to which we shall allude later.

Man, then, must respond to God's love so that divine love can achieve its aims. This response is faith: "God so loved the world . . . that everyone who believes . . . may have eternal life." Faith, therefore, which means acceptance of Christ, is acceptance of the concrete manifestation of God's salvific love.

1 Jn 4 presents faith in the same way but with greater clarity. Verse 9 reads: "In this was manifested God's love for (*en*) us: that God sent His only-begotten Son into the world that we may live through Him." Christ's coming to save us is, therefore, the great and unique manifestation of God's love for us. After the brief development of another idea, John sets about explaining how man accepts the offer of God's love in Christ. "The Father has sent the Son as Savior of the world. If anyone confesses that Jesus is the Son of God, God dwells in him and he in God" (14 f.). In other words, by confessing Christ as the Son of God come into the world, i.e., by accepting Him as God's revelation and offer of Himself to men, man comes to share God's intimacy: "God dwells in him and he in God." This "confession" of Christ is, of course, faith. Since faith means acceptance of Christ and Christ is the concrete manifestation of God's love for us, faith means acceptance of God's love for us. However, John does not merely let us draw this conclusion for ourselves. He states explicity: "[By confessing Christ] we have known and believed the love which God has for (*en*) us" (16a).

THE LOVES OPPOSED TO FAITH

Love of the Darkness—Jn 3: 16-21

Jn 3:16-21 not only treats of man's response to God's love by faith, but also indicates what it is that holds men back from making that response. Man refuses to respond to God's love because of another love. Opposed to faith stands love of the darkness. John explains man's refusal to believe in these words:

---

10. Matthew and Luke, however, do not explicitly call God's kind treatment of the wicked "love."

"The light has come into the world, yet men have loved the darkness rather than the light, for their works were wicked (*ponēra*). For everyone who does evil (*phaula*) hates the light and does not come to the light that his works may not be accused, but he who does the truth comes to the light that his deeds may be made manifest, for they have been performed in God"; or: "that his works may be shown to have been done (*hoti... estin eirgasmena*) in God."

Christ declares Himself the light of the world (Jn 8:12; 9:5; cf. also 12:46). The evangelist, too, describes Christ in the same way (e.g., Jn 1:9). The metaphor is well chosen to describe Him whose role is to reveal or manifest God to men. Refusal to accept the light that has come into the world merely means refusal to accept or believe in Christ. Motivating this refusal we find love of the darkness.

Darkness in its ordinary acceptation means absence of light; hence in John it should mean the absence of the light which is Christ. And in fact, it is precisely the world without God—without the manifestation of God which is Christ—that is in the darkness. At Christ's coming "the light shines in the darkness" (Jn 1:5). Men are free to leave the darkness and come to the light (cf. Jn 12:35 f.). If they refuse, they remain in the darkness. The darkness, then, is man's state without Christ and therefore without God. To remain in the darkness means to remain by one's own choice in the sad state of man without God (Jn 12:46; cf. 1:5). To walk in the darkness means to live and act in accord with this state of separation from God (1 Jn 1:6; Jn 8:12; 12:35; cf. 1 Jn 2:9-11).

Our verses suggest in addition that this state of man without God is a state of man's own making. Verse 19 points out that "men have loved the darkness rather than the light, for their works were wicked." To explain the connection between love of the darkness and evil-doing, John continues, "Everyone who does evil hates the light" and flees from it so as not to have his evil deeds accused. Men's unwillingness to have their evil works accused means attachment to these works, refusal to give them up, or at least unwillingness to undergo the humiliation involved in having these works shown to be evil.

Darkness, then, is simply the state resultant on a man's attachment to works done in the opposition to God. In accord with a principle which John later treats 'as self-evident and fundamental, the principle that a person loves what is "his own,"[11] we may consider love for the darkness on the part of evil men as simply love for a state of their own making, love for what they have or are apart from and without God. Because of attachment to what they have independently of God, they refuse to accept the offer which God's love makes to them of a share in His life.

Love for the Glory of Men—Jn 12:43

The twelfth chapter of John's Gospel, the conclusion of his account of Christ's public ministry, echoes the thoughts which the passage we have been examining presents at the ministry's start; it also considerably clarifies many particular points; among others, the nature of the love opposed to faith. In 3:16-21 we find a pair of clearly defined and diametrically opposed series. At the head of one stands God, who out of love sends His Son into the world as the light of men, i.e., as His offer to men of a share in His divine life; at the head of the other stands the darkness: all that men have independently of God. At the term of the one lies eternal life: an unending share in divine life given by God; at the term of the other lies (eternal) loss incurred by men: the sad fate of being forever left with what man has without God. Between the principle and the term of each series intervenes an act of man: acceptance of God's offer through faith in Christ the light leads to eternal life, while attachment to what is opposed to God (and Christ) but proper to man without God results in eternal loss. In Jn 12 the same pair of contrary series occurs. At the head of one stands the Father offered to the world by and in Christ the light (44-46, 49 f.; 35 f.); at the head of the other stands the darkness (35 f.,

---

11. If the apostles were "of the world," the world would surely cherish them since they would be "its own" (Jn 15:19). The same holds true of Christians in general (1 Jn 3:7-15). See also Jn 8:42-47, where this principle underlies the explanation given of the Jews' lack of love for Christ.

46). At the term of one lies salvation or eternal life (47, 50); at the term of the other lies judgment or condemnation and loss (v. 48). An act on man's part intervenes to link the principle and term of each series: in the one, faith in Christ; in the other, remaining in the darkness, which results in not believing or rejecting Christ (44-48). The principal difference between the two passages lies in the great emphasis which the later passage (ch. 12) lays on the enormity of men's criminal rejection of God offering Himself to them in Christ—an emphasis easily explained by this chapter's role as epilogue to the account of the public ministry, which itself has been hardly more than the story of a long series of repeated refusals to believe in Christ on the part of men. Because John here insists more on men's refusal to believe, he naturally gives a fuller explanation of their rejection of Christ or their remaining in the darkness. Refusal to believe and the will to remain in the darkness come from love for the glory of men.

> (37) Now, though He had worked so many signs in their presence, they did not believe in Him, (38) that the word which the prophet Isaiah spoke might be fulfilled, "Lord, who has believed our report, and to whom has the arm of the Lord been revealed?" (39) This is why they could not believe, because Isaiah said again, (40) "He has blinded their eyes, and hardened their hearts, lest they see with their eyes, and understand with their hearts, and be converted, and I heal them." (41) Isaiah said these things when he saw His glory and spoke of Him. (42) Yet, even among the rulers many believed in Him; but because of the Pharisees they did not acknowledge it, that they might not be put out of the synagogue. (43) For they loved the glory of men more than the glory of God.

The two citations from Isaiah in vv. 37-41 show that God had already predicted men's disbelief in the Old Testament. Verse 42a qualifies the situation as not being one of total disbelief: many of the Jewish leaders themselves, John notes, were convinced of the truth of Christ's claims, though they refused to profess this conviction.[12] Verse 42b gives the reason: "because of the Pharisees . . . that they might not be put out of the synagogue." And verse 43 analyzes this fear of exclusion from the synagogue as fear of losing human glory: "For they loved the glory of men rather than the glory of God." The ultimate reason for their unwillingness to profess faith in Christ was their love for the glory of men.

This present passage, though the only text which ascribes refusal of faith directly to a *love* of glory, is not the only one which mentions the glory that prevents men from believing in Christ. In three other places Christ finds the obstacle to faith in men's concern over glory (Jn 5:41-44; 7:18; 8:50). By comparing these passages with our own, we can form a clear idea of the nature of this glory. 5:41 and 44 present it as honor, praise, or approval given by men. After declaring that He does not seek glory from men, Christ demands from His hearers: "How can you believe [in me], since you receive glory from one another. . .?" 7:18 and 8:50 describe the man who seeks such glory as a man interested in self-advancement or self-exaltation: he who "speaks of himself" (i.e., according to 5:43, on his own authority or to win credence, admiration, and the like for himself) is seeking "his own glory." Since according to 5:44 seeking such glory necessarily implies abdicating all desire for the glory that comes from God, the "glory of men" must mean honor or exaltation given a man by other men independently of God. Love for the glory of men is a man's love for a (false) greatness, a greatness enjoyed apart from God. Like man's love for the darkness, i.e., for his state without God, a state of his own making, it is love for something which man has independently of God. This love of something possessed

---

12. Is this "belief" in Christ on the part of many of the Jewish leaders to be understood as the faith that makes disciples? So it would seem, but it is evidently only incipient and imperfect faith, even more imperfect than that of the disciples, since, by refusing even to manifest itself outwardly, it does not go so far as theirs. Jn 8:30 ff. furnishes us with a parallel case where many "believe in" Him and then immediately reject Him when He explains His claims a little further, even taking up stones to put Him to death.

independently of God prevents acceptance of God's offer of himself in Christ.

Love for One's Own Life—Jn 12:25

In 12:25 another mention of culpable love occurs: "He who loves (*ho philōn*) his life (*psychēn*) loses it, and he who hates his life in this world will keep it for (*eis*) eternal life (*zōēn*)." The word *psychē* can be rendered either as "life" (present physical life) or, following Semitic usage (*nephesh*), as "self." Whichever rendering we adopt, the sense remains substantially the same: it is love for self or love that would spare self which leads to losing eternal life.

In this verse Christ enunciates the New Testament paradox of self-renunciation and self-denial,[13] which the Synoptics report in a slightly different way (Mt 10:39; 16:25; Mk 8:35; Lk 9:24; 17:33). The differences between their version and John's help clarify the exact meaning of the principle. The Synoptics' contraries are sacrifice of self (losing one's life, *psychē*) *for the sake of Christ* (all the texts just cited except Lk 17:33) and seeking to save self. John's opposites are loving one's life or self *in this world* and hating it. John's hating the life one has in this world corresponds to their sacrificing self for Christ's sake. His love of self is equivalent to their seeking to save or spare self. Self-love, a love which values what a man is and has in this world above Christ Himself, leads to losing eternal life. The love that Christ condemns in Jn 12:25 is this inordinate love of self in preference to Himself.

The immediate context does not set this self-love in opposition to faith; faith is not even mentioned. Evidently, however, if this love results in losing eternal life, it must, like the love in Jn 12:43, be opposed to the faith by which a man lays hold on eternal life.

The fourth Gospel, then, mentions three loves as opposed

---

13. In Jn 12:23 ff. Christ enunciates this principle and applies it both to Himself (in His impending passion) and to His disciples (who must follow Him). The Synoptics apply it to the disciples only but give it immediately after noting that in taking up his cross the disciple is merely following Christ.

to faith: love of the darkness (3:19), love of the glory of men (12:43), and love of self in this world (12:25). The first is the sinner's love of his unhappy state of separation from God: an attachment to self and what the self has independently of God. The second is love for self-exaltation—but for a glorification of self independent of the glory that comes from God. The third is a man's love for what he is and has in this world in preference to Christ. In short, all three of them are inordinate self-love, love of self independently of God. This is the love which results in hatred of Christ the light (Jn 3:20) and makes acceptance of Him by faith impossible.

Love of the World—1 Jn 2:15 f.

In his first epistle too, John speaks of a love that excludes union with God (and therefore excludes the faith which makes union with God possible): love of "the world and what is in the world." To understand this love, we must first understand John's notion of "the world." In his account of the last discourse and especially in the first of his three epistles, he presents the world as the personification of the human forces which oppose the realization of God's salvific designs (1 Jn 3:1, 13; 4:4 f.; 5:4 f., 19). He explains this opposition by the activity of God's arch-adversary, the devil, who holds full sway over the world (1 Jn 3:8, 10; 4:4 f.; 5:18 f.). Only faith in Christ which unites a man with God, can conquer the world and "him who is in the world" (1 Jn 5:4 f.; 2:13 f.; 4:4). Love of the world, then, means love of the forces that oppose God's aim to give Himself to men. It therefore necessarily excludes faith and union with Him.

To define the world merely by its opposition to God is to define it negatively. In our present text, however, John presents a positive definition.

> (15) Do not love the world or the things that are in the world. If anyone loves the world, the love of the Father is not in him; (16) because all that is in the world, the lust of the flesh and the lust of the eyes and the pride of life, is not from the Father, but from the world.

In verse 15 John forbids love of the world to Christians. In verse 16 he justifies the prohibition by noting the irreconcilability of love of the world and love of the Father; love for the world and what is in it means love for what is by its very nature opposed to God, what by its very nature is not and cannot be "of (*or* from) the Father." To show this irreconcilability John needs only to list the things that the world contains: the longing of the flesh, the longing of the eyes, and the haughty airs of this life. The first two are evidently craving for self-satisfaction; the third is self-exaltation. The remark that these three are "not of the Father" identifies them as a self-love that seeks the self's satisfaction of exaltation independently of God or without regard for Him.

In John's first epistle as in his Gospel the culpable love which serves as the great obstacle to faith and union with God is inordinate self-love. Termed love of the darkness or love of what is in the world, it means the sinner's love for his sad, godless state—a state of unbridled self-seeking of his own making. Called love of the glory of men or love of one's own life (or self) in this world, it is just as clearly love of something for the self independently of God. This is the love which by its very nature makes union with God through faith impossible and even leads to hatred of Christ the light.

THE LOVES ASSOCIATED WITH FAITH

Love for the Glory of God—Jn 12:43

In several Johannine passages, we find opposed to the self-love which impedes faith a contrary love closely associated with acceptance of Christ. One text which shows us these contrary loves in opposition is Jn 12:43. When explaining why many of the Jewish leaders, though convinced of Christ's mission, refused to profess faith in Him, John says, "They loved the glory of men rather than the glory of God." The obvious implication is that, had they loved rather the glory of God, they would not have hesitated to proclaim themselves believers in Christ. Love for the glory of God, then, stands allied to faith and opposed to love for the glory of men.

Since love for the glory of men is love for honor or approval from men, love for the glory of God would seem to be love for honor or approval given by God. In the very texts in which Christ blames the desire of glory from men, He praises or justifies seeking the glory that comes from God (Jn 5:41, 44; cf. 8:50, 54). However, the expression "love for the glory of God" can equally well convey the idea of love for glory given *to* God: had the Jewish leaders preferred rather to give glory to God than to receive it from men, they would have professed faith in Christ. Nor is this idea of giving glory to God absent from the fourth Gospel.[14] If we hope to determine the precise meaning John wishes this love of the glory of God to have, we must examine what notion he has of the glory of God and of giving glory to God or receiving it from Him.

The word *doxa*, deriving from *dokeō*, occurs regularly in the LXX for the Hebrew *kābôd*. In Old Testament usage the "glory of God" is usually an outward manifestation of the transcendent divine excellence. In the New Testament the Book of Revelation contains the expression with precisely this Old Testament idea. Thus the glory of God illumines the earth (Rv 18:1) or the new Jerusalem (21:11, 23), or it fills the heavenly temple with smoke (15:8). The transition from a manifestation of the divine excellence to the excellence itself is easy and natural. We find the transition made in the expression "to give glory to God." Men give glory to God or glorify Him by admitting or acknowledging His excellence (Rv 11:13; 14:7; 16:9; 19:7): they glorify Him by recognizing His glory. Fundamentally the same idea of the glory of God is found in the fourth Gospel.

Divine glory is the divine excellence proper to God. The Son of God made man has it but, like everything which He has, He has it from the Father; His glory is the glory which the Father also has and which the Father has given Him as Son (Jn 1:14; 17:5). Christ "manifests His glory" by manifesting His own proper excellence, i.e., by showing Himself to men for

---

14. See Jn 9:24: the Pharisees demanded that the blind man cured by Christ "give glory to God" by denying that Jesus, whom they branded as a sinner, had performed the miracle. The man would have glorified God by acknowledging that in His holiness He had not cooperated with a sinner (cf. 1 S 6:5).

what He really is: the Son of God made man (Jn 1:14; 2:11; 11:4). Now His very carrying out of His salvific mission, as we saw above, includes leading men to faith or to the recognition of Him for what He is. By simply carrying out this mission, therefore, He reveals His identity (and therefore His excellence) to men; in other words, that He manifests His glory. "The Word was made flesh ... and we have seen His glory, the glory which He has as only-begotten Son from the Father: *doxan hōs monogenous para patros*" (Jn 1:14).

This manifestation of the Son's glory is of itself a manifestation of the Father's glory; for the Son's glory is only the same divine excellence which the Father has and which He has received from the Father as Son (Jn 7:18; 14:13; 17:4, 6). In theological terminology the two have one same divine nature, in which divine excellence lies, but the Son has received it from the Father: by passing on the one divine nature to a consubstantial Son, the Father gives this Son the excellence or glory which is His own. As soon, therefore, as the Son's excellence is known, the Father's is necessarily known. "He who has seen me has seen the Father" (Jn 14:9). The Son become man—become visible or manifest to men—is necessarily a manifestation to men of the Father's divinity, since His own divinity is also the Father's. The Father, therefore, is necessarily glorified with the Son; the two cannot be glorified separately because the glorification, i.e., the manifestation of the excellence, of either one is of itself a manifestation of the excellence or glory of the other.

With this in mind we can understand what John says about the glorification of the Son by the Father and the Father by the Son. The Father glorifies the Son in that He communicates His own excellence or glory to the Son and, sending Him into the world, manifests it in Him. But by that very manifestation of the Son's glory he also manifests His own glory or glorifies Himself (Jn 11:4, 40; 12:23, 28; 13:31 f.; 17:1). The Son glorifies the Father by "manifesting the Father's name," i.e., the Father's identity or excellence, but by so doing He necessarily manifests His own glory at the same time (Jn 17:1; cf. 1:14; 7:18; 8:50, 54), since this very same "name" or excellence "the Father has given Him" (17:7, 11 f.). All this is true especially of

Christ's passion and resurrection, which appear both as Christ's own glorification by the Father (Jn 7:39; 12:16, 23 [v. 28 shows that the passion is included]; 13:31 f.; 17:1) and as Christ's principal means of glorifying the Father (cf. especially 13:31 f.; 17:1 f.). By the very same act the Son is honored and glorified by the Father and honors and glorifies the Father, because the glory, the excellence, that is manifested is the one same glory possessed by both.

What is true of the relations of the Son and the Father is true also of the relations of the disciples and Christ. If the Father has given glory to Him, Christ has given that very same glory to them (Jn 17:22). Through Christ they have a share in God's life, divinity, excellence—in His glory. They therefore have glory from God which is a share in God's own glory. By living as Christians should, the disciples manifest, in the very way in which they live, the life, the divine reality, which they have from Him. This outward manifestation in their daily actions by the disciples of the divine life within them glorifies Christ (Jn 17:10) and the Father (15:8) or, in other words, manifests the divine glory or excellence in which they have received a share (17:22). In short, the disciples' Christian lives glorify God because they are a manifestation of divine life or glory.

On the other hand, God "honors" (a rare word in John and apparently equivalent to "glorify") the disciples by uniting them intimately with Christ, by letting them "see," i.e., share in, *Christ's* glory (cf. 17:24). The Christian life is a share in the divine life (or divine excellence). The disciples have this Christian life from God, who does not give it to them once and for all (i.e., at their initial acceptance of Christ) but continually communicates it to them. God's giving them this share in His own life (or excellence or glory) is obviously a "glorification" of them by God. When, therefore, they do anything that manifests their union with Christ, the disciples not only honor or glorify God (by manifesting His divine life, or glory, in their action); they *are glorified* by God (who is giving them this share in His life or glory).

If we ask, then, whether love for the glory of God refers to the will to glorify God or the will to have glory and approval from Him, we must answer that it is both. God is glorified by the very thing by which He glorifies us: by our living and manifesting His own life, His own glory, in which He gives us a share.

In our text, then, love for the glory of God is man's disposition and will to have a borrowed glory, a glory that comes from God and whose possession glorifies God (and, we might add, this is really the only kind of glory that befits or is even possible for a creature, a being which is by its very definition totally dependent on God for all that it is and has). Love for the glory of God stands in quite clear opposition to the inordinate self-love by which a man seeks honor for himself independently of God. Any such desire for an independent glory excludes of itself all readiness to accept a borrowed glory from God. On the other hand, readiness to receive a share in God's glory evidently inspires and makes possible the faith which accepts Christ for what He is: the Son of God come to give men a share in God's life and glory.[15]

Love for the Light—Jn 3:19

In the verse just studied (Jn 12:43), the Jewish leaders refused to make profession of faith in Christ the light because they "loved the glory of men rather than the glory of God." A closely parallel text occurs in Jn 3:19, where men refuse to draw near to the light come into the world because they "have loved the darkness rather than the light." If those who reject the light love the darkness rather than the light, then the obvious implication is that those who accept the light have the contrary disposition: love of the light rather than the darkness. "Now this is the judgment: the light has come into the world, yet men have loved the darkness rather than the light, for

---

15. Certain Johannine texts (e.g., Jn 2:11; 1:14 compared with 1:7-13) make faith man's response to the manifestation of Christ's glory. This is only another way of expressing the idea around which Jn 1-12 centers: the Word, the Son, comes into the world as God's manifestation and offer of Himself to men, and men must accept Him by faith for what He shows Himself to be (and is).

their works were evil." The context identifies the men who come to the light by faith (the men, therefore, who love the light) as those who "do the truth," those whose works have been "done in God" (v. 21). Works "done in God" must mean works done under divine inspiration and guidance or at least done in accord with God's will. Men who have "done their works in God" have had or have something of God within them (His passing inspirations or at least acts that have fulfilled His will). They are responsive to His advances and therefore prepared to accept His offer of Himself in Christ. Comparing this readiness to accept Christ with the evil man's stubborn clinging to the darkness or love of the darkness, John calls it love of the light.

Coming to the light (by faith) means fully accepting God's offer of Himself in Christ. But by accepting this offer a man gives up his own independent life in order to become God's child and share in and live His life. The love of the light which lies in readiness to accept God's offer in Christ implies nothing less than the will or readiness to have a borrowed glory, a glory given by God. In other words, love for the light implies love for the glory of God.

Love for Christ—Jn 8:42-47

Jn 8:42 also speaks of a love which only those have who come by faith to Christ the light. It is no longer love of the light, however, but explicitly love of Christ.

(42) Jesus therefore said to them, "If God were your Father, you would surely love me. For from God I came forth and have come; for neither have I come of myself, but He sent me. (43) Why do you not understand my speech? Because you cannot listen to my word. (44) The father from whom you are is the devil, and the desires of your father, it is your will to do. He was a murderer from the beginning and has not stood in the truth because there is no truth in him. When he tells a lie, he speaks from his very nature, for he is a liar and the father of lies. (45) But because I speak the truth, you do not believe me. (46) Which of you can convict

me of sin? If I speak the truth, why do you not believe me? (47) He who is of God hears the words of God. The reason why you do not hear is that you are not of God."

The context is practically the same as in 3:19. In 8:43-47 the Jews refuse to believe Christ's words; in 3:20 men refuse to come to Christ the light. In 8:44, 47 Christ's hearers reject Him because they are "of (*ek*) the devil" and not "of (*ek*) God," i.e., they have the devil for father, follow his example, and do his desires; in 3:19 men do not come to the light because they love the darkness and do evil deeds. On the other hand, in 8:47, 40, 42 the man who has God as father—the man, then, who has something of God within him—loves Christ and listens to and accepts God's words as they are spoken by Christ. So too in 3:19, the man whose works have been "done in God" (under God's inspiration or in accordance with His will) loves the light and comes to it. There is, however, a difference between the two passages: chapter 8 *explains* the connection between love for Christ and readiness to put oneself at God's disposal, while chapter 3 only *implies* it. Those who are of (*ek*) God "love me," Christ says, "for from (*ek*) God I have gone out and come" (8:42). The man who is "of God" or has God as his father loves Christ precisely because Christ Himself is "of God." This man· accepts Christ (by faith) as coming from God, as God's manifestation and offer of Himself to men, as God's offer of a share in His own life to men; he accepts Christ so as to accept God. His love of Christ is nothing other than love for the glory of God.

Love of God—Jn 5:40-44 and 1 Jn 2:15

After having examined these loves which accompany faith, we may well ask ourselves whether they are not all simply manifestations of love for God. Love for the glory of God, in the sense of readiness to accept a share in God's life which will glorify Him, seems nothing other than benevolence or love for God Himself. Love for Christ as God's manifestation and offer to men of a share in His glory amounts to love for God who reveals Himself in Christ. John himself actually presents the "love of God" as being the ultimate explanation of these loves which accompany faith. The phrase occurs in his Gospel in 5:40-44. The genitive is, of course, ambiguous. The love *of* God can mean *God's own* love (with which God Himself loves), love *from* God (come from or given by God), or love *for* God. Since John seems deliberately to avoid the more natural and unequivocal verbal phrase "to love God," his use of the noun phrase bears investigation.

Christ declares the Jews' rejection of Himself a proof that they do not have the "love of God" within them. "I know you," He tells them, "that you do not have the love of God in you" (Jn 5:42). The proof follows: "I have come in my Father's name, and you will not receive me." If they had the "love of God," they would accept Him and show interest in the glory of God (v. 44). Since acceptance of Christ and especially concern over God's glory imply benevolence towards God, we would naturally tend to interpret this love of God as love *for* God. The only reason for hesitating is the somewhat unusual expression. John could easily have said, "You do not love God." He preferred, "You do not have the love of God in you." This somewhat awkward construction with the genitive seems all the more unusual in view of the fact that the noun *agapē* occurs with relative rarity in the fourth Gospel. Besides, John speaks of the disciples' loving God (using the verb with direct object) in only one place in the whole of his writings (1 Jn 5:2), the climactic passage which explains the full depths of his concept of love. We may wonder, therefore, whether he does not here deliberately choose a somewhat ambiguous circumlocution in order to reserve the unambiguous expression for then. Perhaps he wishes to imply to his readers that his thought has deeper meaning than the merely obvious sense suggested by the context.

The "love of God" reappears in 1 Jn 2:15: "If anyone loves the world, the love of the Father is not in him." Here, as in Jn 5:42, it stands in unequivocal opposition to love *for* the world. But here too John expresses his meaning by the same ambiguous phrase: "the love *of the Father* is not in him."

CONCLUSION

In Christ God offers Himself to men out of love. Christ is the concrete manifestation of God's love in the world. To believe in Christ means to accept Him as God's offer of Himself; in other words, it means to comply with the advances of God's love. Those who love themselves inordinately, who desire a glory independent of the borrowed glory they can have from God in Christ or who love the evil which they have apart from God, can only reject the offer of God's love and refuse to believe. Only those who love God's glory and who therefore love Christ, the manifestation and offer of that glory, will accept the advances of God's love. These are the men who have the "love of God" within them.

JOHN'S DOCTRINE OF THE SPIRIT;
A SUMMARY OF HIS ESCHATOLOGY

Bruce Vawter

At first glance, the Spirit seems to play a smaller part in John's conception of *Heilsgeschichte* than in that of the Synoptics. There is nothing in John corresponding to the statement that after Jesus' baptism the Spirit "drove him forth" into the desert and on to his public ministry (Mk 1:10-12); neither is there anything corresponding to the Lucan description of Pentecost (Acts 2:1-11). Although we note in John that the Spirit is present at the baptism of Jesus (see Jn 1:32), the Spirit is introduced as a sign to John the Baptist rather than as the guiding force in Jesus' ministry. We can add to this the fact that in 1 Jn references to the Holy Spirit are quite vague and problematic (1 Jn 2:20, 27, "anointing"; 1 Jn 3:9, "seed"). Indeed, the term "Paraclete," used for the Holy Spirit in the Gospel, refers to Jesus in 1 Jn 2:1. This difficulty can probably be answered satisfactorily on the score that the fairly rigid Johannine vocabulary of the Gospel had not as yet stabilized itself when the epistles were written.

At all events, it is by no means correct to say that the Spirit has been subordinated in John's theology. What is true is that John has treated of the Spirit in a unique way. In doing so, he has brought out, perhaps more consistently than any other New Testament author, the implications of the New Testament revelation that the Spirit of God is more than a personification—that he is a true person standing in relation to the Father and the Son.

As T. W. Manson has pointed out, that which is most remarkable about John's theology is his use of the name "Father" for God (107 times in John; 12 times in 1 John). "The whole system of his thought centers in the experience of God as

Father. It is this experience which becomes the central and creative dogma of his Christianity. It is in the light of this experience that he sees what light is and what darkness is, what is truth and what lies, what love is and what hatred." This expression of intimacy had been adopted by the primitive Church from the language of Jesus, who had in turn derived it from Judaism and stamped it with his own distinctive use. It is in light of the major Johannine theme of God as Father that we see a partial reason for the distinctive treatment of the Spirit. In John, the Spirit is presented less as the divine power that has directed Jesus' ministry than as the divine power that continues and completes it; the Spirit is, as it were, the perpetuation of Jesus' presence among his followers. Correspondingly, the Spirit is the principle of the divine sonship that Jesus has made possible for men.

As is often the case, in this conception John resembles Luke more closely than any other New Testament author. From the earliest times Acts has aptly been called "the gospel of the Spirit" because of its outline of worldwide witness (another Johannine theme) under the impetus of the Holy Spirit (Ac 1:8). Whereas Luke had, besides the Gospel, a second volume in which to develop the role of the Spirit in the Church, John has had to compress this era of salvation history into the Gospel pattern. Furthermore, there is a difference in the two treatments of the Spirit. Luke's emphasis is on the Spirit as power, bringing the Church into its Catholic destiny; John's emphasis is on the Spirit as sanctifier and principle of the life of the Christian.

Paul also attributes to the Spirit the Christian's share in the postresurrection life of Jesus—in 1 Cor 15:45 and, at least indirectly, in 2 Cor 3:17, the Spirit is Jesus himself; in Rm 8:26 and 1 Cor 12:4 ff., the Spirit is distinct from Jesus. Perhaps the closest Pauline parallels to John's doctrine are in Gal 4:6; Rm 8:14-27 where we are told God has sent the Spirit of his Son into our hearts, and in virtue of this we recognize God as our Father. John's development of these ideas lies in several directions: in strengthening the idea of sonship (Paul: "adoption of sons"), in a more precise determination of the distinct function of the Spirit ("in Christ" and "in the Spirit" are often synonymous in Paul), and in assigning to the Son a greater role in the sending of the Spirit. In doing so he has initiated a more elaborated triadic theology (i.e., a theology of three divine salvific agents: Father, Son, and Spirit), though it still remains largely functional (or preferably, "soteriological") rather than ontological. As indicated these precisions about the Spirit are largely those of John rather than of 1 Jn.

The Spirit is the principle of the new life that Jesus has come to give (Jn 3:5-8) and is operative in virtue of Jesus' glorification (Jn 7:38-39; 1 Jn 3:24; 4:13). He is sent by the Father in the name of Jesus (Jn 14:16, 26), which is to say that he is the gift of Christ himself, sent by him from the heavenly Father to abide with his disciples forever (Jn 15:26; 1 Jn 2:20, 27). He is called "the Spirit of truth" in that the life that he gives is a share in the divine existence itself. The life that was revealed in Jesus is perpetuated in and communicated by the Spirit, and in the Spirit man's longing for truth is to be satisfied. This means in practical terms that the Spirit makes possible the God-given knowledge that comes to man by faith (Jn 16:13). In even more practical terms, John like Paul sees the activity of the Spirit manifest in the preaching of the word by the Church through which the saving power of Christ is brought to mankind.

The designation of the Spirit as the Paraclete is distinctively Johannine in the New Testament (only Jn 14:16, 26; 15:26; 16:7—in 1 Jn 2:1 it refers to Jesus). The term is brought into the Gospel without introduction, so that we must determine its meaning from its usage there. We are aided by Jewish usage that had already transliterated the Gk *parakletos* into Hebrew as *p^eraqlît* (*Pirke Aboth* 4-11); in fact, it is likely that in this form it was used originally by Jesus himself. "Paraclete" means "helper," "advocate": that Jesus is our advocate with the Father is a common Christian conception (Heb 7:25; Rom 8:34); therefore it is easy to see how John can call him our Paraclete (1 Jn 2:1). The Holy Spirit is "the other" Paraclete (Jn 14:16) whose activity begins with the return of the Son to the Father, and whose activity remains till the end of time. The activity of the Paraclete is to reveal the mind of Christ (16:13) even as Christ revealed the mind of the Father (14:10): "He will not speak on his own authority". Yet the Paraclete will glorify the Son (16:14), just as the Father has glorified the Son and the Son the Father. In other words, the Spirit stands in the same relation to the Christian of the Johannine church (and of all times) as that in which Jesus stood to his disciples during his ministry. The Spirit, that is to say, the Son and the Father in the Spirit, is the route by which man enters into the way, the truth, and the life proclaimed by Christ. Thus we are reminded that it is not by the words of the "historical" Jesus alone that we live, but by the words of Jesus as made known by the Church enlightened by the Spirit (16:13: "He will teach you all the truth"; cf. 14:25-26). In Rv, too, the Lord speaks to the living Church through the Spirit (cf. 2:1, 7; 2:8, 11; 2:12, 17; etc.).

REALIZED ESCHATOLOGY

In the context of the foregoing, the peculiarities of the Johannine "realized eschatology" can be seen in their proper perspective. In Jewish thought the coming of the Spirit was an eschatological idea. Given John's theology of the Spirit, his eschatology could hardly be other than "realized."

The New Testament testifies to a continued expectation of the parousia unbroken from the quite primitive formulations preserved in Acts 3:12-26 down to what appear to have been some of the latest of the New Testament writings (as in 2 Pt 3:1-13). To this pattern John forms no exception (cf. Jn 5:28; 1 Jn 2:28). It is quite obvious, however, that all of John's emphasis (in Jn, if not in 1 Jn) is on the here-and-nowness of salvation rather than on the salvation that is to be consummated in the last days. In this emphasis he has been followed by most of subsequent Christianity.

Neither, however, was John entirely isolated in New Testament times. Paul, too, particularly in his later writings, began to dwell on the present realities of salvation rather than on the salvation to come. Both Paul's conception of the Holy Spirit as the "down payment" (*arrabōn*) in the history of salvation (2 Cor 1:22; 5:5; Ep 1:14) and his ability to speak of the resurrection of Christians as already having taken place in Christ (Col 3:1) fit into this pattern. Even a book as heavily weighted in favor of future eschatology as Rv can speak about the possession of the Spirit as a present reality. Further, the "first resurrection" of Rv 20:4-6 corresponds adequately to Paul's concept of the here-and-now participation in the resurrection of Christ. It was doubtless the primitive Church's consciousness and experience of the presence of the Holy Spirit, rather than the "delay" of the parousia, that was above all responsible for the development of "realized eschatology."

(A) THE CHURCH AND THE SACRAMENTS

It is in the Spirit that man encounters the way, the truth, and the life that the Son has brought as the Father's gift into this world. But how and under what conditions does one possess the Spirit? John's answer to this is simple: The Spirit is to be had in the Church. It is in the preaching and the teaching of the Church, inspired and guided by the Spirit, that the word of God and therefore the Word of Life is encountered. The truth that makes men free resides in the community which exists as the result of Jesus' exaltation (Jn 8:28-32) and is presided over by the Spirit. This is the house of God, in which the Son lives with his disciples in the Spirit (14:2-4; cf. 2:19-22). The word of God is accepted by faith as it is transmitted by the Church's ministry (1 Jn 1:5; 2:7). Here men find the way that leads to eternal life and is the beginning of that life (1 Jn 2:17).

Sacraments

In the Church, moreover, men find not only the teaching of Jesus, his words, but also his works of salvation. Salvation is not a matter of human activity following on divine inspiration; this is not the meaning of faith. Salvation is the acceptance of a divine activity that continues to do its work in those who believe. The works of Christ that the Spirit perpetuates in the Church are chiefly the sacraments.

John is mainly concerned with the sacraments of Baptism and the Eucharist, the two sacraments that are most intimately connected with the life of the Church and are the pre-eminent "signs" of that life. However, this is not to say that he would

have limited the divine life in the Church to these two "signs."
On the other hand, it would be unrealistic to expect to find in
his writings the precisions of sacramental theology that un-
folded only in later times through the developing doctrine of
the Church.

The sacraments draw their efficacy from the sacrificial death
of Christ (Jn 19:34). Jesus Christ is Savior not simply by having
been declared the Messiah at the time of his baptism ("through
water"), but by having fulfilled his mission in death on the
cross ("through blood"); therefore, as the object of faith, he
must be confessed as one who has come "not in the water only,
but in the water and the blood" (1 Jn 5:6). John customarily
writes on several levels, making his narrative of historical events
significant to his readers in respect to the enduring Christian
realities. And so, "water and blood" also means the continuing
witness given water and blood in the Church through the Spirit,
that is, in the sacraments of Baptism and the Eucharist: "Therefore there are three who testify, the Spirit and the water and
the blood, and the three make up one" (1 Jn 5:7). The Spirit,
then, rather than the water only, gives the new life of Baptism
(Jn 3:5).

The Word become flesh gives his flesh and blood for the
life of the soul (Jn 6:53-58), and it is the Spirit that makes this
possible (6:63). It is by the gift of the Spirit that the Church
exercises its power to forgive sins in the name of Christ (20:
21-23). The condition of the Church expressed in the figure
of the branches drawing life from the vinestock is also a sacramental image connected with the coming of the Spirit (15:1-27).
The frequency with which water is mentioned in Jn (2:6;
4:10, 23; 5:25) has as at least part of its explanation John's
preoccupation with Baptism, just as his stress on "flesh" in
reference to the incarnation (1:14) is not made without regard
to the Eucharist.

Worship

Christ is encountered through the Spirit also in the worship
of the Church. Christian worship necessarily had quickly distinguished itself from its Jewish origins by reason of the essen-

tially different eschatological perspective. When Jesus told his disciples that he would not leave them orphans but would return to them in the Spirit (Jn 14:15-21), he was proclaiming the fulfillment of the kingdom in Old Testament language parallel to that of Lk 6:20. Christianity now consciously distinguished itself from the Synagogue, so much so that John refers consistently to "the Jews" in the third person as alien to the Church. Christians had their own Lord's day to replace the Sabbath (Rv 1:10), and their own liturgy to replace the feasts of Judaism. In his description of the Last Supper (Jn 13-17), John may have echoed the basic Christian liturgy: sermon, prayer, and Eucharistic banquet. Liturgical songs have been preserved in such passages as Rv 5:9-10, 12, 13; 12:10-12. The role of the liturgy as a re-creation of the historical events of salvation under the guidance of the Spirit is part of the Spirit's function of "reminding" the Church (Jn 14:26). This is the worship of God "in Spirit and truth" (4:23); this is prayer in Jesus' name (14:13).

Christian Living

Pervading all, however, is the presence of the Spirit manifested in Christian life. This does not exclude, but neither does it simply mean, the extraordinary manifestations of the Spirit in charismatic activities. These have their part to play, certainly, in the life of the Church (cf. Rv 1:10), but they can be ambiguous and must always be tested by the criterion of known Christian truth (1 Jn 4:1-3). For John as for Paul the more obvious way in which the Spirit is present in the Christian virtues, specifically fraternal charity, is manifest in the Christian community, and in the consciousness of the forgiveness of sins and of fellowship with God (1 Jn 2:3; 3:6, 23; 4:8, 12-21; 3 Jn 11). Life, after all, can be verified only in living actions, and the life with which John is concerned produces actions that can only be divine in origin. Just as Jesus' words and deeds were the proof of his origin from the Father, the words and deeds of Christians show forth the presence of the Spirit of the Son, the Spirit who has brought the eschatological peace that Jesus promised (Jn 14:27).

184 A COMPANION TO JOHN

Church Order

There is not a great deal in John on the organization or "constitution" of the Church. The literary form of the Gospel more or less precluded this; and, in any case, both Jn and 1 Jn have put all their emphasis on the life of grace lived in the Church rather than on its externals. However, such an organization is presupposed in the sacramental and liturgical concerns of John, as well as in the references to doctrinal authority (1 Jn 2:24; 4:6). Whether "the Presbyter" of 2 Jn 1 and 3 Jn 1 uses the title in the ecclesiastical sense familiar from Acts and the Pastoral Epistles is not certain; the discourteous Diotrephes of 3 Jn 9, however, is most likely the chief presbyter of the church with which the Epistle is concerned. The supplementary ch. 21 in John manifests the concern for Peter's primacy in the Church shown by other New Testament documents. Rv supposes a local church organization which is also implied in 1-3 Jn; and the figure of the woman in Rv 12 is certainly ecclesial.

(B) JUDGMENT

Judgment was eminently an eschatological idea in Jewish thought. Even in paganism the idea of a divine judgment itself had become widespread, though not necessarily in an eschatological context. Paul is represented in Acts 17:31 as preaching the judgment of the world as a concept that would be understood and accepted by the Stoics and Epicureans of Athens. For the Jew, such terms as "judgment," "the day of the Lord," and "that day" had become synonymous, deriving from the earliest days of prophecy (cf. Am 5:18), designating the definitive intervention of God in history in the end-time. It is significant that this prophetic idea figures so largely for John who has identified the eschatological Prophet of Jewish expectation with Jesus.

John's concept of the judgment is in accord with the rest of his eschatology and would have appealed to the non-Jewish mentality as well as to the Jewish. "That day" is the day of Jesus' glorification (Jn 14:20), which in turn, is simply God's applying on behalf of man the glory that the Son has possessed from eternity (17:5) and that has been made manifest in the incarnation. Without denying the final judgment of traditional eschatology (5:45), John nevertheless insists on the present realities of judgment, on the importance of the existential moment of decision that every man must make regarding an acceptance or rejection of the light.

It is for this reason that we can understand the apparent paradox that, although the Son has not been sent to judge the world, he still says, "For judgment have I come into this world" (9:39). Judgment, that is, condemnation, is far from being the purpose of the incarnation. But the coming of Jesus is and ever will be the occasion of judgment, in view of the decision with which man is faced. Man must choose whether to accept or reject the way, the truth, and the life that have been revealed to him in the Son by the Spirit. In making his decision, man judges himself. The "division" caused by the appearance of the Light among men, a characteristic of the Johannine accounts of Jesus' preaching to the Jews of Palestine (10:19-21; etc.), continues in the time of the Church for which John wrote and in our own time as well. And thus the beginning of John's theology is also its end, even as Christ is truly the alpha and the omega (Rv 1:8; 2:8; 21:6; 22:13). The Light continues to shine in the darkness, for Jesus is the eternal "I am". He who died now lives, and is communicated by the Spirit in the Church. Judgment is not tomorrow or the next day, but now, because of him who was and is and is to be (Rv 1:4).

CHRISTIAN MORALITY ACCORDING TO JOHN

Rudolf Schnackenburg

Johannine theology, which has left its mark on the gospel and three epistles of John, finds its focus in Christology. The main reason for the composition of the last canonical gospel may very well have been to give Johannine churches a picture of Christ which showed them in the earthly activity of Jesus the glory of their Christ already shining, that eschatological revealer and mediator of salvation through whom alone true information and knowledge of God and his world, genuine communion with God and share in the divine life, are to be obtained. This picture of Christ is outlined against a background of the intellectual trends at the turn of the first Christian century, and is addressed to a Christendom for which Christ's message had already become an interior and well-pondered possession, but which also had problems in its intellectual dealings with the world around it (Judaism, Hellenism, Gnosticism) and in defending itself against false teachers from its own ranks (1 John). The reflection on what is proper to, and characteristic of, Christian faith in an atmosphere that is intellectually alert and religiously full of life, involves as a consequence that the theological lines are more sharply drawn, the view is deeper, the thoughts simplified but directed to what is essential and permanent. As regards moral teaching that means that less prominence is given to more specialized questions such as we find in Paul's dealings with his churches, but there is a gain in comprehensive vision of principles and this is to the advantage of the picture of the world and of man, the understanding of reality and of salvation. In our age which has raised the question of the actual concrete human situation and directed attention more closely to man's historical lot, this Johannine message deserves increased reflection, all the more so as it has been given a special interpretation in terms of existential theology by R. Bultmann.

In contrast to the synoptic gospels in which the message regarding the kingdom of God involves God's claim on man, the emphasis in St. John's gospel becomes a Christological one. The summons to man follows from John's own claim as God's eschatological envoy. Because Jesus is the Messiah in a sense that transcended all expectation, because he is the Son of God equal in nature to the Father (20:31), he in his person reveals the Father (14:8-11; 8:19; 12:45), and he designates himself as salvation (8:12), as the way (14:6), as life (11:25; cf. 6:35, 48, 51). As a consequence, however, he only makes the one demand, that men should believe in him (3:16, 18, 36; 5:24; 6:29), follow him (8:12; 12:26), keep and observe his word (8:51 f.; 14:15, 21, 23; 15:10). The clear recognition that only one has "descended from heaven" and that only one "ascended" again in order to provide access for all to the heavenly world of light and life, namely the Son of man (3:13, 31; 6:33, 50 f., 58, 62; 20:17), illumines at the same time the hopeless situation of the man in this world who trusts to himself (3:18, 36; 8:24; 12:35), and the only possibility of salvation, which is to pass from the domain of death to God's circle of light and life (5:24).

Thought of this kind presupposes God's infinite distance from all the transitoriness of creatures, the frailty of what is earthly (the antitheses σάρξ — πνεῦμα 3:6 f.; γῆ — οὐρανός 3:31; κάτω ἄνω 8:23), and takes as an established fact that the "world" has as a matter of history turned aside to evil. This thought, however, is only presented and sustained because God in the meantime has overcome the gulf and taken the initiative in deliverance by sending his Son into the world (3:17; 12:47). The great eschatological event has taken place: the eternal Logos himself has become "flesh" (1:14), the heavenly witness and revealer has appeared on the earth (1:18; 3:32 ff.; 8:26), he who lives from a divine source has come in order to give life forever to the world enslaved to death (4:14; 5:21, 25 f.; 6:33, 51, 56; 7:38; 10:10; 11:25 f.). Against the dark background of a "dualist" view of the world, the Christian message of salvation stands out all the more brightly. Besides, Johannine the-

ology, despite dualistic modes of expression, is far removed from
any extreme dualism. It is true that there is an opposition of
contrasted concepts, life and death, light and darkness, truth
and falsehood, freedom and slavery (only in John 8:31-6), being
from above and being from below (8:23), children of God and
children of the devil; but they are not traced back to two
equally strong primordial powers, or understood metaphysically;
it is not a cosmological dualism or one of principles. It is never
forgotten that all that was made was created by God and by
the Logos (1:3), that to God and the Son of God there belongs, even before "the foundation of the world" an inviolable
glory (17:5) and that God is always stronger than his adversary "in the world" (1 John 4:4). The "world," is not, as in
Gnosticism, the "plenitude of evil" (*Corpus Hermeticum* VI,
4), but is only full of evil tendencies such as the "concupiscence
of the flesh, the concupiscence of the eyes and the pride of
life" (1 John 2:15 ff.). What belongs to the body and to matter
is not bad in itself or of less account in contrast to the soul
and the spirit, but only weak and frail, so that even the Logos
could become "flesh" (John 1:14) and "all flesh" (a Semitic
expression for "all human beings") could be called to share
in eternal life (17:2). The "dualistic" perspective borrowed by
John derives from an historical conception of the "world" which
has shut itself against God, developed away from him (1:5)
and placed itself under the rule of the "evil one" (1 John 5:19),
that is to say, Satan, the "prince of this world" (Jn 12:31; 14:30;
16:11). There are no "children of the devil" by nature, but
human beings who show themselves to be such by their desires
and deeds (Jn 8:44). "He that commits sin is of the devil, for
the devil sins from the beginning" and through sin the "children
of the devil" are manifest (1 Jn 3:8, 10).

This sharply contrasting opposition of two classes of men
strongly recalls the Dead Sea manuscripts which speak of the
"sons of light" in antithesis to the "sons of darkness". Those
who joined the community of Qumran were obliged to "love
all the sons of light, each according to his lot (= place) in God's
community and hate the sons of darkness, each according to
his guilt in God's vengeance" (*1 QS* I, 9 ff.). The sons of light
armed for the eschatological combat against the sons of dark-

ness (*1 QM passim*). There is instruction about the two kinds
of spirits according to which each class walks (the "spirits of
truth and falsehood"), and in accordance with which men's
deeds are determined. Each of these opposed classes of men
is placed under a spiritual ruler ("an angel"): "In the hands of
the prince of light lies rule over all the sons of truth, they
walk in the ways of light; in the hands of the angel of darkness
lies rule over the sons of falsehood and they walk in the ways
of darkness" (3:20 f.). But even this dualism which itself extends
into what is supra-human and cosmic, is subject to faith in the
biblical God and creation. God "created the spirits of light and
darkness" (3:25), and he retains dominion: "But God in the
secrets of his understanding and in his glorious wisdom has set
time (or, an end) to the continuance of falsehood; in the time
of visitation he will destroy it for ever" (IV, 18 f.). The descriptions, though to a certain extent they sound deterministic,
leave no doubt that it is a matter of the moral decision of
men, in whose hearts "the spirits of truth and falsehood struggle"
(IV, 23), and that they are not absolved of responsibility. This
dualism of Qumran whose more specific nature and origin is,
of course, still disputed, is certainly close to Johannine thought,
at least in its formal structure and moral aspect. What is special
and distinctive in Johannine theology derives from the sending
of God's Son into the world. By his call, the sole intention of which
is to serve the deliverance of all men, he summons men to a decision and this brings about a separation among them (Jn 3:
18-21; 8:47; 9:39; 12:44-50; 18:37).

This Johannine antithetical mode of thought not only places
Jesus' mission in the clearest light from the point of view of
the theology of redemption, by teaching that is to be understood as the outcome of God's love overcoming all distances
(Jn 3:16; 1 Jn 4:10), but also has important consequences for
moral theology. Decision concerning faith in regard to the
"Light" who has come into the world, calls for clear and reso-
lute turning away from all works of darkness. "For every one
that does evil hates the light and comes not to the light, that
his works may not be reproved. But he that does truth comes
to the light, that his works may be made manifest; because
they are done in God" (Jn 3:20 f.). To this "Light" the whole

man is transparent and he cannot conceal his moral attitude; belief and "doing the truth" are very closely linked. Just as believing acceptance of Jesus as the revealer who incorruptibly announces God's word and truth presupposes a pure disposition only concerned with God's honor (5:40-4; 8:43 c.; 12:43), so also "faith" signifies submission to all that Jesus teaches and prescribes as his commandments. "My doctrine is not mine, but his that sent me. If any man will do the will of him, he shall know of the doctrine, whether it be of God, or whether I speak of myself" (7:16 f.). This saying refers in the first place to belief. God's will, the only "work" that he demands, is to believe in him whom he has sent and to whom he has testified (6:29); but belief in this unique plenipotentiary of God, in whom God himself speaks, also involves faithfully holding to his words and commandments, which are summed up in the precept of mutual love (8:31, 51 f.; 14:15, 21), and of abiding in his love (15:7, 10). This very accomplishment of Christ's commandments becomes a confirmation for the believer that Jesus is the savior who comes from God, a concrete proof of experience of the truth of belief in Christ. From it there follows the closest conceivable connection between religion and morality, between knowing God and keeping the commandments, between communion with God and brotherly love, as the First Epistle of John shows by its rejection of a pseudo-gnosis that was morally a failure. What Jesus aimed at establishing and achieving by his double command of love of God and the neighbor, the single structure of a moral religion and a religious morality, the obligation of all religious endeavor to authenticate itself by pure moral action, and at the same time the grounding of all moral activity on the nexus with God, was confirmed in a new way by John's Christological perspective. His Christ who lives in complete unity with the Father, subject to him in love and obedience, seeking his honor only and fulfilling his command (7:18; 8:29, 55; 10:17 f.; 12:49; 14:31), requires of his disciples the counterpart of this, and is their direct example and guide: "If you keep my commandments, you shall abide in my love; as I also have kept my Father's commandments and do abide in his love" (15:10). He draws his own into loving community with the Father (17:26), but also expects that they will produce the fruits of this communion with God bestowed by him (15:8 f., 16 f.).

Just as the Johannine presentation of Jesus' eschatological mission and message brings out with incomparable urgency the unity of the requirement of faith and love, it also emphasizes the negative judgment on unbelief and sin, and manifests the inner connection between them. Although the evangelist knows the old Jewish concept of sin (5:14; 9:2 f., 34), sin only appears in its full horror when men refuse to believe and follow the Son of God who takes away sin (cf. 1:29). Anyone who in inexplicable blindness (9:39; 12:38 ff.) bars this, the sole way to deliverance, falls a victim totally and entirely to the dark domain of the "world". He remains in his sins and will die in his sins (8:21, 24). Only Jesus, the divine bringer of life, can lead him out of the lower world of death and ruin (3:16, 36; 5:24). Consequently, unbelief is sin absolutely as such. That is not only clearly stated in a saying regarding the Paraclete (16:9), but also forms the tacit presupposition of other passages in which instead of the many particular sins, only "sin" is mentioned (8:12; 9:41; 15:22, 24; 19:11).

John had reflected a great deal on the dark power of unbelief. How was it that so many people, and precisely those who should most of all have recognized Jesus as the Messiah, namely the leading circles among the Jews at that time (Pharisees, Scribes, high priests), shut their hearts to this messenger of God from the world of light and life? And although Jesus had done everything to bring them to belief? "If I had not come and spoken to them, they would not have sin; but now they have no excuse for their sin. . . . If I had not done among them the works that no other man has done, they would not have sin; but now they have both seen and hated me and my Father" (15:22, 24). It was a terrible, active and aggressive unbelief. From it developed blind hate against the man sent by God, which did not rest until the latter was bleeding to death on the cross. How could men rage in such a way against God and their salvation? Precisely because they belong to that world hostile to God with which Jesus and his own have nothing to do (15:18 f.); they come from "below" just as Jesus is from "above" (8:23). Because in this way it might sometimes seem as though this unbelief were due to lack of grace (6:44, 65) and to a hardening imposed by God (9:39; 12:39 f.), it is stated in other passages that these obstinate enemies are themselves guilty of their own unbelief. They seek only their own honor, not the honor of God (5:44; cf. 12:43). They are already sunk in evil deeds and darkness (3:20 f.), and share the desires of the liar and murderer from the beginning (8:44). To his unbelieving "brethren", too, Jesus declares that the world hates him because he has given testimony of it, that its works are evil (7:7).

John makes these judgments in view of the attitude of men to the historical Jesus in whom he confesses the Messiah and the Son of God. But in addition his judgments gain additional weight for his readers also, the Church of his time, and are important in general for the psychology and evaluation of unbelief. Unbelief in regard to Jesus Christ is and remains a dark, terrible enigma, a mystery of iniquity (cf. 1 John 3:4), in which the essence of sin is manifest. Sin is not to be regarded superficially as an offence, an individual action or an omission of good; it springs from the whole attitude of a human being towards God, and only becomes visible in its true form to the eye of faith, as the great power hostile to God in the life of man and the course of history.

This narrower and yet profounder concept of sin which reveals the nature and historical range of evil, this antithesis between the world of evil and devil and God's world of light which is penetrated by his holiness (1 Jn 1:5; 2:10), gives to moral exhortation great seriousness and confronts those who hear it with a strict alternative. He who loves his brother dwells in light and there is no scandal from him (or in him?) but he who hates his brother is in darkness, not knowing where he is going because the darkness has blinded his eyes (1 Jn 2: 10 f.). There is no middle way between belief and unbelief, love and hate, any more than there is any other choice except that between salvation and perdition. He who has the Son possesses life; he who has not the Son does not possess life.

The clear, radiant motives, however, predominate: knowledge of God's will to save (Jn 3:17; 12:47), confidence in his saving power (1 Jn 4:4), faith in the victory already won by

Christ which is asserting itself and ceaselessly prevailing (John 16:33; 1 Jn 5:4 f.). "The darkness is past and the true light now shines" (1 Jn 2:8). Yet the Church in the world is not spared conflict. Great tribulation is laid upon it and the individual Christian must also struggle with temptation, weakness and sin.

The Synthesis of Moral Teaching
in the Commandment of Faith and Love

After reading Paul, who in his letters decides moral problems of the most varied kinds, the Johannine message seems simple and uniform: faith and love, and that is all. The reduction of all requirements to these two fundamental attitudes is deliberate and has its ground in the Christological focus. Belief in Jesus the Messiah and Son of God is the only means and the only possible way to attain life; love, however, especially active, fraternal love, is the necessary consequence of adherence to Jesus in faith. John does once, in fact, summarize the "commandment of God" in the words, "that we should believe in the name of his Son Jesus Christ, and love one another" (1 Jn 3:23). Comparison of this with the synoptic gospels makes it appear even more impressive. Of Jesus' basic requirements for entry into the kingdom of God, only one has survived: faith. But this has acquired quite a different fullness and profundity from what it had in the synoptic gospels. "This is the (only) work of God: that you believe in him whom he has sent" (Jn 6:29). In this reply to the Jews, Jesus was not meaning an achievement, a performance, like the Jewish works of the law, but rather was merely taking up the words of his interlocutors and explaining to them that instead of all the many human endeavors they had been prepared to undertake (v. 28), there is one fundamental decision to be made: to believe in him, whom God had sent. In the Johannine writings we frequently hear of the commandments of God; but this does not indicate a rehabilitation of legalism. St. Paul himself could not have formulated the difference between the old and the new order of salvation more succinctly than it is expressed in the prologue to John's gospel: "For the law was given by Moses; grace and truth came by Jesus Christ" (1:17). When he speaks of the commandments of God or Christ it is with the sole intention of indicating the binding character of faith and love. Faith rightly understood also includes love for God, Christ, and the brethren, and the fulfillment of the moral duties springing from love.

More precisely, Johannine faith has assimilated two commandments of the Jesus of the synoptic gospels: repentance and discipleship. It is noteworthy that the word "repent" does not occur in the Johannine writings (apart from the Book of Revelation). But we must remember that in consequence of Johannine dualism, faith implies determined renunciation of the "world" hostile to God, rejection of all the works of darkness. The believer steps completely out of the dark realm of death into the bright expanse of the divine life (Jn 5:24). Anyone in this light, must also walk in light, that is, holy and without sin (1 Jn 1:6 f.; 2:9-11). In the moral judgment of condemnation passed on the disbelief of the "Jews" (Jn 3:19-21; 5:44; 7:7; 12:43), there is contained the idea that they would have needed "repentance" in the sense of the first three evangelists, in order to begin to believe in Jesus. But these opponents, whose minds are closed to the word of God, are blind and obdurate. John's gospel nowhere describes or mentions an act of conversion (not even with the Samaritan woman in chapter four); but it does bring before us people who possess an outlook of a kind that disposes them to belief: Nathanael, who was at first sceptical, but whom Jesus called a "true Israelite . . . in whom there is no guile" (1:47); the Samaritan woman, who had fallen very deeply into sin, but who was a soul seeking God and thirsting for salvation (ch 4); the man born blind, who would let neither remonstrance nor terrorization obscure his realization of Jesus' majesty and holiness (ch 9); Martha, the sister of the dead Lazarus, who in spite of her severe shock on the human plane did not become confused about Jesus' person and mission (11:20-27); Jesus' close disciples themselves, who were so often puzzled and yet loyally continued in his company (6:66-69). They were all people whom Jesus did not have to accuse, as he accused his faithless enemies, of seeking their own glory, but not the glory of the one God (5:44; 12:43). Even the gloomy picture of the Jewish leading circles is somewhat relieved by the mention of the two councillors, Joseph of Arimathea and Nicodemus (19:38 f.). If Jesus had believed that it was impossible for a man to turn to faith, he could not have cried to the multitude until the last moment, "While you have the light, believe in the light, that you may be the children of light" (12:36).

Johannine faith binds the believer to adherence to Jesus, not always in that closest of bonds, that of the disciple, sharing in Jesus' wandering life and continuing his preaching, but, nevertheless, to a real "discipleship", as John himself could call it by using the word in a wider sense. Jesus once cried out to a great multitude of people who were ready to believe, "If you continue in my word, you shall be my disciples indeed" (8:31). Expressions synonymous with "believing" in this gospel are, "keeping Jesus' words" (8:51), "hearing" and "keeping" them (12:47), and "following" Jesus (8:12; cf. 1:9 ff.). Unbelief leads immediately to the end of one's "walking" with Jesus (6:67). The use of "keeping Jesus' words" (12:47) shows that adherence to him in faith also makes moral demands. Because faith is obedience (3:36b), perfect self-submission to the Son of God, it must lead to loving observance of all his instructions (14:15, 21, 23).

' The believer must be resolved to accept even the ultimate consequence of following Jesus: he must be prepared for suffering and martyrdom. There is one text in the gospel of St. John which directly recalls the words of Jesus in the synoptic gospels on following the way of the cross (Mk 8:34 ff.; Mt. 10:38 ff.): "he that loves his life τὴν Ψυχήν shall lose it: and he that hates his life in this world keeps it unto life eternal (εἰς ζωὴν αἰώνιον). If any man minister to me, let him follow me. And where I am, there also shall my minister be" (12:25 f.).

These words are not addressed directly to the Twelve, but are, it would seem, deliberately left undefined. Moreover, the saying has been recast by John. The addition "in this world" is new, and correspondingly the promise "unto life eternal". The synoptic saying is more pithy, the Johannine clearer: compare the two different words for "life". John contrasts "this" cosmos of death with the true, divine realm of life. The second saying about "ministering" (with synoptic parallels at Mk 9:35 ff.;

10:43 ff.; Mt 23:11) is already looking forward to Jesus' highest ministration of love in the washing of the disciples' feet and the sacrifice of the cross as it is interpreted in the gospel of John (13:1, 12-17). Another wholly Johannine idea here is that Jesus' servant will be where he himself is, that is, in the heavenly world of glory, into which Jesus leads the way for his followers (14:3; 17:24).

This text is all the more significant because just before it Jesus had applied to himself the image of the grain of wheat, which must fall into the soil and die, if it is to bring forth fruit. Here the Johannine Christ too is requiring of his disciples that, uniting themselves as intimately as possible with his own destiny, they should follow him even to death. What glory for the disciple whom the Lord deems worthy to follow him even to martyrdom (Jn 21:18). In conjunction with the prophecies of sufferings for the disciples (15:18-20; 16:1-4), John 12:25 f. is enough to show that John, too, was aware of the severity of serving Jesus, of the radical nature of his demands. He does not, however, offer the disciple a more fully elaborated moral doctrine. It seems to him enough to believe in a lively and unfading way in Jesus, and love unto death (21:15-17). However, these words about love require special attention too.

It is only in the gospel of John that Jesus speaks of love for himself.[1] Faith and discipleship are perfected only in love, but this love of the disciple for his Master does not appear as a commandment, but as the consequence and fruit of true faith. The "first farewell discourse" (ch 14) is especially informative on this point. The whole of the first part of this (14:1-14) is concerned with the necessity and power of faith in Jesus, which makes the disciples proof against all the shocks of the coming hour of darkness (13:19; 14:29; 16:4). When such faith is fully mature, it leads to a living community with Jesus. The second part of the discourse, treating of the mystical communion of the disciples with Jesus and the Father (14: 18-24), replaces faith by love. The exhortation in these verses is that love for Jesus must be confirmed by keeping his commandments. So then effectual love grows out of the actual mysti-

---

1. 8:42; 14:15, 21, 23, 24, 28; cf. 21:15f.

cal union with him. This emerges even more clearly from the
discourse in chapter fifteen, where John writes that the disciples
should remain in Jesus (vv. 4 ff.), especially in his love (v. 9 f.),
that is, they should do everything to preserve the love and community given them by Jesus.

Not even the first part of the great commandment, to love
God with all one's heart and soul, is to be found in John's
gospel in that form. Most of the texts which people used to
like to interpret as referring to actual love for God are probably
intended to refer to divine love, God's love, that is, to the love
essentially characteristic of those who are God's and of which
they have been made capable by the love they have received
from God. John is not merely thinking here of the willingness
of human beings to love; he is convinced that the fire of love
has to be enkindled by God himself. If God himself has begotten them "from above" and filled them with his holiness and
love, they are, of course, to respond to him both in attitude
of mind and in their actions. It is in this way, through the
cooperation of God and of man, that God's love "is perfected"
in the Christian (1 Jn 4:18), "his charity is perfected in us"
(4:12) and we have "perfect charity" (4:18). Of those who
are not God's it can be said that "you have not the love of God
in you" (Jn 5:42). John is profoundly convinced that our love
is a gift from God (1 Jn 3:1; 4:10). If we allow ourselves to be
moved to a corresponding love and to obedience, the love of
God will be bestowed on us even more fully (Jn 14:21, 23).
At the moment of his departure, Christ prayed that the Father
would draw us ever more deeply into communion with him
(17:23, 26).

Strictly speaking, in John the plenitude of the moral commandments is summed up not in the double commandment
to love God and one's neighbor, but in the "new" commandment to love the brethren alone. A single text in the first
Epistle seems to contrast love for God with love for the "world":
"Love not the world, nor the things which are in the world.
If any man love the world, the charity of the Father is not in
him. For all that is in the world is the concupiscence of the
flesh and the concupiscence of the eyes and the pride of life,
which is not of the Father but is of the world" (1 Jn 2:15 f.).

In reality this text is meant neither to warn against certain vices nor to comprise all virtues in love for God. It is a dualistically colored warning against toying with the world, that perilous temptress, and coming to terms with her, a warning in keeping with general early Christian paraenesis. At every stage John remains faithful to his single-minded and urgent call to faith and love, a call that contains all that God requires of his children in this world.

*Active Love for the Brethren as the Proof
of Communion with Christ and God*

The exhortation to love of the brethren is the characteristic feature of Johannine moral teaching. In the fourth gospel, even when Jesus is speaking of his commandments (14:15, 21), his primary aim is to urge on his disciples' love for the brethren (13:34; 15:12, 17). "To keep Jesus' word" (14:23, or "words" v. 24) means the same thing, except when it refers to faith (8:51 f.; 15:20). But in the last resort faith, keeping Jesus' word and loving the brethren are all different facets of obedience to the Son of God. In 1 John 2:3 f., the commandments of God, or the word of God (2:5), are explicitly interpreted as relating to the old and yet new commandment of brotherly love (cf. 2:7-11). The (moral) message brought to Christians from the very beginning has been that they should love one another (3:11).

But why does Jesus call this crucial commandment a "new" commandment? Was not fraternal love already axiomatic in Judaism? Was it not sincerely practised in many Jewish communities (the "fellowship" of the Pharisees, the monastic communities of the Essenes and Therapeutae, the Damascus sect and the closely-related brotherhood at Khirbet Qumran), and indeed in many pagan, Hellenistic religious societies? Only the answer to this question, what the "new" element in Christian love of the brethren was, brings understanding of Johannine thought. Jesus adds the words "as I have loved you" (13:34; 15:12) and so provides the key to understanding: because he has loved his own in the world to the uttermost (13:1), so giving them an example (13:15), his disciples, acting explicitly as his disciples (13:35), should love one another in precisely the same way. Jesus is their precursor, their model, their master and their teacher. The act enshrining and revealing in an unparalleled way this loving attitude of Jesus, expressing his love and making it fruitful, was his voluntary loving sacrifice upon the cross (10:11, 15, 17 f.; 15:13).

Probably, within the framework of the Johannine narrative, the washing of the feet is intended to be the pre-eminent "sign" of this and is to be seen (perhaps in addition to another interpretation cf. 13:10) as a model for love only in connection with Jesus' sacrificial death. The sacrificing of oneself for one's brethren, serving them selflessly in accordance with the great pattern of Jesus may be, in John's mind, the "new" element in the commandment to love. Otherwise John could not have written, "Again a new commandment I write unto you; which thing is true both in him and in you, because the darkness is passed and the true light now shines" (1 Jn 2:8).

It is also remarkable how strongly John emphasizes the example of Christ in his own moral exhortation (1 Jn 2:6; 3:3, 7; 4:17). And above all he draws from Jesus' highest proof of love the conclusion "We ought to lay down our lives for the brethren" (1 Jn 3:16). In these words he bases the interpretation of the "new" commandment of love on faith, for only the believer realizes the uniqueness of the love of God expressed on the cross of Golgotha and the compelling force with which it binds us. There God revealed out of the primordial depths of his own nature, a love which the world did not know, and enkindled a movement of love that brought something new into the world (1 Jn 4:9 f.). In obedience to his Father (Jn 10:18; 14:31), Jesus, the bearer and revealer of the divine nature, expressed this divine love in action. The result is that his commandment to love one another "according as I have loved you", cannot but seem to be something new.

Consequently what is new in the Johannine commandment of love must consist in two things, the profoundly understood idea of discipleship, namely, that of following Jesus' example and model to the utmost, in his loving disposition and activity, which is binding on the disciple and, closely connected with this, the eschatological novelty of such an attitude. For John such unselfish love which sacrifices itself to the utmost, has only been made possible and realized by God's initiative, by the eschatological mission and sacrifice of his Son, which is the consequence of his incomprehensible, paradoxical love for the sinful world. The "new" commandment has "become a reality in him (Christ) and in you, because the darkness is past and the new light is already shining" (1 Jn 2:8). In Jesus the love of God has become visibly perceptible and has entered this world as a divine power lightening the darkness and it is received, continued and put into practice by his disciples who are really worthy of the name. "We know that we have passed from death to life (that of God), because we love the brethren" (1 Jn 3:14). It is understandable how urgent the call for brotherly love is, since it is to manifest the new state of affairs that God has brought about.

In addition there were also historical grounds why John should esteem brotherly love so highly and make it the characteristic mark of those who are disciples of Christ and begotten of God. In his first and second Epistles at least he was warding off certain false teachers whose tendency was clearly towards gnosticism. They altogether despised the divine commandments (1 Jn 2:3 ff.) and even claimed to be in communion with God without moral obligations of this kind (1:6 ff.; 2:9 ff.). They also seem to have maintained that they loved God, but John would have nothing to do with such bare assertions: "If any man say: I love God, and hates his brother, he is a liar. For he that loves not his brother whom he sees, how can he love God whom he sees not?" (4:20). Thus, outwardly perceptible love of the brethren becomes a proof of the interior love for God that cannot be directly tested. John deepens this thought (which can already be found in the writings of the noble Jew Philo)[2] still further, by his teaching about faith. Christians are the children of God in a very real sense (3:1), for, through baptism, they have been "begotten of God". "Every one that loves him who begot, loves him also who is born of

---

2. *De Decal.* 120: "It is impossible for the invisible God to be honored by those who dishonor the visible and near at hand." The saying relates to respect for parents.

him" (5:1), that is, loves those who, like himself, are born of him, or in other words, his brothers: it is a fact and law of nature. But for the Christian it is also the express wish and will of his Father (4:21; cf. 3:23; 2 Jn 4). If in general it is true to say that the children of God must have love as a sign, as it were, of their relationship with God, "who is love" (1 Jn 4:7 f., 16), so too this love must be made apparent in the concrete, in love for the brethren. In its nature their love is very similar to that revealed to us as proper to God's own essence by the mission and death of his Son (4:9-11), a completely unselfish, generous, merciful love, a love seeking the salvation of others, a love that for the most part does not correspond to the "natural" feelings of men, and surpasses all other human kinds of love.

One often hears references to Johannine mysticism. It is indeed true that this great theologian did make our communion with Christ and God the central point in his thinking. But so that there should be no misunderstandings, no pantheistic, ecstatic, or magical mysticism, or any that fuses God and man, he demanded love of the brethren as the expression and realization of our exalted communion with God. "No man has seen God at any time. If we love one another, God abides in us; and his charity is perfected in us" (1 Jn 4:12).

But in spite of all his "mysticism", John also sees God as our Lord and judge. As a result of his sins, even the Christian's conscience may still prick and disturb him. Doubts can appear, if we belong wholly to God at all. It is then, however, that we recognize, through the operation of active, practical love, that we are "of the truth" (that is, participate in the divine nature) and calm our heart in the sight of God with regard to everything for which it condemns us, because God is greater than our hearts and knows everything (1 Jn 3:19 f.). John is not saying here that loving good works on our part can outweigh previous guilt; his purpose is rather to give us a criterion for our participation in the life of God.

Fraternal love expressed in action is so great, so important, so indispensable, it is, as it were, the outer mark of our divine sonship, the unmistakable sign of our union with God. A simple act of true love is a rock on which the dreamer founders, but those heavily burdened or in doubt find respite. Here John the "mystic" shows himself to be a very practical Christian realist.

The concrete demands of John's brotherly love were already appreciated within the framework of the charitable life of the early Church. But is it not true to say that in John the commandment to love one's neighbor is narrowed down into love of one's brethren? It has frequently been asserted that this is so, yet closer examination of the texts shows that it is not so. For John, love is the completely universal characteristic of the children of God, in contrast to hate, the token of the "world" (1 Jn 3:13 f.). If he is reproaching the "world" for its hatred towards Christians, it would be unintelligible of him to limit the Christian's love to the circle of the community of the Church. He nowhere preaches hate or speaks of revenge. By comparing love for our human brethren whom we can see, with love for the invisible God (4:20), he is giving the title "brother" a comprehensive meaning; in the next verse he seems to be referring to Jesus' great commandment. Clearly, then, John has expressed the synoptics' "love of one's neighbor" as "love of the brethren", and hence he cannot be using this in any exclusive sense. All John does, is to point first to the community of his brethren in the faith, as a sphere in which the Christian may express his love. But in doing so, he does not mark any frontier. The fact that he orders that heretics be expelled and refused even a greeting (2 Jn 10 f.) is due to his anxiety about the faith. It is self-evident, however, that he did not mean to forbid Christians to play the part of the Good Samaritan. We should not expect to find all Christ's teachings repeated in these occasional writings. But fresh prominence is given to one new duty, hospitality to brethren who are travelling and support for wandering missionaries (Jn 2-8). This passage reflects the changed, more complex situation of the Church at the end of the first century. A certain shift of emphasis is perceptible here, but no fundamental change in charitable attitude and practice. St. John is not only a loyal guardian of Christ's inheritance preserving his spirit but also a disciple of the Lord illumined by the Holy Spirit, giving added profundity to the commandment of love and raising it to be the ruling principle of Christian morality throughout all ages.

CHRISTIAN SPIRITUALITY IN JOHN

W. K. Grossouw

By "spirituality" we have consistently understood a specific spiritual posture and *élan vital,* from which undoubtedly all sorts of practical attitudes and consequences follow, but which nonetheless primarily signifies a structuring and directing of the *spirit.* Never is this word in a more congenial context than in an effort at sketching the piety of the last Gospel, no matter how briefly; for the fourth Gospel is distinctively unwordly, limitless and "spiritual." The same may be asserted correctly concerning the spirituality of the other Gospels and of the entire New Testament, but the conviction that religion is basically a matter of the spirit and of interior posture is nowhere expressed more clearly than in the Gospel which already in early Christianity was called "pneumatic" or "spiritual."

From the earliest ages there has always been the feeling that the Gospel of John has a unique character, which distinguishes it not only from the older Gospels but also from the epistles of Paul. In the New Testament, it occupies a place totally its own. Only the letters which bear John's name breathe a similar atmosphere. When we ask, however, in what precisely this Johannine spiritual climate consists, the answer is not easily come by unless a person is satisfied with poetic classifications, and is prepared to speak with Dostoevsky of "the white Christianity of John." Actually, very different solutions have been suggested from even the earliest periods. The Gnostics of antiquity felt at home in this Gospel, or at any event had immediate recourse to it, seeing there an opportunity to impose their own interpretation. Fathers of the Church such as Augustine pointed emphatically to its symbolism. Long before the advent of modern criticism it was recognized that its theology was as important as its history. In our day some seek the explanation of the properly Johannine element in its affinity to what they call the superior religion of Hellenism or to Gnosticism; others point to its Jewish-Hebraic character, to its strongly cultic or sacramental fabric, or to its Old Testament and primitive Christian background. The amazing thing is that not only do all these theories contain at least an element of truth (as happens in most instances), but that the first and the last impression which the reader of the fourth Gospel carries away with him is one of an outstanding strong spiritual unity and of great consequences issuing from the viewpoint it proclaims. The writer succeeded in completely absorbing the influences which he had himself experienced piecemeal, in uniting his material into a closely-knit structure, and in creating a work which leaves an incomparable impression of unity of spirit, language and atmosphere. It is marked not only by its own character, but by the possession of its own spiritual personality.

This originality, which is so difficult to define but so easy to perceive, is also to be found in Johannine spirituality. What strikes us first is its *unworldly character*. We may recall here the well-known admonition of 1 Jn 2:15-17: "Do not love the world, or the things that are in the world ... because all that is in the world is the lust of the flesh, and the lust of the eyes, and the pride of life; which is not from the Father, but from the world." But what is meant here is much more than merely an admonition to flee from the wicked world.

If we may summarize the Sermon on the Mount as the program of the Synoptic way of life, we see there an exalted ideal which seems hardly capable of full achievement, but we can still recognize in it some consideration for human relationships and human society. There are instructions for marriage, for association with those who are not disciples or even enemies or persecutors, instructions concerning oaths and the use of money and property, and even regarding certain practices of piety. Of all this there is no trace in the Gospel of John. Society and the world—understanding this term in our sense—leave him apparently indifferent. There is not a single pronouncement on detachment from riches or on the giving of alms, about which the Synoptic Gospels have preserved so many logia. There is nothing which may be compared to the sentence: "Give to Caesar the things that are Caesar's." In John, Jesus says to Pilate: "You would have no power at all over Me were it not given from above" (19:11). Looking at the matter superficially, it would seem that we have here the same thought as Paul's "There exists no authority but from God" (Rm 13:1). But this is only apparently so. Rm 13:1 is a positive evaluation of earthly authority, whereas Jesus' saying in John means only that no earthly tribunal has proper jurisdiction over Him who was sent "from above."

In the fourth Gospel there is no moral teaching. There is naturally no system of ethics anywhere in the New Testament, but the basis is there, and there are rules of behavior which were susceptible of further development and application. In Paul we even come across initial indications of family and social morals (1 Th 4:11-12; 2 Th 3:6-13; Col 3:18–4:1; Ep 5:22–6:9; 1 P 2:18–3:7, etc.). In the fourth Gospel there is only one commandment to regulate human relationships—love; and *agape* is mentioned only so far as this exists between brothers and sisters in Christ, as will be explained in due time. All this does not mean that John wants to reject traditional morality, as some Gnostics maintained. Traces of ethical evaluation can 'be found in 3:20-21, and in the first epistle: "My dear children, these things I write to you in order that you may not sin" (2:1; 3:4; 5:17). But these are vague and general indications, and it can hardly be asserted that the attention of the evangelist is fixed on these matters. He does not seem to be concerned with those things which preoccupy the majority of people—cares, worries, money, and earthly position. In this sense he is truly "unworldly."

But then, what does he mean by the *world?* He uses this term very often, and its usage is extremely typical of his whole bent of mind. But what he denotes by it is only partially synonymous with our customary moral terminology when we speak of worldly people and of the dangers of the wicked world, and so on. In John these things lie on a deeper level; they stand in wider scope. The Greek spirit, not only in the so-called classical period but also at the height of the Stoa until far into the Christian era, did not regard *kosmos* as the

neutral and unqualified "world" of the universe, but simultaneously as order, regularity, a harmonious whole, the totality
of being, actually divinity itself, as manifest to the human
reason, as something which encompasses and embraces man
in an accommodating and a dignified manner. For the perspective of the Old Testament and thus also for the upright
Jew it is sufficient to cite the very first sentence of the Bible:
"In the beginning God created heaven and earth." The world
is created by God; it is therefore completely subject to Him,
and proclaims the glory of its Creator. "The heavens proclaim
the glory of the Lord." The transcendent God of the Bible
can in no way be identified with the world; but neither is
there any trace of an irreconcilable opposition, of an unalterable antagonism between God and the world. According to
the Scriptures one could never say without qualification that
God is good and the world bad. The Old Testament does not
suffer from a guileless optimism; it fully acknowledges the
existence of evil, of sin and suffering, but it does not personify evil, it does not make it independent from the one
Creator. In one or another way, indeed in a way which astounds
us and which we are bound to interpret philosophically, it
brings even evil into direct relationship with God. For the
Lord is good and merciful, but He is also just and omnipotent;
in a word, He is *The Lord,* and nothing happens independent
of His will.[1] "I am the Lord, and there is none else: I form
the light, and create darkness, I make peace, and create evil.
I, the Lord, am the one that does all these things" (Is 45:7).
"Shall there be evil in a city, which the Lord hath not done?"
(Am 3:6).

---

1. Or permission, we add quickly. But the Scriptures do not distinguish
explicitly between willing and permitting, between direct or indirect caus-
ality. Christian theology has been operating on the basis of the data of
revelation (Scripture and Tradition) with the aid of Greek methods and
concepts. But this does not mean that theology is a sort of synthesis between the Bible and Greek thought. In the present instance, for example,
Catholic theology continues to consider the mystery of evil, as does the
Bible, in the light of the one, totally dominating mystery of the self-reveal-
ing God who created all things and guides and governs the world in its
entirety. It does not destroy, so to say, the contact between God and evil,
as Greek philosophy, certainly in its leading tendencies, was compelled to do.

Much could be said about these and various other texts, but they all show without ambiguity that the perspective of the Old Testament on the world was unified and consistent. The Jewish concept was so sublime because it totally accepted this world, which it saw realistically both with its miseries and its pleasures, and placed it before the face of the one God as "the work of His hands." The Greek spirit, which could view evil only as a deviation, irreconcilable with metaphysical "goodness," really did not know what to do with it. Consequently, evil had no place in the Greek world-picture except as an anomaly to be overcome and transcended at all costs. For the Greek, the world meant correct order, uniformity, and beauty. Even in biblical thought, evil remains a puzzle; but the Scriptures do not shy away from the paradox which does not isolate evil from the all-good God. The origin of evil is not eliminated, any more than it is separated, from the ⌐per mystery of faith—God, who has disclosed Himself to u⸀ This does not solve the problem but it does place it in the context of revelation, thus making it possible to accept by faith an incomprehensible mystery.

In its effort to solve the mystery of evil, the human mind came upon yet another solution, which when followed to its final conclusion leads to radical *Gnosticism.* If one abstracts from all sorts of small differentiations in its manifold manifestations, one may equate Gnosticism with the mentality which, though having its origin in the East, spread quickly in the period contemporaneous with John and exercised great influence on the religious thought of many. At the same time it must be affirmed that it expressed an existentialist posture, a certain way of looking at life and the world, which is part of common human possibility and is thus not limited to any particular historical era. As a matter of fact, it recurs regularly, whether in the form of different religious sects, such as the Manicheans and the Catharists, or in individual religious experience. In its more radical form it is characterized by a dualism which accepts two principles entirely independent and opposed to each other, good and evil, from which all beings have their origin with their unalterable character or "nature." Evil is thus personified; not merely separated from the "good" God, but made equal with Him, either entirely or at least as being of equal birth, and set up against Him as an autonomous fountainhead of the hierarchy of evil. A whole system of irreconcilable opposites is then constructed on this division; light is put into opposition to darkness, spirit to matter, God to the world.

Gnosticism does not ignore in any respect these concepts so dear to the Greek; quite to the contrary, these notions are equally important to the Gnostic, but with an entirely different emotional value. Precisely because of its regularity, the cosmos now becomes the sum of evil; the compelling force of matter and bondage; blind fate, to which the chosen, Gnostic man is subjected because of his body, but from which he can escape with his divine quiddity. "The world is the plenitude of evil" (*Corpus Hermeticum*, VI, 4). For Gnosticism redemption therefore consists in overcoming the deceitful appearance of all matter, in freeing the spark of light from the darkness of the body; in ascending from this world to the realm of light; and *gnosis*—a religious "knowledge" of the true self, its origin and destination—is the only means for accomplishing this.

If now we return to the fourth Gospel and the epistles of John in order to investigate the meaning and role of the concept "world," we must first observe that here the term occurs very frequently and apparently plays a more important role than in the rest of the New Testament. At the same time we discover, and this is a matter of even greater importance, that we can no longer be satisfied with the simple and evident meaning which the notion of world has in the Old Testament and to a large extent also in the Synoptic Gospels. No less than ten times in John do we meet the expression "this world." This is a point of great significance, for it always suggests the existence of another world, which is the true world, that of God and of the divine reality. "World" is therefore synonymous with "the lower things," the realm here below. The Redeemer who brings revelation has His origin in a realm "above" (8:23). In innumerable places we read that He "comes into the world," that "He was sent into the world," and that He leaves it by "passing out" of it. Passing out of the world is synonymous with going to the Father (13:1, etc.). The disciples, likewise, do not belong to the world, but have been taken out of it. Perhaps this is stated more impressively nowhere than in those extremely simple sentences of the highpriestly prayer: "And I am no longer in the world, but these are in the world, and I am coming to You, Holy Father.... But now I am coming to You; and these things I speak in the world.... I have given them Your word: and the world has hated them, because they are not of the world, even as I am not of the world. I do not pray that You take them out of the world, but that You keep them from evil. They are not of the world, even as I am not of the world" (17:11-16).

This cosmos is therefore an expanse, the all-inclusive place of men and their behavior and the stage for the drama of the redemption. But it is also humanity itself; humanity which does not yet believe, which must be saved, which still can be saved. "For God so loved the world that He gave His only-begotten Son.... For God did not send His Son into the world in order to judge the world, but that the world might be saved through Him" (3:16 ff.). But generally the term signifies that sector of humanity which refuses to believe and rejects revelation. This world cannot receive the Comforter (14:17). Those who believe do not belong to this world but are necessarily hated by it (15:18; 17:14; 1 Jn 3:1). The world does not "understand" them. Between this world and God there is an irreconcilable opposition. Christ does not pray for it (17:9). It is anti-God and anti-Christ. "All that is in the world, is not from the Father" (1 Jn 2:16). Christ "overcame" the world (16:33); the believer is also victorious over it by his faith, by his supernatural knowledge (1 Jn 5:4). It is subject to a master, "the ruler of this world" (12:31; 14:30; 16:11). It "is wholly in the power of the evil one" (1 Jn 5:19). It is also a spiritual realm, an impersonal source of unbelief. They who reject revelation are "of the world and speak of the world" (8:23; 1 Jn 4:5). Just as the Lord knows His own, it also has "what is its own" (15:19).

As we examine this whole picture it would seem that the dualism is perfect and we ask ourselves wherein lies the difference between the Johannine view of the world and that of

Gnosis. Is not the evil one, who was a murderer from the beginning and the father of lies (8:44; 1 Jn 2:13-14; 3:8-12, etc.)
equipped with all the paraphernalia of the wicked Demiurge?
There are, however, a number of texts which we have not yet
cited which will, as if at the last moment, save John's view
from being Gnostic. He says expressly that the world was created
by the Logos, that is, by Jesus Christ (1:3, 10; cf. 17:24). He
also says that God loved the world (3:16; 1 Jn 4:7 ff.); the
unknown God of Gnosticism cannot love it. And finally, the
evangelist leaves open the possibility that the world will do
penance and have its sins forgiven (1:29; 14:31; 17:21; 1 Jn
2:2; 4:14), whereas the Gnostic world, because of its eternally
immutable character, cannot do penance nor have its sins forgiven.

From this it follows that we may not interpret in a Gnostic
sense his many statements on the world, no matter how dualistic
they may seem. That the whole world is subject to the evil one
does not mean that it was not created by God, nor that un-
believers are inevitably surrendered to the power of the devil.
But it does mean that the cosmos of John is a "world" of tensions
with a wide range of implications which are barely compatible
with each other, extending from an almost completely neutral
concept of the world to one which signifies mankind persistent
and rigid in unbelief. And it is precisely this last, extremely
pregnant, sense of the word which preserves it from dualism
properly so-called. For the world in this sense means mankind,
standing alone by its own choice because of its refusal to believe in Jesus; it does not mean human nature. In spite of
appearances to the contrary resulting from his way of speaking,
the universe of John is not static, it has not been previously
determined and arranged according to unchangeable categories
of good and evil; it is in motion, revolving about the only possible
central point, which is Christ, and it is (let me repeat again)
personal relationship to the Lord which determines this position.
"He who believes in the Son has everlasting life; he who is unbelieving toward the Son shall not see life, but the wrath of
God rests upon him" (3:36). Only those who refuse to believe
in Christ and hate their brothers as did Cain are children of
the devil (8:44; 1 Jn 3:8); by their deeds they manifest their
own character, but their deeds are the consequence of their

own choice. But the ruler of this world remains subjected to the power of the humble Redeemer.[2]

The question remains: Why does the evangelist express himself in this manner, why is his "world-view" drawn in colors that are so much darker than those of the other Scriptures,[3] and why do they show such a striking resemblance to Gnosticism, notwithstanding their basic differences? The answer can only be that the spiritual movement which we call Gnosticism was a part of the times and did not leave him unaffected. It seems quite probable that his ultimate purpose in writing the Gospel— the same applies to the longer epistle, for that matter—was not merely to make a Christian appeal to the followers of this religion which toward the end of the first century was exerting a strong and widely-spread influence as an amenable spiritual atmosphere rather than a uniform doctrine; he wants to convert and correct at the same time, and to show that the Gnostic world-view can acquire real meaning only if it is centered on the incarnate Logos, and thus becomes essentially changed.

Some time ago Romano Guardini, in a very fine little book,[4] presented the hypothesis that by nature the evangelist himself tended to a dualistic outlook and had an inclination, as it were, toward a sort of Gnostic psychology, traces of which can still be detected in his writings, such as absolutism, preference for stark contrasts, keen attention to the essence and origin of things. But he overcame this dangerous inclination through his encounter with Jesus; in place of the irreconcilable conflict of essences, there came the unifying relationship to this unique, personal center. Guardini also fosters the opinion that in the striking emphasis on fraternal charity in the Johannine writings we can discern an indication that love for an individual concrete person was not particularly attractive to his natural disposition. Whatever the case may be, it is certain that he had an inner affinity to Gnosticism and that his peculiar outlook on the world

---

2. To understand the character of the evangelist we should note that in his Gospel Satan plays an important role as a spiritual power, but he makes no mention of the many exorcisms which we read of in the Spnoptics.

3. With the exception of a few later Pauline texts which tend in the same direction (Ep 2:2; 6:12; Col 2:8, 20).

4. *Das Christusbild der johanneischen Schriften, Würzburg,* 1940.

is not the result of his apostolic interests alone. The manner in which he evaluates the world is so vigorous and consistent that it reveals a personal concept of the term, 'an idea of the world that is directly opposed to the original Greek notion, which, without being in conflict with the Old Testament or primitive Christian apprehension of the world as a creature of God, can nonetheless not be entirely explained in its specific connotations by derivation from the latter.

We have given more consideration than usual to this one important image because it was necessary to clarify in a singular particular detail what is involved also in many others: the very special nature of Johannine thought and the resultant unique character of his spirituality. Furthermore, the cohesion between the various ideas in the fourth Gospel is so strong that whenever one goes a little more deeply into one he always faces the whole. It is impossible to treat his great ideas individually and successively. Every effort to bring a certain portion into the light necessarily directs our attention to the whole. What we called the unearthly character of Johannine spirituality may also be pointed out as its peculiar nature. It is absolute, seldom shaded; it is compressed into a few fundamental realities. It is consequently also universal, precisely so far as it is not enclosed by concrete, accidental circumstances, but takes place entirely on an existential level.

Naturally, the Gospel is not independent of the historical situation of Jesus' life; but the evangelist is constantly anxious to have the timeless element shine through the historical, and to show in the concrete relationships of Jesus to the Jews and to the disciples the essential relevance of revelation to the world and to the faithful. The Samaritan woman and the crowds of Galilee illustrate the tendency of the masses toward materialism (4:15; 6:26-29). In Nicodemus we see the hesitation and doubt of the well-intentioned intellectual. The "Jews"[5] especially, are a type of human pride and spiritual self-sufficiency, the repre-

---

5. In the fourth Gospel the Jews must not be simply identified with the Jewish people; "historically" speaking they are the spiritual leaders who reject Jesus; "typically" speaking they represent the "world" because they, even while appealing to the Scriptures, oppose themselves to the revelation which has come in Jesus.

sentatives *par excellence* of the world which rejects revelation and is worthy of condemnation.

In the second part of the Gospel (chs. 13-17), it is true, the disciples find themselves in the historical situation of the final gathering and the approaching farewell, but at the same time they clearly represent the Church after Jesus' glorification. They are representatives of all believers who have never seen Christ. "If you love Me, keep My commandments" (14:15). And what are these commandments? Faith in Jesus and fraternal charity! In other words, both the disciple at the farewell and the Christian standing without Jesus in the world, who ask, "How can I still love You?," are directed to keep the commandment. Intimacy with Jesus is realized in this world by fraternal charity, and this is "earthly" only so far as it expresses itself in a willingness to help, in the form of genuine solicitude and the gift of earthly life; for, by origin, it too is from above. These chapters tell us that a purely human relationship of love toward Jesus is no longer possible. They declare moreover that this has never been the case. The sentiments which the Twelve experienced before the departure of the Master was not true love. The farewell, the departure—that is, the glorification of Jesus—and the sending of the Spirit first made true love possible. But in its realization in this world, this consists in fraternal charity, and in faith as an immediate and personal relationship to the Lord. And yet faith is directed to the absent and glorified One who has no need of our solicitous love. "Blessed are they who have not seen, and yet have believed."

The piety of the fourth Gospel, in its fullest dimension, is Christocentric. "These things are written that you may believe that Jesus is the Christ, the Son of God, and that believing you may have life in His name" (20:31). His spirituality, if we may use that term yet once more, has been reduced to this one absolute and is therefore identical with Christian existence itself. It is above all a devout contemplation, a belief, an acknowledgment that Jesus is who He is: the one, the way, the truth and the life. Whoever knows Him, knows God, because He is the perfect revelation of the Father. "This is eternal life, that they may know You, the only true God, and Him whom You have sent, Jesus Christ" (17:3). For John, "life" consists in knowing—in a positive, supernatural, divinely given knowledge, which is really a *gnosis*, a knowledge of God, an awareness of the invisible and eternal Father through the Logos of His Son. "Whoever has the Son, has life"; and one "has the Son" by believing in the testimony which the Father has given concerning Him (1 Jn 5:11, 12). This knowledge and acknowledgment of Christ as the light, as the bread of life, as the vine, and the shepherd, that is to say, as the unique and perfect salvation of man, necessarily includes the acknowledgment that man of himself is powerless and that his gods are nothing. "Without Me you can do nothing" (15:5). This constitutes Johannine self-denial; it is entirely on a spiritual level.

It is this constant relationship to Christ in whom we have been given the fullness of life and salvation, which preserves the fourth Gospel from the pessimism of the Gnostic concept of the world. Just as Paul overcame Pharisaism as an existential possibility, not only by vehemently contradicting it but by positively transcending it with the doctrine of justification through faith, so John gives the Christian answer to the "Gnostic" question which belongs to the perennial human problems: there is an unbridgeable chasm between good and evil; a complete separation of spirits is possible. But the demarcation which sets off these worlds irrevocably is established only by every man's personal decision, by his choice of either giving or refusing faith. Faith in the Logos who became *flesh* directs man's attention to the material world, which through the Incarnation is filled with God's own glory.

The spirituality of the fourth Gospel exists entirely in personal relationship to Christ and in "having the Son"; for whoever has the Son, has life, the only true life, the life which is "eternal." The problem of the possibility of Christian existence is then reduced to the problem of the possibility of this relationship to Jesus. How can a real and living bond arise between the Lord and the man who has never seen Jesus? This is one of the important questions which set the background for the Gospel and the first epistle. John wrote for a generation which had never met the Lord here on earth, for readers who, for the greatest part surely, did not belong to the Palestinian milieu which was the scene of Jesus' activity. How could they, and how can we, acquire relationship with Him who is the life, the way, and the truth? The answer of the fourth Gospel is that this is possible through faith in Christ and love for all the brothers and sisters in the Lord. This faith and this love do not exist in a purely idealistic and abstract realm; they cannot be separated from the historical existence of Him who became man. Even after the ascension, all Christian generations are linked with the earthly revelation of the glory of God which has taken place in Jesus.

It is the peculiar genius of the evangelist to be able to develop a subtle plot with simple words. Direct relationship to Christ begins by *faith*. John repeats endlessly: faith in Jesus, faith in His name, faith that He is, etc. But he also speaks about seeing and contemplating Christ, and about knowing Christ. Some insight into the interconnections between these three ways of understanding is indispensable for grasping his purport. The easiest approach is a short review of the ways he applies the different Greek verbs meaning "to see" to the notion of viewing Christ.

First there is a merely empirical seeing of Jesus, which has no connection with faith and really is no seeing at all, but rather a blindness, as Jesus says, to the unbelieving Jewish leaders who, together with His own disciples, had been eye-witnesses of His deeds: "For judgment have I come into this world, that they who do not see may see, and they who see may become blind" (9:39). Secondly, there is also a different kind of seeing on the part of the eye-witnesses. This is accompanied by faith and therefore sees in the scandal of the "flesh" the "glory" of the Only-begotten. "And the Word was made flesh, and dwelt among us. And we saw His glory—glory as of the only-begotten of the Father—full of grace and of truth" (1:14). This is put forth even more clearly in the introduction to the first epistle, where an appeal is made to all the senses to witness to the corporeal reality of the Logos: "I write of what was from the beginning, what we have heard, what we have seen with our eyes, what we have looked upon and our hands have handled: of the Word of Life.... What we have seen and have heard we announce to you, in order that you also may have fellowship with us" (1:1-3). This is seeing as both witnessing and believing taken together. This was the privilege of the contemporaries of the Lord, of the disciples who had been called to come forward as authentic witnesses. And it was they who were able to recognize the "sign" in His miracles. Thirdly there is faith, which is *contrasted* with bodily seeing and is pronounced blessed. Jesus said to Thomas: "Because you have seen Me, do you believe? Blessed are they who have not seen, and yet have believed" (20:29).

It is not without reason that this pericope about Thomas, who could not believe without seeing and touching, is used as the conclusion of the fourth Gospel, thus ending the whole with a most exalted confession in the Lord: "Thomas answered and said to Him, 'My Lord and my God!'" The evangelist is evidently appealing here to the faith of that later generation for which he is writing, and which had not seen. To arouse and deepen this faith is really the sole reason for writing his book (20:30-31).

This faith, however, *our* faith—which in a certain sense is the crowning of the whole Gospel and of the whole Scriptures and is connected with a direct, personal seeing of the Lord— may not be regarded as a purely spiritual vision. It is this too; and if you will, it is such principally. Faith is aroused deep within us by God Himself. "No one can come to Me unless the Father who sent Me draw him, and I will raise him up on the last day. It is written in the prophets, 'And they all shall be taught of God.' Everyone who has listened to the Father, and has learned, comes to Me" (6:44-45).[6] This faith is spiritual insight: "Now this is everlasting life, that they may know You, the only true God, and Him whom You have sent" (17:3; see 14:7-9, etc.). But it is always connected with and joined to the bodily vision of the One-who-became-flesh, so that in this point, too, we come across the polarity of spirit and flesh which is

---

6. In characteristic fashion this text continues as follows: "not that anyone has seen the Father except Him who is from God (i.e., Jesus Himself), He has seen the Father." Contemplation, that is, direct knowledge of God is reserved for the next life; see 1 John 3:2, "We shall see Him as He is." This is the true blessedness of salvation, and we may consider this (strictly) eschatological seeing of God (in Christ) as the fourth way of knowing God, when added to the three already mentioned above.

distinctive of the fourth Gospel. As is evident from the texts that have been quoted above (1:14; 1 Jn 1:1-3), our faith rests upon the actual seeing of eye-witnesses, on their testimony which continues in the preaching of the Church. And we may add here entirely in the spirit of John that our faith, too, goes hand in hand with a bodily contemplation of the divine glory in the form of flesh; for in the celebration of the liturgy and in the experience of the sacraments we see and hear and touch with faith, as did the apostles.

Linguistic statistics generally have interest only for specialists. But perhaps it will be of some import to others to know that the verb "to believe" occurs almost a hundred times[7] in the fourth Gospel, three-fourths of which occur in the first twelve chapters, which are dedicated to the revelation of Jesus to the world and the judgment of the world. For John, just as for Paul, the act of faith is a decision by which a person decides in favor of God who has revealed himself in Jesus, and thus escapes the judgment which has already been pronounced on the world. Whoever refuses to believe simply adds this condemnation to his own imputability; he is already condemned and need not wait for the "final" judgment (3:18, 36, etc.).[8]

One of the most distinctive features of Johannine thought consists in what may be called his anticipation of eschatology. He assures the Christians who toward the end of the first century were still anxiously looking for the Parousia—on this state of mind see the second epistle of Peter—that even before the second coming we may rightly speak of judgment, and that the believer will possess eternal life before the final resurrection. The decision, which involves both a discernment of spirits and

---

7. Ninety-seven times, to be exact. At the same time it is most strange that the substantive *faith* is entirely lacking. A similar phenomenon can be noted with the words "to know" and "knowledge." Whereas the verb forms for "knowing" are used very frequently, the substantive *gnosis* (knowledge) is not used at all, not even in the epistles. However, this is readily understandable, once we realize that the evangelist wants to avoid the term because of its pejorative connotation.

8. This must naturally not be considered an irrevocable judgment. True to his own mannerism, John speaks about an absolute and essential attitude of spirit. Whoever with full knowledge and deliberation actually rejects grace and persists in this attitude "is already judged."

a judgment, is a matter of the present. John has all this in mind with his word *krisis*. For him, as well as for the Apostle of the Gentiles, faith is the distinctive mark of the Christian life even *after* conversion. "You believe in God, believe also in Me," Jesus told His disciples in His farewell address (14:1). In Christianity, faith in God and faith in Jesus are on equal level. In the fourth Gospel we have left deism behind more than at any other time. John declares categorically: "No one has at any time seen God. The only-begotten Son, who is in the bosom of the Father, He has revealed Him" (1:18).

Whatever the Christian believes, therefore, has reference only to the Son; He is the essential object of our *Credo*. The disciple believes that Jesus is the Holy One of God (6:69), the Christ, the Son of God, who came into the world (11:27; 20:31, etc.); that God sent Him, that He is in the Father and the Father in Him (14:10), in one word: *that He is* (8:24; 13: 19). This is repeated with an impressive monotony; and this is really the sole content of Jesus' preaching in the fourth Gospel, namely, that God speaks to us through Him, through His words and through His "deeds," that He is the one who brings revelation and at the same time *is* Himself the revelation in the most literal sense of the term. For this reason Johannine faith, as well as that of Paul, includes personal relationship to the Lord. One cannot believe in His message without believing in Him. One cannot believe His words, one cannot believe that all He says is true without accepting Him wholly, without having trust in Him, without embracing Him and subjecting oneself to Him with loving surrender, for He himself is the message. He is wholly present in His word and in His deeds, which themselves are "words" (14:10). This is what John calls "believing in His name," accepting Him for everything He claims to be, "receiving" Him (1:12) such as He is. For this reason everyone who believes, has eternal life, even now.

The Johannine doctrine on love, agreeing essentially with the other books of the New Testament, is outstanding in three aspects: its absolute character, its strong emphasis on fraternal charity, and its censure of every indiscreet "exercise of love toward God." Concerning the last it has been said that Paul almost never speaks about loving God. John goes much farther on this point. It would seem that in his first epistle he wants to warn against illusions of a (false) mystical love for God. Notwithstanding the avoidance of the word "gnosis," one nevertheless gets to hear about the marks of the true Gnostic throughout the entire epistle. The writer carries on a silent but positive and direct polemic by means of what may be called phrases of definition or of description which mark the style of this letter: "He who says that he knows Him, and does not keep His commandments, is a liar" (2:4). "He who knows God, listens to us" (4:6). The criteria of real gnosis and true love for God are faith in the incarnation and active fraternal charity. "For this is the love of God, that we keep His commandments; ... and this is His commandment"—in the singular!—"that we should believe in the name of His Son Jesus Christ, and love one another, even as He gave us commandment" (5:3 and 3:23).

The necessary interconnection between these two ways of Christian life is indicated nowhere more clearly than in this passage of the first epistle: "If anyone says, 'I love God,' and hates his brother, he is a liar. For how can he who does not love his brother, whom he sees, love God, whom he does not see? And this commandment we have from Him, that he who loves God should love his brother also" (4:20-21). John therefore unquestionably acknowledges the possibility of a real love of the Christian for God, but he is not so effusive on the point as is our devotional literature, which seems to insist on placing constantly on our lips the most ardent aspirations of the saints. John always adds the commandments in the same breath, and it is always the Johannine commandments of faith and brotherly love which give reality to and incarnate the love of God which would otherwise appear so immaterial. The faith which he has in mind is specifically faith in the true incarnation of the Lord (1 Jn 4:2; 5:5-6; 2 Jn 7); and his fraternal charity is one of action and reality (1 Jn 3:18) toward one whom we "see," which means toward one who belongs to our human world, which cannot be idealized.

A Christian must not want to me in heaven before his time, but must remain a man among men. John will have no part in a love which wants to go directly to God without dealing with the incarnate Logos and the tangible, crass reality of human society. He rejects Gnostic spirituality, which reserves its love for immaterial, celestial essences: "To love the God of heaven and heavenly creatures means to tender them continuous respect. . . . Man is composed of a double nature so as to be able to answer to his twofold task, namely, of being in a state where he can simultaneously have a care for earthly things and love the divinity" (*Aesculapius*, 9). The Christian attitude toward man comprises more than "care"; it consists of a love which is directed toward another in his whole concrete reality.

For this reason the emphasis of John's preaching rests on brotherly love. It is more accurate to use this term rather than the expression "love of neighbor." The last is naturally not excluded from John's intention, but he speaks only of the mutual love of Christians. "He who loves his brother abides in the light" (1 Jn 2:10). "For this is the message that you have heard from the beginning, that we should love one another" (3:11). And there are the words of the Master in the Gospel: "A new commandment I give you, that you love one another: that as I have loved you, you also love one another" (13:34). "This is My commandment, that you love one another as I have loved you" (15:12). The precept of love of neighbor is the summation of the "New Law" of Christianity. It is characteristic of John that he places the sayings of Jesus on brotherly love in the context of the farewell address, where the world is excluded and the traitor has departed (13:30-31); in the intimacy of Jesus' last stay "with His own" (13:1). That the evangelist does not mention love for those who are outside or for enemies is not so much the result of a feeling of partiality as the consequence of an exalted and profound insight. It is also consistent with his view on the world, as we have already explained. The world John speaks of, when thought out thoroughly to its last implication—as John loves to do—is an obstinate refusal to believe in Jesus, and *as such* it can have no share in true love. This apparent exclusiveness, however, is primarily a consequence of his sublime idea of *agape*, which both in origin and in intrinsic nature surpasses the purely psychological and even moral level. It is not only a gift of God, it is a sharing in God's own being. Whoever excludes himself from the fellowship with God, which has been offered us in the self-revelation of the Word, simply cannot receive it. *This* love is simply inconceivable without the notion of reciprocity; whoever rejects the Son toward whom the

Father's love is primarily directed (3:35, etc.) cannot possibly be the object of *agape* in the full sense of the term.

In the preceding part we have already shown wherein lies the fullness of John's notion on love. Here we can do no better than transcribe 1 Jn 4:7-21: "Beloved, let us love one another, for love is from God. And everyone who loves is born of God and knows God. He who does not love does not know God; for God is love. In this has the love of God been shown in our case, that God has sent His only-begotten Son into the world that we may live through Him. In this is the love, not that we have loved God, but that He has first loved us, and sent His Son a propitiation for our sins" (vv. 7-10; one must naturally read the whole passage). For John, as well as for Paul (Rm 3:21-26; 5:5-8; Ep 5:1-2, etc.), the sending of the Son, which culminated in the death on the cross because of love, revealed to us *in actu* who God is and what we are to think of Him. Paul prefers to speak about the grace and mercy of God; John refers to love; but they both mean the same.

Jesus, dying on the cross so that the world might live,[9] is the incarnate and therefore revealed love of God. He shows us God's essence. "God *is* love," not as a state of self-contained quiet, but an overflowing, self-sharing life which communicates itself with the Son, and through Him with every man who is willing to believe in this revelation of love. We did not know this love of God before God showed it to us in Jesus (1 Jn 3:16; 4:9-10). The initiative belongs to God alone, from whom the *agape* descends via the Lord to man. And the love which is in God, reveals itself among Christians as brotherly love. The mutual love of Christians is more than a moral obligation; it is above all a sharing in the divine love; it is a mark of the new life (1 Jn 3:14), of having been born of God (4:7) and of the true gnosis. But with all this sublimity, or better, because of this supernatural origin, it remains real and active. "He who has the goods of this world and sees his brother in need and closes

---

9. The evangelist does not distinguish the death on the cross from His glorification; the Son of Man who was raised on the cross is already the glorified one, who draws all things to Himself by His Spirit and condemns the unbelieving world with its rulers (cf. 3:14-15; 8:28; 12:31-33; 14:30; 16:11; 19:37).

his heart to him, how does the love of God abide in him?"
(1 Jn 3:17). It is the tangible manifestation to the world of
what Christianity really is and intends to be. Without it, all
preaching remains but an idle word, as the history of the Church
has shown on innumerable occasions. "By this will all men know
that you are My disciples, if you have love for one another"
(13:35). It is the achievement which the Lord expects from
His disciples (15:1-7), His last word, His testament, the unworldly peace which He left us (14:27).

THE JOHANNINE SACRAMENTARY

RAYMOND E. BROWN

The question of sacramentality through symbolism is one which deeply affects the interpretation of the Fourth Gospel. Yet, in approaching this question, one encounters two very different scholarly evaluations. On the one side, there is the antisacramental (or at least nonsacramental) school led by Bultmann and most of the German scholars. On the other, there is a type of ultrasacramentalism which sees a symbolic reference to some sacrament or other in virtually every chapter of John. This view is championed by Cullmann[1] and by many of the French and British scholars.

Our purpose in this essay is to re-examine the methodological principles behind the theory of Johannine sacramentality and, in particular, to distinguish relatively well-founded examples of sacramentality from the less defensible suggestions. We believe that there is true sacramental symbolism in John; nevertheless, unproved applications of this symbolism have served only to bring the whole principle of symbolism into disrepute.

We recognize, of course, that in pursuing such an investigation we are to some extent dealing in categories and precisions that may be foreign to John. Whether we confine our study to baptism and the Eucharist, or include the complete sacramentary, we may be overprecise in the question we are asking, namely, are there references to the sacraments in John? For would the author of John have distinguished precisely between sacraments and sacramentals?[2] His was a general insight that the

---

1. His *Urchristentum und Gottesdienst*, which appeared in 1944, has had tremendous influence through its translations. We shall cite it as *Early Christian Worship*, tr. by A. S. Todd and J. B. Torrance (London, 1953).
2. Henri Clavier, "Le problème du rite et du mythe dans le quatrième évangile," *Revue d'histoire et de philosophie religieuses*, 31 (1951), 287,

lifegiving power of Jesus was effective through the material symbols employed in the deeds and discourses of the public ministry.[3] Now we know that in the course of time some of those material symbols were recognized by the Church as permanently valid signs communicating Christ's grace (the sacraments), while others were recognized as having only a lesser or temporary significance. We shall take advantage of this distinction and confine ourselves to the sacramentary in the strict sense; yet we must recognize that this precise delineation is more our own than the Evangelist's.

The Nonsacramental View of John

Those scholars who see a minimal sacramental interest in John have based their case on literary criticism. Bultmann[4] finds in John three clearly sacramental passages: 3:5 with its reference to water, 6:51b-58, and 19:34-35 (passages referring respectively to baptism, Eucharist, and to both sacraments together). Otherwise John does not mention the institution of the sacraments, and places all emphasis on a personal union with Jesus. For Bultmann,[5] then, John basically ignores the sacraments and serves as a corrective to that tendency in the early Church which would see the sacraments as a means of salvation. The three sacramental passages are additions made by the ecclesiastical redactor, a censor postulated by Bultmann who made corrections in the Gospel to conform it to the Synoptic tradition and Church usage.

---

thinks that in Jn we have a generalization of sacramentalism in the direction of sacramentals. He thinks that the evangelist did not want to confine sacramental references to two particular rites like baptism and the Eucharist.

3. The Johannine concept of miracle as a "sign" borders closely on this. If men could really see and believe the revelation of Jesus portrayed in a material "sign," they could receive life eternal.

4. *Das Evangelium des Johannes*, 16 ed. (Göttingen, 1959). See also *Theology of the New Testament*, 2, 2, tr. by K. Grobel (London, 1955), pp. 3-14.

5. *Das Evangelium*, 360: "Although the Evangelist tolerated the Church's use of baptism and the Eucharist, he remained suspicious of it because of the misuse to which it was subject, and therefore he did not speak of it. In truth the sacraments were superfluous for him."

While many have rejected Bultmann's view of John as basically antisacramental, there has been a wider acceptance of at least a nonsacramentality or of a peripheral sacramentality. Eduard Schweizer doubts whether or not one can prove that the three sacramental passages are redactionary. In any case, their sacramentality is merely anti-Docetic and only helps to show the reality of the Incarnation. In John there is no stress on the sacraments in themselves, but only as witnesses to Jesus, and sacraments are not a central thought. Helmut Köster maintains that even if 6:51b-58 and 3:5 ("water") are secondary, there is already a cultic and sacramental element in the other parts of Chaps. 6 and 3. Yet the Evangelist is interested in sacramentality only insofar as it leads back to the reality of Jesus. In John there is nothing like the metaphysical viewpoint that characterizes the sacramentality of Ignatius of Antioch.[6] Eduard Lohse agrees with Bultmann that the three sacramental passages are redactionary and that the original Gospel had no sacraments. But this does not mean that the Evangelist was antisacramental. Rather the Evangelist's interest was centered on *martyria*: he wished to emphasize contact through witness with Jesus, and this main purpose did not call for any sacramental stress.

Despite certain disagreements, most of the above-mentioned discussions are focused on the three sacramental passages singled out by Bultmann. The question of wider sacramental symbolism is, for the most part, regarded as unproved and almost unworthy of detailed rebuttal. The underlying methodological principle seems to be that if the Evangelist had intended sacramental significance, he would have expressed it more clearly.

---

6. Gunther Bornkamm, "Die eucharistische Rede im Johannes-Evangelium," *Zeitschrift für die neutestamentliche Wissenschaft*, 47 (1956), pp. 161-169, maintains, on the other hand, that the interpolation 6:51b-58 is much more sacramental than the rest of ch. 6 and much more Ignatian. Wilhelm Wilkens, "Das Abendmahlszeugnis im vierten Evangelium," *Evangelische Theologie*, 18 (1958), pp. 354-370, tries to refute Bornkamm's arguments and to show that the passage is truly Johannine and not an interpolation. Yet he agrees with E. Schweizer on the anti-Docetic, peripheral character of Johannine sacramentality.

The Ultrasacramental View of John

This school approaches John from another standpoint. Albert Schweitzer maintained that the exegete had to consider the whole New Testament ethos. The theory that Old Testament prophecy had a fulfillment in the New Testament created a sensibility to typology. Therefore, it was natural for John to present Jesus' words and actions as prophetic types of the Church's sacraments, and the significance of these types would be easily recognizable to the Christian readers of the Gospel. Schweitzer began a trend; it was for Cullmann to go through John in detail and establish the case for sacramentality. Cullmann stresses that we know something of baptism and the Eucharist as essential parts of early Christian worship. Therefore, he maintains, both the Evangelist and his audience must have been familiar with these sacraments. Since the Evangelist's purpose was to ground the community's faith in the historic Jesus, what more natural than for him to show a basis for the sacraments of baptism and the Eucharist in Jesus' words and works? Of course, this sacramental reference would be understood only in the postresurrectional period in which the Evangelist and his audience were living. As Cullmann proceeds through John incident by incident, he seeks to find some internal indication that sacramental symbolism was intended by the Evangelist. In fact, however, he often seems to fall back on the principle that since a passage could have been understood sacramentally, it was intended sacramentally. His treatment was answered incident by incident by Wilhelm Michaelis, who maintained that in virtually every case Cullmann had not proved the existence of sacramental symbolism.

The Swedish scholar Alf Corell[7] also takes a deeply sacramental view of John, although he does not see as many sacramental references as Cullmann does. Corell believes that just as there is a strong influence of the Jewish festal liturgy on John (in the direction of replacement), so there is influence of the Christian sacramental liturgy, i.e., baptism and the Eucharist. As Protestants, Cullmann and Corell would confine the

---

7. *Consummatum Est* (Swedish ed., 1950; English ed., London, 1958).

sacramental references to just two sacraments; the Catholic scholar Bruce Vawter[8] would enlarge the sacramentary. He suggests the possibility of a reference to a sacramental anointing, similar to extreme unction, in the anointing of the feet (Jn 12), and to matrimony in the Cana scene (Jn 2).

The British commentaries on John have tended to be more prosacramental than the German. Edwyn Hoskyns[9] presents some interesting researches into Church history and liturgy to back up the sacramental interpretations of the narratives of the healing of the blind man (Jn 9) and of the washing of the feet (Jn 13). Even the more critical commentary of C. K. Barrett[10] states ". . . there is more sacramental teaching in John than in the other Gospels." He traces this to several Johannine categories of thought which are favorable to sacramentalism, e.g., symbolism and emphasis on the material circumstances of Jesus.[11]

Paul Niewalda has given us the most recent and complete defense of sacramental symbolism in John. He frankly admits that by the ordinary tools of exegesis one cannot prove that the Evangelist intended to refer to the sacraments by means of material symbols. And so he suggests a different exegetical approach. Niewalda shows that a dependence on some type of symbolism or deeper meaning was in vogue in all types of literature at this time, and that our earliest Christian records (liturgy, Church art, the Fathers) witness to the use of fixed symbols for the sacraments. Therefore, he maintains that when these traditional symbols are encountered in the New Testament and, in particular, in John, they should be interpreted as

---

8. "The Johannine Sacramentary," *Theological Studies,* 17 (1956), pp. 151-166. David M. Stanley, S.J., has also shown himself very favorable to ultra-sacramentalism in his series of articles in *Worship,* 32-35, (1957-1961).

9. *The Fourth Gospel,* 2 ed. (London, 1947), esp. p. 363 and p. 443. R. H. Lightfoot, *St. John's Gospel* (Oxford, 1956), also accepts much sacramental symbolism in Jn.

10. *The Gospel according to St. John* (London, 1958), p. 69.

11. Clavier, *art. cit.,* 287, has the same view; he asks how could Johannine thought ignore sacramentalism (i.e., the use of exterior forms as a means of grace) when it makes a fulcrum of the Incarnation?

references to the sacraments. The author of John was a child of his time: symbolism would have been part of his literary technique, and he would have used the same symbols as his contemporaries. Rudolf Schnackenburg objects to this principle on the grounds that most of the early Christian witnesses are later than John and may represent a more developed symbolism. Water, for instance, certainly plays a more symbolic and sacramental role in Tertullian than it does in John. Schnackenburg, who is a moderate sacramentalist, has his own method of procedure; first he studies the clearly sacramental texts in John and establishes from them an estimate of the sacramentality of the Evangelist with which to approach the more obscure texts.

Consideration of the Methodology of These Views

The study of all the arguments for and against Johannine sacramentality suggests that a balance may be achieved through a better methodological appreciation on both sides.

First, the literary criticism of the nonsacramentalists should not be neglected. This pertains chiefly to the three definitely sacramental passages stressed by Bultmann: 3:5; 6:51b-58; 19:34b-35. Too often, if we take Jn 6 as an example, supporters of the sacramental position satisfy themselves by proving that the chapter is a unity. Against Bultmann, and quite correctly, they point out Eucharistic indications in the earlier part of Chap. 6. To some this would prove that the Eucharistic section belongs to the rest of the chapter. Yet why could it not have been added to the chapter by someone desiring precisely to clarify the Eucharistic undertones of the rest of the discourse? The unity could be purely a literary or logical one.

What the recognition of Eucharistic elements in other parts of Chap. 6 does prove is that Bultmann's concept of the ecclesiastical redactor is false. There is every evidence that the sacramental section has a certain harmony with the rest of the discourse and was not simply superimposed by an act of ecclesiastical censorship to make John conform to sacramental ideas.[12]

---

12. Clarence T. Craig, "Sacramental Interest in the Fourth Gospel," *Journal of Biblical Literature,* 58 (1939), 32, pointed this out a long time ago. He stressed that we cannot discover a redactor's addition by isolating

Nevertheless, while we may rule out such a theory of arbitrary redaction, we cannot exclude editorship in the history of the composition of John. E Schweizer and Ruckstuhl, by the use of stylistic characteristics, have devastated the source theory of John as posited by Bultmann and others. There is too much literary homogeneity in John to posit the simple combination of totally distinct sources. Yet this homogeneity cannot rule out subsequent editorship *within* the Johannine tradition. The Last Discourse is, perhaps, the best example of this: it is all quite Johannine, but it certainly shows signs of editorial modifications.

With this in mind, we cannot dismiss the possibility that some sacramental sections in John (e.g., 3:5 and 6:51-58) are editorial additions of Johannine material, designed to bring out the real sacramental undertones already present. This would account for the surface unity of the sections, and yet allow for the startlingly deeper sacramentality of the specific additions. Thus there would be truth in the remarks of the non-sacramentalist that certain specific sections do have clearer sacramental emphasis than the rest of the Gospel. In our view, this theory weakens Schnackenburg's criterion of using the clearly sacramental sections as a canon for judging the sacramental symbolism and interest of the rest of the Gospel.

Second, we must discuss the claim of the nonsacramentalists that Johannine sacramentality is of a peripheral character, or introduced only as part of anti-Docetist apologetic. This peripheral sacramentality is contrasted with "Hellenistic" or "Ignatian" sacramentality, which gives independent value to the sacraments.

Here, too, there is a methodological difficulty. Most of those who hold this view (see above) have confined their study to the three so-called clearly sacramental passages of the Gospel and to 1 John 5:6-8. Now there probably is an anti-Docetist emphasis in 1 John 5:6-8 and in John 19:34b-35; the author is stressing the bloody death of Jesus as the Christ. The water and blood bear witness to the humanity of Jesus. Another

---

ideas that seem to us to contradict the main position of the Evangelist. "It is quite another thing to demonstrate that they were contradictory to him."

section, 6:51b-58, may have some claim to be considered as anti-Docetist, although this seems less clear to us.[13] Yet it is only in these two or three sacramental passages that there is any emphasis on the connection between anti-Docetism and sacramentalism. The many other sacramental passages claimed by Cullmann, Niewalda, and others have no such particular bent. Thus, if any truth can be granted to even a part of the claims of the ultrasacramental school, this very specialized aspect attributed to Johannine sacramentality would disappear, and anti-Docetism would become merely one aspect of a larger sacramental picture.

As for "peripheral sacramentality" in general, a great deal depends on the definition of terms. No exegete with a sense of history expects to find a fully developed Scholastic sacramentalism in John. And it is probably true that even between the time of John and that of Ignatius of Antioch there was some development of sacramental theology. Yet, in evaluating Johannine sacramentality, we must remember that the purpose of the Evangelist was different from that of an author like Ignatius. The Evangelist cannot treat of the sacraments as such, but only inasmuch as they are reflected in the words and works of Jesus.[14] Therefore the claim that in John the sacraments are emphasized only insofar as they help unite the Christian to the historical Jesus is a bit naïve. What other role could the sacraments play in *a gospel?* Any reference to the role of the sacraments in the postresurrectional Church can only be through prophetic typology or some other secondary sense, if the author is to maintain his purpose of telling the significance of what really happened between the baptism of Jesus and His resurrection. Thus, most of the exegetes who interpret John sacra-

---

13. The stress on "feeding on" Jesus' flesh may help to prove His humanity, but 6:55 ("My flesh is a real food, and my blood a real drink") seems to put more emphasis on the true nourishing value of the flesh and blood, rather than on any anti-Docetist motif. There is nothing particularly anti-Docetist about 3:5.

14. Schnackenburg says that for John the sacraments take the work of salvation once performed by Jesus, re-present it, and apply it to all believers after the coming of the Spirit. The self-revelation of Jesus as the source of truth and life stands in the foreground of the Gospel; the Church and the sacraments stand in the background as a continuation of that work.

mentally are quite correct methodologically in seeing any sacramental reference as the second of a twofold meaning present in the words and works of Jesus. For example, if we posit some historical tradition behind the Nicodemus incident, then we must allow a primary nonsacramental meaning to Jesus' words, a meaning which Nicodemus could have understood. The reference to Christian baptism can only be secondary, at least chronologically. Johannine sacramentality fits into the Gospel's oft-repeated confession that the deeper meaning of these things was not understood until afterward. In this sense, then, Johannine sacramentality is "peripheral," but such a description tends to be misleading.

Nor does the fact that John omits the institutions of baptism and the Eucharist mean that the Evangelist was not interested in the sacraments. That Jesus Christ instituted the sacraments is a dogma of the faith. But there is nothing of faith about when He instituted baptism. St. Thomas connects the institution of baptism to Jesus' own baptism in the Jordan, a scene which John does not narrate but at least implies (1:33). Estius connects the institution of baptism to the Nicodemus scene (3:5), in which case John would be the only one to have recorded the institution. More frequently, perhaps, theologians follow Tertullian and Alexander of Hales in connecting the institution of baptism to Mt 28:19, "Go . . . baptizing them in the name of the Father and of the Son and of the Holy Spirit," words not recorded by John (nor by Mk, nor by Lk—are these also nonsacramental?). Many scholars today, however, suggest that the Trinitarian formula as given by Mt came into the Gospel from liturgical usage. Therefore, in not connecting the institution of baptism to any precise words, but in seeing references to baptism in many of the words and works of Jesus, John may be representing the original, imprecise outlook of the earliest Christian theory.

The Eucharist presents a more complicated problem. Tradition places the institution of the Eucharist at the Last Supper. But did the early Church preserve the precise words of Jesus as words of institution? Behind the four accounts in Mt, Mk, Lk, and 1 Cor, scholars see two basic traditions, that of Paul (Lk) and that of Mk (Mt), both with claims to antiquity. And while John does not record the scene of institution at the

Last Supper, the words of 6:51, "The bread that I shall give is my own flesh for the life of the world," may stand quite close to the Semitic original of Jesus' words at the Last Supper, since many claim that Jesus probably spoke of His flesh rather than of His body. Thus the argument against Johannine sacramentality from the failure to record institutions is not as impressive as might first seem, and probably reflects more of modern theological interests than of those of antiquity.

Third, we must consider the methodology of the sacramentalists and answer the fundamental question: Is it necessary to have some internal indication that the author himself intended a symbolic reference to the sacraments? As we have said, most of the ultrasacramentalists approach the problem from the viewpoint of what the Evangelist's audience could have understood. Yet that is a very delicate instrument of exegesis, or rather an instrument that is used with much more ease in eisegesis.

A few considerations seem in order. We grant that we cannot approach John with the idea of accepting only the symbolism that is clear to us today. Certainly Niewalda is correct in pointing out that some type of symbolism (typical sense, secondary sense, *sensus plenior,* or whatever hermeneutical tag we may give it) was in more general vogue in New Testament times than it is in our own. And there are indications all through John that the author was prepared to carry his symbolism quite far. Who would have dared to interpret 21:18 and its vague reference to Peter's stretching out his hands as a symbol of his crucifixion, if the sacred writer did not make it specific? Or, if one prefers to avoid chapter 21, the same may be said of the equation of the Temple and the body of Jesus (2:21), and of the Spirit and water (7:39).

Now it may be objected that these symbols show that the Evangelist can and does explain symbolism when he employs it, and that therefore we should confine ourselves to just those symbols that he explains. But is there anyone who believes that "the Lamb of God," which John does not explain, does not have some symbolic reference, whether it be to the Suffering Servant or to the paschal lamb, or both? And since the water-Spirit equation is not specified until chapter 7, are we to believe that in none of the earlier passages water refers to the Spirit?[15]

Thus it might be more precise to say that the symbols the Evangelist explains are precisely the very difficult ones that might otherwise have been overlooked. To confine the Gospel's symbolism to them would be arbitrarily to prejudice our exegesis.

Niewalda's investigation of the symbols used in the early Church for the sacraments can serve as a negative criterion in exegeting John. If there is no clear indication in the Gospel itself that a passage has symbolic reference to a sacrament, and if there is no evidence in the early Church that the passage was understood sacramentally, then we may well rule out a sacramental exegesis. A sacramental symbol that the Evangelist intended to be easily understood without explanation should have left some trace in art or in liturgy or in the writings of the Fathers. Without such assurance, we may suspect that we are dealing with modern imaginative eisegesis.

Let us consider, for instance, Cullmann's interpretation of the foot-washing scene in chapter 13 as a symbol of the Eucharist. Jesus specifically holds up the foot washing as an example of humble and loving service to one's brethren (13:15). Nevertheless, in this scene many have seen a symbolic reference to a sacrament or sacraments. Verse 10 reads: "He who has bathed does not need to wash, except for his feet." The first clause, says Cullmann, "can surely have only this meaning; he who has received Baptism, even when he sins afresh, needs no second Baptism." While we would not attribute to this exegesis the certainty that Cullmann gives it, we believe that some symbolic reference to baptism is solidly probable, and it was well known in antiquity.[16] But Cullmann goes on to maintain that

---

15. We do not suggest that every mention of water refers to the Spirit; but since the Spirit gives life (6:63), we would find difficulty in dissociating the "living water" of chap. 4 from the Spirit.

16. Elsewhere we have listed our reasons for seeing a reference to baptism. But this symbolism must be interpreted loosely (we certainly do not mean that this scene is the baptism of the disciples). It is a secondary symbolism, perhaps gained by the fusion of two accounts; in the primary significance we have an example of love, and that is what must be repeated. But the washing, considered as bathing (v. 10), also symbolizes baptism in the sense that it flows from the power of Jesus (compare 13:3 with Mt 28:18-19) and is necessary if we are to have a share with Him in the next life (13:8).

the clause "except for his feet," which is of doubtful authenticity, is a symbol of the Eucharist, a sacrament which is meant
to be repeated. This is a view shared by Goguel, Loisy, W.
Bauer, and Macgregor, who point out the connection between
the washing of the feet as a symbol of love and the Eucharist
as the sacrament of love. Now antiquity may have seen a reference to penance in this text, but not to the Eucharist. The
lack of external support makes the exegesis suspect, especially
since foot washing is scarcely a natural symbol for the Eucharist.
The statement in v. 14 that the disciples must wash one another's feet would be an exceedingly strange form of a command to repeat the Eucharist. And so, on the basis of our
criteria, we would reject this interpretation.

Fourth, if thus far we have accepted some of the criteria
of the sacramentalists, and if, in particular, we can employ
Niewalda's criterion of traditional symbolism as a negative check,
we cannot accept it as the sole positive criterion that he makes
it. We agree that the author need not have explicitly explained a symbol, but can we rule out the need for some indications in the text or context? Exegesis is still the determination of the author's intent, and not primarily the determination
of the audience's understanding. We agree fully with Schnackenburg that the examination of how others understood the Gospel
a century later cannot serve as a sole criterion of interpretation. (On that principle, could we not determine the literal
meaning of the Old Testament through its usage in the New
Testament?) Such a criterion is especially open to question
when we are dealing with something like symbolism, which
lends itself to imaginative development.

Let us take an example. For Niewalda, both the healing
of the man at Bethesda in chapter 5 and the healing of the
blind man in chapter 9 are symbols of the cleansing and healing
wrought through baptism. There is good patristic and liturgical
evidence for this interpretation of both.[17] Yet, what a difference
of internal indication!

---

17. Niewalda marshals the evidence. Both scenes are connected with
baptism in catacomb art. For chap. 5, Tertullian and Chrysostom are among
those who see baptismal reference; for chap. 9, Irenaeus and Chrysostom.
For the lectionary evidence, see Hoskyns, *op. cit.*, pp. 363 ff.

a) The main theme of chapter 9 is the opening of the man's eyes to what Jesus really is, in contrast to the blindness of the Pharisees (9:35-41). That baptism was spoken of as "enlightenment" (*phōtismos*) is seen in the New Testament (Heb 6:4; 10:32) and in the earliest patristic evidence.[18] If we turn to chapter 5, we find that the main theme concerns the Sabbath. The dramatic role of the man who was healed is reduced to a minimum. He recovers his health, but he receives no particular gift of understanding. His healing is simply the occasion for the Sabbath dispute.

b) In chapter 9 there is a specific connection between blindness and sin. The disciples think that physical blindness is an index of sin (9:2). Jesus denies this, but points out (9:4-5) that the healing of this blindness will demonstrate how, as the light of the world, He overcomes night, which is certainly a symbol for Satan's power. At the end (9:41) we hear that the Pharisees are spiritually blind and remain guilty of sin. Thus the whole context lends itself easily to a symbolism of baptism removing sin. On the other hand, the only reference to sin in the Bethesda story is the direction to "sin no more" in 5:14. This direction merely establishes the same connection between Jesus' power over sickness and His power over sin that is common to many miracles in the Synoptics. No figurative aspect of the healing is brought out as in chapter 9. True, the discourse that follows is concerned with the power to give life, but this is in the light of the rabbinic theology that God continues to give life *on the Sabbath*.

c) The man in chapter 9 is healed by washing in water (9:7). The man in chapter 5 is healed by the command of Jesus. In fact, this healing is contrasted with the healing that might have been accomplished by washing in the pool.

d) A symbolism is specified in 9:7 which connects the healing waters with Jesus. Siloam means "sent," and in John Jesus is the one sent. There is no such definite symbolism in chapter 5. Some have pointed out that the name of the pool is

---

18. Justin, Apol. 1, 61: "This bath is called enlightenment." Notice that the New Testament references are from Heb, an epistle with strong Johannine affinities. See C. Spicq, *L'Epître aux Hébreux*, 1, 2nd. ed. (Paris, 1952), pp. 109-138.

"Bethesda," which means "place of mercy." Actually, we know that the Hebrew form of the name was *byt šdtyn*, which does not refer to mercy. It is true that there could be a play on the Greek form of the name, but the manuscript evidence is very uncertain as to which is the real Greek form (Bethesda, Bezatha, or Bethsaida). In any case, the man was *not* healed in this pool. Another symbolism, suggested by Tertullian, labors under similar difficulties. A reference to baptism is seen in the angel's stirring of the waters and giving healing power to them (even though these waters do not heal the man!). It is well known that the verse that concerns the angel (5:4) is not found in any early Greek manuscript and is probably not authentic.

And so, while Niewalda's external criterion may fit both chapter 5 and chapter 9, there is no parity in the internal indications pointing to sacramental symbolism. It is quite plausible that the Evangelist may have intended a secondary reference to the healing and enlightening power of baptism in chapter 9, but he has left no real indication of a similar intention for chapter 5. Therefore, in our judgment, we should reject the claim for baptismal symbolism in chapter 5.

These observations have led us to two relatively clear criteria for judging the presence of sacramental symbolism in John. While there need be no clear identification of the symbolism, there should be some internal, contextual indication. This should be corroborated by the external criterion of good attestation for the sacramental interpretation in early Church art, liturgy, or literature. Now, of course, the combination of these two criteria will give us varying degrees of certitude in our exegesis. At times, as in chapter 9, the evidence may be strong enough to be reasonably probative. At other times, the internal evidence will be somewhat elusive, and the most we can have is a probability. If either criterion is totally unfulfilled, we should reject any sacramental symbolism, rather than allow ourselves to be victimized by accommodation.

Application of the Criteria

We shall not attempt to apply these criteria to every example of sacramental symbolism that has been proposed for John;

some examples would obviously meet the criteria, some would obviously not. Let us take, however, some of the more difficult examples.

First, the baptism of Jesus in the Jordan (1 Jn 1:19-34). In this scene Cullmann sees the historical origin of Christian baptism and "a pointer to the baptism of the Christian community." This is fairly evident. Jesus' baptism by John marked the beginning for the public proclamation of God's dominion. For His followers, baptism was the means by which men were incorporated into this dominion. The two baptisms were joined because the apostolic kerygma, which began its narrative with the baptism of Jesus, put a demand on the listener to be baptized. The question we wish to decide here, however, is whether *in John's account* there is any special baptismal symbolism beyond that which is the common heritage of all the Gospels. We should point out from the start that the external criterion is difficult to apply here, for references to the baptism of Jesus will not always specify John's account as the precise source of the symbolism.

The suggestion that John's account, in particular, specifies that Christian baptism will be a baptism communicating the Spirit is not too impressive. This is far clearer in the Synoptics (Mk 1:8; par.), where a baptism with a Holy Spirit is directly contrasted with a baptism with water. This contrast is not found in John, since 1:33 stands by itself.

Cullmann maintains, however, that John's 1:26 really presents a deeper insight than the Synoptic contrast, for John contrasts John's baptism in water and the person of Jesus: "I am only baptizing in water, but there is one among you whom you do not recognize." The true significance of Christian baptism, Cullmann maintains, is achieved in the person of Jesus Himself—a truth foreshadowed in John. Actually, the supposed contrast in v. 26 does not exist. The contrast there is between John the Baptist and the one to come after him. The interrogators have demanded to know what the exact role of the Baptist is and why he is baptizing. He tells them that they should not worry about him, but about the more important one-to-come who stands in their midst.

Does the fact that John 1:33 says that the Spirit rested on Jesus symbolize that Christian baptism will communicate a permanent gift of the Spirit? John 1:33 is a reminiscence of the Suffering Servant passage in Is 42:1; and the Suffering Servant theme in the baptism of Jesus is found in all the Gospels (Mk 1:11 also echoes Is 42:1). We might add that the descent of the Spirit on Jesus at the baptism, as described in the Synoptics, is also permanent (see Mt 4:1, where the Spirit conducts Jesus into the desert). Again there is no distinct sacramental symbolism in the Johannine account.

According to Cullmann, Corell, and Niewalda, John like Paul connects Christian baptism with the death of Jesus, for the Baptist points Him out (1:29) as "the Lamb of God who takes away the world's sin." Thus, in a baptismal context, Jesus was marked out as one to die for sin. We admit that the Evangelist thinks of the baptism as revealing Jesus to be the Suffering Servant, the Lamb of God (even though John does not specifically draw this causal relation, for John does not describe the baptism of Jesus as such). Likewise, we admit that the designation of Jesus as the Lamb, at least in its Gospel sense, refers to His death. But how does the fact that Jesus' baptism pointed to His death also signify that from His death would flow Christian baptism? It is true that the Lamb of God who will die for sin (1:29) will also baptize with a Holy Spirit (1:33), but one must admit that there is no hint in John of the connection of the two ideas. Is there any more or less connection in the Synoptics between Jesus as the Suffering Servant (Mk 1:11) and baptism with a Holy Spirit (Mk 1:8)?

Thus the special baptismal symbolism attributed to John's account of the scene lies in extremely complicated exegesis— exegesis which finds little support in the Gospel itself.

Second, the Cana scene (Jn 2:1-11). Vawter[19] suggests for this scene a symbolic reference to the sacrament of matrimony, or at least to marriage as a sacred institution in the sense of Eph 5:25, which compares it to the union between Christ and the Church. Vawter stresses the presence of Mary at Cana as

---

19. *Art. cit.* (*supra*, n. 14), p. 164.

the "woman" and draws on what is, in our opinion, the very plausible relation to the figure of the "woman" at the cross (Jn 19:26) and in Rv 12. He thus sees Mary as a symbol of the Church. "The presence of Mary-the-Church at this wedding forecasts the sacramental nature of Christian marriage once the glorification of Jesus is accomplished." Jesus and the Church are present at this marriage, the two terms of the comparison in Ep 5.

In applying our external criterion to this suggestion, we find that most of the ancient evidence connects Cana with the Eucharist or baptism. However, a few of the Fathers[20] do see in the Lord's presence at Cana a tacit attestation of the sanctity of marriage against any encratitic extremes. By way of internal support, Stanley[21] reminds us of the wedding symbolism present in the Old Testament, where marriage symbolizes the relations between God and Israel. Thus, for him, the mention of the wedding at Cana could symbolize the relations of Christ and the Church, which in turn could point to Christian marriage.

In our judgment, neither the external nor the internal evidence for a symbolic reference to matrimony is strong. The wedding is only the backdrop and occasion for the story, and the joining of the man and woman does not have any direct role in the narrative. In the Vawter-Stanley hypothesis we still have an obvious difficulty: Jesus and Mary-the-Church are only present; there is no union between them to symbolize matrimony as in Ep 5. Perhaps our objections smack too much of modern logic, but the proposed symbolism does not seem to have made any particular impression in antiquity either, at least in the form proposed by Vawter and Stanley. We cannot allow, then, any more than a remote possibility to the symbolism.

The Eucharistic reference of changing the water into wine is better supported. Niewalda points out its early occurrence in a fresco in an Alexandrian catacomb, where it is linked to the multiplication of the loaves. St. Irenaeus says that "Mary

---

20. The Fathers mentioned this scene in their treatises on marriage, but that is not exactly the same as seeing the scene as a symbol of Christian matrimony.

21. "Cana as Epiphany," *Worship*, 32 (1957-1958), pp. 83-89.

was hastening the wonderful sign of the wine and wanted before the [appointed] times to partake of the cup of recapitulation."[22] Internally, too, there are many possible hints of Eucharistic symbolism. The changing of water to wine occurs before Passover (2:13), as does the multiplication of the loaves (6:4) and the Last Supper. Thus before Passover we have a wine miracle and a bread miracle; these might be seen as taking the place of the Eucharistic institution, which John does not mention.

There is a probable connection with the death of Jesus in the mention of the hour that was to come (2:4) and would only begin at the Last Supper (13:1). The water becomes wine, as the wine would become blood. The wine at Cana is praised as "the quality wine," the wine of the new dispensation kept until now; and this wine is the means of Jesus' manifesting His glory (2:11 and 17:5). All of these indications, though far from conclusive, do have special significance when we realize that, for the Jew, wine was the blood of the grape.[23] Thus, on the basis of our criteria, we would allow a good probability for the Eucharistic symbolism of Cana.[24]

Third, the cleansing of the Temple (2:13-22). Cullmann suggests this as the other half of the Eucharistic symbolism that we have seen at Cana: there the blood, here the body, of Christ. The Temple does stand for the body of Jesus (2:21); nevertheless, scarcely the Eucharistic body, which in John is referred to as "flesh." That this ingenious theory proposed by Cullmann has no real internal support is obvious, nor is there

---

22. *Adv. haer.* 3, 16, 7: ". . . conpendii poculo," i.e., as F. Sagnard, O.P., explains it (*Sources chrètiennes,* 34, pp. 295-297, n. 1), the cup "which sums up and concentrates in it the mysteries of salvation, in a striking 'epitome' of the marvels of grace . . . it is the cup of the Eucharist, 'the wonderful sign of the wine' of which Cana is the figure . . . in intimate connection with 'the hour of His passion.'"

23. Gn 49:11; Dt 32:14; Sir 50:15.

24. Naturally, any sacramental symbolism is secondary. The principal idea seems to be that the old has passed away in favor of a new creation; the replacement of the Jewish purifications; and the plenitude of wine as a sign of the messianic days.

an echo in tradition for Eucharistic symbolism in the cleansing of the Temple.

Also to be rejected is A. Schweitzer's suggestion that the Temple scene is a reference to baptism because it is a fulfillment of Ezk 47:1-12, where water flows out from the Temple. While the threatened destruction of the old Temple and its replacement with a temple of messianic nature may have been a fulfillment of a whole battery of Old Testament passages, there is no reason to single out Ezk 47 in particular, or to think that the stream of water mentioned there was in the Evangelist's mind.

Fourth, a baptismal symbolism has been suggested by Niewalda for the walking on the water (6:16-21), the Good Shepherd discourse (10:1-18), and the Lazarus story (11:1-45). All of these meet to some extent his criterion of traditional symbolism. However, they do not meet any criterion of internal evidence. We can see how Lazarus' return to life might be connected in Christian thought with rebirth by baptism, especially in the light of Paul's theology (Col 2:12), but the Evangelist, who knew both ideas, makes no attempt to connect them. Likewise, the connection of baptism and incorporation into the Shepherd's flock is a logical deduction but scarcely an exegetical one.

Fifth, the anointing at Bethany (12:1-11). Vawter sees here a symbolic reference to the anointing of the dying. In John this scene does not serve to prepare for the physical burial of the Lord, as it does in the Synoptics, for there is a real burial described in John 19:39-42 which would make such preparation otiose. Rather, the anointing of chapter 12 prepares for the type of burial we hear of in 12:24, the burial of the seed in the ground so that it may bear rich fruit. Thus the anointing has a connection with the glorification and exaltation of the Lord. Then Vawter tells us: "The day of Christ's burial is the day of the Church." This is somehow connected to the suggestion that the anointing in John may symbolize the sacrament of final anointing referred to in James 5:14-15. We must humbly admit that the logic of this connection escapes us, unless perhaps the author means that the sacrament of anointing predicts our resurrection as the anointing at Bethany predicted Christ's. However, as has been seen more clearly in recent years, the sacrament of anointing was primarily directed against sickness, not against death. This, plus the fact that the anointing at Bethany was with perfume (*myron*) and not oil (*elaion*), removes any internal indications of a symbolic reference to extreme unction. As far as we know, there is no ancient tradition to support such symbolism.

Sixth, the allegory of the vine (15:1-8). Many have seen a Eucharistic reference here. Tradition seems to give good support to this symbolism, beginning with the blessing over the chalice reported in the *Didache*: "We thank you, our Father, for the holy vine of David your servant, that you have revealed to us through Jesus your servant."[25] Such an early connection of the vine and the Eucharist is impressive.

There is internal evidence, too, for sacramental symbolism. The figure of the vine is placed in the setting of the Last Supper; and even if the Evangelist did not mention the Eucharist at the Supper, we can scarcely believe that he did not know of its place there. The disciples have just drunk the Eucharistic wine-made-blood, "the fruit of the vine" (Mk 14:25). The primary stress in the description of the vine and the branches is on unity; this is also one of the signal effects of the Eucharist in early Christian theology (1 Cor 10:17).

There are similarities between the vine-and-the-branch passage and the Eucharistic section in 6:51-58. The branch must abide in or remain on the vine; in 6:56 we hear: "The man who feeds on my flesh and drinks my blood *abides in* me and I in him." Cut off from the vine, the branch will wither because life comes to the branch through the vine; in 6:57 we hear: "The man who feeds on me will have his life through me." The unity represented by the vine demands love (15:9), love so great as to lay down one's life for one's loved ones (15:13). Thus there is a connection between the fruitful vine and the Lord's death. In 6:51 we hear: "The bread that I shall give is my own flesh

---

25. *Didache*, 9, 2.

for the life of the world"; and we note that "give" here is a reference to giving in death. And so it seems that "I am the real vine" (15:1) is very close to "I am the living bread" (6:51). In their primary meaning both metaphors may refer to divine wisdom as the source of life, but both may also have a secondary reference to the Eucharist. Thus, we believe that the proposed Eucharistic symbolism of chapter 15 meets our criteria satisfactorily.

Seventh, the draught of fish and the meal in chapter 21. The catch of 153 fish in 21:6-8, 10-11 is, as Lk 5:1-11 teaches us, probably a symbol of the mission of conversion, i.e., the fish caught symbolize those converted by the disciples as fishers of men. This is reinforced by the emphasis that the net which was the instrument of the catch was not torn (21:11), a symbol which can be interpreted in reference to the Church. Peter's role as the shepherd in 21:15-17 would fit into this general picture.

Now, since this conversion logically implies baptism, are we to think that the Evangelist had baptism specifically in mind? There is evidence for this in antiquity. The internal case for baptismal symbolism would be strengthened if St. Jerome's interpretation of the number 153 is correct. In his commentary on Ezk 47:9-12, he sees a connection between the scene in John and that of the fish caught in the miraculous stream that flows from Ezekiel's Temple. If John had the Ezekiel passage in mind with the number 153, then the miraculous stream of baptismal water flowing from the new temple which is Christ (Jn 7:38; 2:21) could have been meant. However, this type of exegesis is quite complicated and tentative; it would not allow us to characterize the baptismal interpretation of the scene as more than possible.

A similar case can be put forward for Eucharistic symbolism in 21:9, 13, with its meal consisting of fish (*opsarion*) and a loaf of bread, to which Jesus invited the seven disciples (21:2). Niewalda points out that the representation of a meal with seven at table appears in a Eucharistic context in catacomb art. There are difficulties, of course: there is no mention of wine at this meal, nor is the symbolism of the fish (*ichthys*) for Jesus Christ really applicable here. However, since the symbolism could be based on the bread alone, these difficulties are probably not insurmountable.

Is there a general basis for Eucharistic symbolism in all the postresurrectional meals in the Gospels? If in the reception of the Eucharist the early Christians awaited the return of the Lord (1 Cor 11:26), they may well have read Eucharistic significance into those meals where the resurrected Lord did appear among men. Certainly the vocabulary used of the meal in John 21 is significant in the light of the multiplication of the loaves (Jn 6:11) and of the words that the Synoptics record at the Last Supper:

Jn 21:13: *"Jesus took the bread* [*gave thanks*: D, Syr[s]] *and gave it to them, and did the same with the fish."*

Jn 6:11: *"Jesus took the loaves of bread, gave thanks, and distributed them to those seated there, and did the same with the fish."*

Mk 14:22: *"And taking the bread, he blessed, broke, and gave it to them."*

If there are Eucharistic overtones in the multiplication of the loaves (and we believe there are, not only in John, but also in the Synoptic accounts), there may well be Eucharistic overtones in the very similar account in John 21. And the description of the postresurrectional meal in John 21 may have reminded the Christian of the Last Supper as well. But again, we cannot go beyond possibility.

With this we can bring our treatment to a close. Obviously we have not solved all the difficulties, nor have we proposed foolproof criteria which will work in every instance. But we hope that we have made a contribution toward bringing the proposed Johannine sacramentary under workable control.

IS THERE A JOHANNINE ECCLESIOLOGY?

RUDOLF SCHNACKENBURG

At first sight the Johannine theology expounded in the Gospel according to John and in the "great epistle" (1 Jn) does not seem to recognize the Church as a theological factor (the term ἡ ἐκκλησία does not occur). For a long time John's Gospel was considered evidence of an individual, spiritualized, even "mystical", Christianity. The "religious individualism" expressed in the call "he that believes in the Son has eternal life", or other such statements (3:16, 36; 5:24 etc.), the "mysticism" that appears to lie in expressions denoting union ("... abides in me and I in him", 6:56; 15:5 etc.), the wrongly interpreted statement concerning "worship in spirit and truth" (4:23), all contributed to such a distortion. Nor is R. Bultmann's existential interpretation, which regards the Gospel according to John as the chief witness on behalf of an already "demythologized" gospel message, capable of grasping the eminently ecclesiological aspect of Johannine theology. Where everything is aimed solely at the "eschatological", concrete decision of the individual in regard to the "revealer" and his word, no place remains for the reality and operation of a redemptive society equipped for, and charged with, conveying the light and life brought into the world by the divine envoy. It is also insufficient to form the link with the community only by the requirement of brotherly love comprised in the moral summons; for then the movement is again solely from individual to society and it is not evident that the individual can realize his Christian life only on the basis of the redeemed community to which he is subordinated. In fact, the idea of the Church is much more deeply rooted in Johannine thought, and indeed is indispensable to this independent, magnificently devised theology, with its concentration on the essential. That has been convincingly shown by recent investigations, and will be confirmed by examination from the ecclesiological point of view.

There can be no doubt that the chief interest of the fourth evangelist is in Christology. The impelling motive for the composition of this late gospel (the traditions of which it is true must go back very far) certainly lies in the author's intention to provide the Church of his time and surroundings with a picture of Christ corresponding to the Church's spiritual condition, but which, in the evangelist's view, was already perceptible in Jesus' words and work (1:17f.; 17:3; 20:31). But is it not inevitable that readers and faithful who were already living at a considerable distance from the historical events should raise the question of the relation in which they stood to the Christ who had brought revelation and salvation to the earth, and ask what function was assigned to the community which they acknowledged? Was the Church only the recipient of Christ's gospel and saving gifts; was it not also the administrator of his bequest, and the executor of his intentions? Closer penetration into John's gospel shows that the Church in fact is assigned a quite definite position in the work of salvation.

In the soteriological revelation saying: "He that believes in the Son has eternal life", the gift from God's envoy appears in the first place to be one made there and then. Yet it is only the Spirit sent from the exalted Christ who confers the divine life to the faithful in a definite and real manner. At the beginning of the individual's way of salvation there is needed in addition to faith, a "generation from on high", that is to say, baptism, in order to enter at all into the sphere of God's life (3:3, 5), and this at the same time places the individual, even when this is not expressly stated, in the array of the other children of God (Jn 1:12f.; 1 Jn 3:1f.), who in the First Epistle of John are recognizable as the orthodox community (2:20, 27f.; 3:9f.; 5:1f.). In defence against the "anti-Christs" the profoundly rooted community-consciousness appears: "They went out from us but they were not of us. For if they had been of us they would have remained with us; but it was to be made manifest that they all did not belong to us" (2:19). If W. Nauck is right in thinking that the basis of the epistle is an exhortation written in connection with baptism and its obligation, the significance of baptism becomes quite clear; but even without this the theological lines are plainly recognizable: baptism is the generation by God which produces children of God; it implants in the believer the "seed of God", that is to say, the Holy Spirit, for a life without sin (3:9) and administers to him the "unction" for perseverance in correct doctrine (2:20, 27). But by the behavior of the children of God, by their true confession of Christ (2:22; 4:2f.; 5:1) and their fraternal love (2:9ff.; 3:14, 23; 4:20f.; 5:2), it is then recognized whether they are really such, or not rather "children of the devil" (3:10). The community represented by the author (3:14) makes the claim to be the true children of God, to possess communion with God (1:3, 6; 2:3 etc.), and refers in this regard to its possession of the Spirit (3:24; 4:13). Spirit and life are only conveyed and preserved, are only operative and fruitful in the community.

That is not, however, as it were a subsequent, supplementary conviction formed in controversy with teachers of false doctrine. The same fundamental theological ideas are already expressed in the Gospel according to John, which is not dominated by this polemic. It is only since Jesus has been raised up that the Spirit has been there for the faithful as life-giving power (7:39). He is released in "streams of living water" which (so verse 37f. should no doubt be interpreted) flow from Jesus' body. This metaphor immediately recalls the scene in John 19:34f., where blood and water come from the open side of the Crucified. If the cognate passage in 1 John 5:6f. is compared with this, the assumption will probably be justified that the evangelist also sees in it a symbol for the sacraments of baptism and eucharist; for according to the passage in the epistle, Spirit, water and blood all become perpetual witnesses whose testimony converges (in favor of Jesus Christ). The death of Jesus becomes effective for salvation by means of the Spirit in the sacraments of the Church. For the holy eucharist we have another passage which fits into this group of ideas. At the end of the discourse on the bread of life in chapter 6, Jesus says: "If then you shall see the Son of man ascend up where he was before (will you be scandalized even then)? It is the Spirit that gives life, the flesh profits nothing" (6:62-63a). This must certainly be interpreted as follows: a Son of man who comes from heaven (cf. however v. 42), returns there once more and shows by that that he is not confined to the sphere of the "flesh" (the earthly human sphere); he also gives his flesh and blood (v. 53), not in the manner of his earthly, natural existence, but after his return to heaven in a way in which his life-giving Spirit is at work. Both sacraments, but similarly the forgiveness of sins as well (20:22f.), are effective through the Spirit proceeding from the exalted Lord. In fact the thought is fundamental for the whole picture given by the gospel that the earthly Jesus continues and only then really fulfills his saving work when he is raised on high. Consequently he asks his Father to be glorified; only when glorified will he be able to use the "power over all flesh" given to him, in order to bestow eternal life on all those "given" to him by the Father (17:2). Only when he is exalted will he "draw all to himself" (12:32) and only after his departure to the Father will the disciples accomplish "even greater works" than himself, clearly in winning over men (14:12). There is also for John a "time of Jesus" and a "time of the Church" characterized by the Spirit, but he does not present them as Luke does in a double work, but views them together in the very words of his Christ. Jesus' gaze is already perpetually turned towards the future in which when glorified he will make his work, completed on earth (19:30), fruitful for all men (12:24, 32; 17:2, 21), through the Holy Spirit (cf. the sayings regarding the Paraclete) and through the activity of his disciples (15:27; 17:18; 20:21).

That this gaze of the Johannine Jesus, fixed on the future, is directed towards the Church, is clear from various sayings and metaphors with which he defines his work. The chief image is that of the flock which not only occurs in the discourses and imagery of chapter 10 but exercises a pervasive theological influence. The faithful, in Jesus' time the disciples assembled around him, are those whom the Father has "given" to the Son and brings to him, and whom the Son does not "cast out" but rather accepts and keeps and does not allow "to be lost" (6:37-39; 17:6, 9 f., 11 f.). If this mode of speech is compared with the pictures of the shepherd in chapter 10 a complete system of thought can be recognized which has also shaped that terminology. God is the real owner of the sheep but he has entrusted them to the shepherd Jesus so that the sheep belong to both, just as, in general, there is a complete community of property between the Father and the Son (cf. in particular 10:26-29; 17:10). The true and good shepherd, Jesus, in contrast to the hirelings (the Jewish leaders), knows and loves his sheep, cares for them and gives his life for them (10:11-15); the sheep who know him follow him and he gives them eternal life (10:10, 27f.). On departing, however, he gives them back again to his Father's immediate care; above all he prays that the Father will preserve them in perfect unity (17:11ff., 22f.). By this metaphor light is thrown on other questions too, such as the call to faith, which results from the Father's free power over grace (6:44, 65); in the present connection, however, it is important that the image of the flock is also maintained for the future. "I have other sheep that are not of this fold; them also I must bring and they will hear my voice and there will be one flock and one shepherd" (10:16). There the perspective opens out to the one Church composed of believing Jews and gentiles. The question regarding the old "Israel" and the call of the gentiles is, therefore, perceptible in John too. "Israel" is still a title of honor (1:31, 50; 3:10; 12:13); only the unbelieving Jews are depreciated, even verbally (οἱ Ἰουδαῖοι is used mostly in a negative sense for the leading Jewish circles), for as the representatives of the "world" hostile to God, they have become haters of Jesus and persecutors of Christians (2:18; 5:16, 18; 7:1 etc.; cf. also 15:8-16:4). Non-Jewish mankind already meets Jesus in very promising representatives (the Samaritan woman 4:39-42; the "Greeks" 12:20c.), and waits as it were to be incorporated in God's flock. Then all national or other modes of thought disappeared; Jewish modes of thought are radically broken. The chosen children of God (not even: the children of Israel dispersed among the gentiles) are scattered all over the world and are to be gathered together into a unity by Jesus' redemptive death which avails for all (11:52). It is solely a question of faith in Jesus the Christ and the Son of God; the departing Lord prays for all who will believe in him through the word of his disciples (17:20f.).

Finally the image of Christ's flock also appears in the "supplementary chapter 21", in the words of the risen Christ to Simon Peter: "Feed my lambs, feed my sheep" (21:15-17). Even if this chapter perhaps did not belong to the original plan of the gospel, it certainly belongs to the evangelist's tradition. The conferring of pastoral ministry on the disciples whose position in the rest of the gospel (perhaps precisely on account of the rivalry with the "disciple whom Jesus loved", cf. 20:6ff.) is not in doubt (1: 42; 6:68f.), cannot be dismissed with a remark that the Johannine picture of the Church is not interested in a constitution, for even in that scene after Easter, it is not the constitution which is the decisive viewpoint, but care for the guidance of the sheep which are deprived of their true and abiding shepherd (10:16). The heavenly protection of the Father, preservation from evil, sanctification (17:11-19), do not exclude earthly direction by a representative of Christ. For John, too, the Church is a reality both of the present world and the next, a society existing in the world but of a kind that is not of this world (17:14f.).

The Johannine picture of the Church is enriched not only by the image of the flock but also by that of the vine and the branches (15:1-8), which concerns as it were the very sanctuary of the Church, its nature and mystery, that is to say, the living union of the faithful with Christ. In this sense it is a parallel to the Pauline idea of the Body of Christ. The Johannine picture, however, has a different basis and depth. If it was borrowed from the imagery of the Old Testament, and there is much in favor of this supposition, it is linked with the idea of God's chosen people; for in the Old Testament Israel is regarded as God's vineyard (Is 5:1-7; 27:2-6), or choice vineyard (Jr 2:21; Ps 80[79]:9-16), which God himself has planted. In that case Christ himself first of all would take the place of Israel as the authentic vine on which believers in him would blossom like living vine branches, bear fruit and glorify the Father. This thought is not of course worked out because it is the need to "abide" in Christ which is to the fore. Nevertheless such an identification of Christ with the "true Israel" and such a concentration of eschatological thought on him as the representative and foundation of the life of the new people of God would certainly be possible, for in him the eschatological hour and salvation are already present (4:23; 5:25), and he has only gone on ahead of his own, where he intends to bring them themselves (14:2; 17:24, and the passages that refer to the Son of man). In the same way he could represent the new "temple", for the logion regarding the building up of the Temple in 2:21 is interpreted as referring to the body of the risen Christ, and the "adoration in Spirit and truth" is fulfilled (4:23f.) from now on (in the Church). But again the identification of Israel and vine, worshipping community and Temple (and certainly the interpretation of the Son of man in a collective sense) is not at all so certain. It remains open to question whether the Johannine Christ may be regarded as a corporate personality (in the sense of the Pauline Body of Christ), who even in his historical work of salvation comprised in himself the society of believers. The Johannine Christ in fact makes a markedly exclusive claim. He, and he alone, is the divine revealer and bringer of salvation (cf. the ἐγώ εἰμι sayings); he is the Son; he demands adherence, by faith, to his person, in order then to give life to the believer and to lead those who are joined to him in that way into the heavenly world. Yet even if the "corporate" interpretation is not insisted on, the eschatological significance of the allegory of the vine remains. For what Jesus says to his band of disciples in view of his departure is after all only realized in the Church. Only in the Church is the abiding in Christ and the promise of Christ's abiding in them possible; the disciples and the later believers could not have understood this in any other way (even as regards the supplementary exhortation "to remain in his love" and as regards brotherly love). Whether there is also a reference to the holy eucharist, as many commentators suppose, need not be inquired here. It is sufficient to recognize the Johannine Church's conception that in it the most profound communion with Christ is accomplished and that this alone permits any fruit to be borne. The Old Testament metaphor of the vine is then transferred to another, the Christian, plane; it is the new people of God which is the fruitful vine, by its union with Christ who gives it life and strength just as God's flock, led by its shepherd Christ, stands in a new light: by its inner connection with him it attains true and full communion with God.

It is for that reason that the Church is so insistently called to unity. Unity is impressed on the Church as an essential characteristic, for Christ draws the Church into the existing indissoluble communion between Father and Son (10:14f.; 17:21); consequently unity must also take effect perfectly and distinguish the Church (17:23), so that the world may believe in the divine mission of Jesus Christ. This idea of unity is hardly derived merely from topical reasons of polemic through the danger of heretics, but belongs to a profound Johannine grasp of the essence of the Church. God's love, which is wholly directed to the Son, also comprises all who are in communion with the Son (16:27) and is, therefore, also to overflow as a unifying force to all who are united with Christ (17:26).

This picture of the Church, however, also reveals some focal points of church life in the Johannine communities or, to put the matter in another way, shows us something of the functional context of John's exposition. They were churches in which liturgical and sacramental life was flourishing. They understood their worship of God as "adoration in Spirit and truth" and themselves as true worshippers filled with the Holy Spirit; their worship was the eschatological culmination of all worship practised until then, transcending even the Jewish service of the Temple (which in the meantime had disappeared) (4:21-23). Their Pasch replaced and fulfilled the Pasch of the Jews (2:13; 6:4; 11:55), for they possessed the true paschal lamb, Christ (19:36; 1:29). They had already inwardly withdrawn themselves from the "festivals of the Jews" (5:1; 7:2), even though they did not deny the historical origin of the redeemer of the world from Judaism (4:22). In the sacraments they possessed testimonies and vehicles of the continuing redemptive act of Jesus Christ (1 Jn 5:6f.), and obtained living and abiding union with the Son of God and through him perfect communion with God (Jn 6:56f.). Whether divine service was celebrated only as celebration of a meal or of baptism, or whether "the community at divine service finds expression as body of the crucified and risen

Christ", as Cullmann seeks to infer from John 2:18, 22, must remain doubtful; but it cannot be disputed that the Johannine Church experienced the word of Christ (Jn 6:63b; 8:31, 51; 14:23f.; 17:14, 17) and the person of Christ (6:57) as present in its solemn worship (comprising word and sacrament) and was even more consciously to experience it through the Johannine writings.

A strong interest was also felt in the Johannine Church for the mission. As well as what has already been quoted, two further scenes may be indicated. The detailed account given of the episode in Samaria (chapter 4) culminates in the conversion of the inhabitants of Sychar. These Samaritans, cut off from Judaism and regarded as half pagans, make a full profession of faith in the "savior of the world" (4:42). The intervening missionary discussion of Jesus with his disciples (4:31-38) is noteworthy. The people of Sychar, approaching over the fields, are a harvest full of promise, and Jesus' gaze moves prophetically into the distance to the day when he will have sent out his disciples. They will harvest where they did not labor; others have already labored before them and they have entered into their labors (v. 38). This vista which is no longer fully intelligible to us, must have had a concrete meaning for the evangelist, perhaps in relation to the mission in Samaria. The "Greeks" who shortly before the Passion came to Jesus and wished to see him (2:20f.), are a sign that the grain of wheat when it dies does not remain alone but brings forth much fruit (v. 24) and that when Christ is lifted up he will draw all things to himself (v. 32). Though the Gospel according to John is not expressly a missionary work, its missionary interest is nevertheless unmistakable.

Finally, the Johannine Church is engaged in a stern defensive battle against an unbelieving hostile world, but is certain of victory (16:33). It carries on the struggle not with weak human powers but in the might of the Holy Spirit: The Paraclete will "convict the world of sin, of justice and of judgment" (16:8, cf. 9-11). How else is sin as such, unbelief in regard to the eschatological envoy of God, revealed than by the Church's preaching and its inflexible faith? How is "justice", the entry of Jesus into the heavenly world of his Father, made plain if not through the testimony of the Church to the resurrection?

And how is it disclosed that "the prince of this world" is already judged, except by the triumphant existence of the Church in the midst of a world hostile to God? The testimony of the Holy Spirit is perceptible in the testimony of the disciples (15:26f.). The same conviction that Jesus' victory is continued in the faithful and manifested before the world is expressed in 1 John 5:4-8 and, similarly, that this is only possible by virtue of the sacraments and of the Holy Spirit.

REFLECTIONS ON THE THREE EPISTLES OF JOHN

J. Ramsey Michaels

First John, the longest of the three Johannine "letters," has few of the characteristics of a real letter. There is no identification of the writer or of the addressees, no greeting at the beginning, no word of farewell at the end. But popular tradition, based on the occasional use of such clauses as, "I am writing to you, little children," or, "Beloved, I am writing you" (1 Jn 1:4; 2:1, 7-8, 12-14, 26; 5:13), has led most people to the assumption that this document is a typical New Testament letter from an apostle to some church that he knows well. For convenience, 1 John has been grouped in the canon with two shorter communications, both of which are unquestionably letters. Second John comes from "the elder to the elect lady" (v. 1), contains a typical epistolary salutation ("grace, mercy, and peace," v. 3), and closes with some personal words and a greeting from "the children of your elect sister" (vv. 12-13). In 3 John "the elder" writes to "the beloved Gaius," expressing his best wishes for Gaius' health and faith (vv. 1-2). Again he closes with a warm, personal greeting (vv. 13-15). The contrast between these two letters and 1 John could hardly be greater in this respect, and yet, because they have been placed together, the title of epistle has become attached to all three.

In actuality, 1 John is more a doctrinal and ethical treatise than a letter in any normal sense of the word. It may have in view a group of churches rather than a single church. Its theology is built securely on the "life in God" theme of the fourth Gospel. At the very outset John writes: ". . . that which we have seen and heard we proclaim also to you, *so that you may have fellowship with us; and our fellowship is with the Father and with his Son Jesus Christ*" (1 Jn 1:3). This statement is crucial for two reasons:

1. The "fellowship" (*koinōnia*) of which it speaks is not simply conviviality or social "togetherness" in the sense that the word "fellowship" is sometimes used today. Rather, it is an expression of that union with God realized in Jesus' resurrection according to John's Gospel. In his resurrection Jesus returns to the Father and also to his disciples, thus uniting them in himself with the Father. This experience is best understood as communion, the sharing of a common life. Just as in the Gospel, it is ultimately a communion both with the Father and with the Son.

2. The "we" of this introductory statement refers to the eyewitnesses of Jesus' life and deeds. Presumably they share in the apostolic witness, here represented by John. From the beginning they had heard and seen and even touched Jesus (1:1). Most vivid perhaps was the memory of that Easter day when Thomas had been invited to touch the wounds of the risen Lord. First John is written in order to extend this immediate perception of Jesus from the apostles alone to all Christians everywhere. Thus the readers would be able to participate in the *koinōnia* which the apostles had experienced with the Father and the Son. First John aims at the realization of Jesus' final words to Thomas, "Blessed are those who have not seen and yet believe" (Jn 20:29).

Such factors as these indicate that the thought of this treatise runs closely parallel to that of the fourth Gospel. Whether 1 John circulated with the Gospel as a kind of postscript designed to point up the same truths in a more didactic form, or whether it embodies a compendium of John's oral teachings in the churches before he wrote the Gospel, we do not know. What is clear in any case is that we are justified in using each of these Johannine writings to shed whatever light it can upon the other.

The special contribution of the "epistle," however, is its proposal of several practical, concrete tests by which the presence of divine life in a man may be discerned. To speak of dwelling in God or enjoying communion with him is not very significant unless it produces results in the way one actually behaves. Just as a prophetic interpretation of Jesus' life and words in terms of their present significance must be solidly anchored in the historic tradition of what Jesus really said and did, so also spiritual assertions about a person's life in Christ must be proven by the creed he recites and by the actions he performs. Flesh not quickened by the Spirit is profitless; Spirit not manifested in human flesh is meaningless. For the sake of convenience, we may designate these two sides of essential Christianity as the *metaphysical* and the *practical*. The term "metaphysical" is here used in a non-philosophical sense simply to denote what (or where) Christians *are*: they are, for example, "in God," or "in the light"; they have communion with God and with one another; they "abide in him"; they are "of God," or "of the truth"; they are "children of God," or "born of God"; they "know God" and "have eternal life." The term "practical" refers to what Christians *do*: they love God and one another; they "keep the commandments"; they "walk in the light"; they confess specific beliefs about Jesus Christ.

A remarkably high percentage of the sentences in 1 John can be bisected into precisely these two divisions. They are both metaphysical and practical, put together in such a way as to show that the two aspects of Christian experience are inseparable. Each depends mutually upon the other. A few statements are sufficient to illustrate what is meant:

Practical	Metaphysical
2:10 "He who loves his brother	*abides in the light.*"
3:7 "He who does right	*is righteous*"
3:24 "All who keep his commandments	*abide in him, and he in them.*"
4:15 "Whoever confesses that Jesus is the Son of God,	*God abides in him, and he in God.*"

Sometimes the point is made negatively, but the basic elements are the same:

Practical	Metaphysical
3:8 "He who commits sin	*is of the devil.*"
3:14 "He who does not love	*remains in death.*"

To John, the practical marks of divine life can be reduced to three essentials: righteousness, love and belief. These criteria are applied to Christian experience several times in a cyclical or spiral fashion. While John's thought seems to go over the same ground again and again, there is in reality a definite progression. The tests of love and righteousness recur throughout the treatise, while the test of belief is concentrated especially toward the end. The whole of John is, however, organized around three doctrinal affirmations which also belong, in the proper sense, to the test of belief:

1. "God is light and in him is no darkness at all" (1:5).
2. "Children, it is the last hour" (2:18).
3. "Jesus Christ has come in the flesh" (4:2).

Ultimately these three propositions reiterate a single message. It is the message of the prologue to John's Gospel and of the Gospel itself as a whole. Each of the three affirmations expresses in its own way the good news of the decisive redemptive event that took place in Jesus Christ. Taken together they constitute the "word of life" which was "from the beginning" and which John declares to his readers (1:1). Each proposition begins a cycle of Johannine thought in which the tests of righteousness and love are applied. These cycles may be used to form a broad outline of 1 John in terms of *walking in the light* (1:5-2:17), *living for the future* (2:18-3:24), and *believing the truth* (4:1-5:21).

First Cycle: Walking in the Light (1:5-2:17)

To those who have become familiar with the New Testament formulations of the Christian gospel, "God is light" comes as a strangely abstract and speculative way of stating "the message we have heard from him and proclaim to you" (1:5). It is a proposition to which a Hellenistic Jew or even an educated pagan could give assent just as readily as could a Christian apostle or prophet. The existence of evil in the world is a problem which haunts virtually every known religious and philosophical system. The aim of many such systems in John's day was to account for evil without imputing its origin to God. In such a framework, the maxim "God is light and in him is no darkness at all" would be both natural and pertinent.

Many statements in 1 John suggest that one of its purposes was to combat heresy within the church. It has often been suggested that this heresy was an incipient form of Gnosticism. This is a broad term covering a number of ancient mythical or philosophical systems that radically separated the true God from the created world as we know it. Gnostics believed that originally there was only the true God who existed in perfection. He was the true Light. He created secondary "gods" (e.g., Mind, Wisdom, or Primal Man) as reflections of himself. But by a series of defections or "emanations" that which the true God had created became more and more estranged from him. The world was not his creation at all, but the handiwork of alienated and fallen deities. Hence the world of matter is darkness. Man belongs to this world, yet also possesses within him sparks of the true light. When a call comes to him from without, from the world of light, he is initiated into the secrets of that world, the secrets of his own origin and existence. He becomes a *gnostic,* one who knows or understands. Thus he is delivered from the material world of darkness and reunited with the ultimate source of his being. Certain similarities between these Gnostic systems and New Testament Christianity are, of course, apparent. As soon as some ventured to identify the Gnostic revealer, the messenger of the decisive call, with Jesus Christ, there came into being a Christian Gnosticism that was to plague the church for centuries. It may be against early examples of such tendencies that John is contending. If so, two considerations must be kept in mind with respect to his use of the "God is light" terminology:

1. The declaration that "God is light" derives its force from the corollary that John attaches to it: "If we say we have fellowship with him while we walk in darkness, we lie and do not live according to the truth" (1:6). Frequently the Christian Gnostic, believing that he had been delivered from the evil physical world, concluded that he was also free from all moral laws that governed human life in this world. What he did with his body was of no import; only the soul counted for anything in God's sight. Against this mentality, John urges that a person's "walk," his practical daily behavior, is crucial. To say

"God is light," as some Gnostics did, while walking in the darkness of sin was to live a lie. 1 John, like 2 Peter and Jude, stands firmly opposed to all such antinomianism. A metaphysical assertion that does not pass muster in the realm of personal conduct is worthless.

2. John's rather philosophical formulation of the gospel in 1 John 1:5, defining God in terms of light, should not be interpreted apart from a different formulation of the same truth in 2:8. There John articulates the message more in the language of redemptive history: "the darkness is passing away and the true light is already shining." Just as in the prologue of the fourth Gospel, it is the *coming* of the light in the historic ministry of Jesus Christ that is decisive (Jn 1:5, 9). Only on the basis of this once-for-all dawning of the light in history can it be said with conviction that "God is light and in him is no darkness at all." Thus "the message we have heard from him" (1 Jn 1:5) belongs to the orthodox Christian, not to the Gnostic. For all their accent on revelation, the Gnostics fell short of a true appreciation of what it meant for God to reveal himself in human flesh. That John has not similarly cut himself off from this historic revelation is apparent from his references to the blood of Jesus (1:7) and to the commandments that Jesus gave (2:3f.), as well as the necessity "to walk in the same way in which he walked" (2:6).

John's first cycle follows a coherent and well-defined pattern. After the initial doctrinal affirmation, the test of *righteousness* is applied in 1:6-2:6. First, a series of five conditional sentences spell out the ethical implications of fellowship in the light (1:6-10). These statements alternate back and forth between the negative (vv. 6, 8, 10) and the positive (vv. 7, 9), confronting the readers with a radical and ultimate choice. In 2:1 the tone changes to one of assurance with the phrase, "My little children." The readers' confidence rests on two facts: their sins are forgiven through the work of Jesus their advocate,[1] and they know God. But the test of righteousness is still being applied.

---

1. The Greek word is *paracletos*, the same term that the fourth Gospel applies to the Holy Spirit. As the Spirit addresses man on behalf of God, so Christ addresses God on behalf of man.

They have this assurance only because they keep Christ's word and walk as he walked.

In 2:7-17 John administers his second test: *love*. The "commandments" (2:3) come to a focus in one commandment which is at the same time both old and new (2:7f.). It is old because it is a corollary of the "word of life" which was "from the beginning" (cf. 1:1), the gospel message that started with Jesus. Yet it is new because it means the passing away of the old world of darkness and the dawning of a new order (2:8). The context indicates that the commandment John has in mind is the one recorded in 13:34 of his Gospel: "A new commandment I give to you, that you love one another; even as I have loved you, that you also love one another." The application of this test of love follows the same pattern that characterized the test of righteousness; first the doctrinal statement is reiterated (2:8); then the ethical implications are spelled out in alternately negative and positive statements (2:9-11); finally there are assurances to the readers (addressed as "little children") that "your sins are forgiven" and that "you know the Father" (2:12-14).

The warnings in 2:15-17 serve as a transition to the next cycle of the author's thought. The announcement that "the world passes away" (2:17) looks both backward and forward: backward to the good news proclaimed in 2:8 that "the darkness is passing away and the true light is already shining," and forward to the doctrinal formulation that introduces the next cycle: "Children, it is the last hour" (2:18). The Christian message, even when couched in terms like these, is not world-denying like Gnosticism, but essentially world-affirming. In Christ the darkness that men call their world has been put to flight, John says. It is "passing away," and a new world of light and love and righteousness is upon us. To "love the world" (2:15) is to attempt to live in the past and in the darkness; to have "love for the Father" is to open oneself to the light and live for the future.

Second Cycle: Living for the Future (2:18-3:24)

If the theme of the first cycle was light, the theme of the second is *life*. This time John develops the doctrinal affirmation at some length (2:18-3:3); then he points out the ethical implications of the doctrine in terms of *righteousness* (in a series of alternating negative and positive statements, 3:4-10), and *love* (3:11-17); finally he adds his customary words of assurance (3:18-24).

In the Jewish world to which John had originally belonged, "eternal life" meant "the life of the age to come." His reference to "the last hour" (2:18), therefore, leads him naturally to a discussion of life. But John had told in his Gospel how Jesus shifted the tense of this eternal life from the future to the present. Jesus' promise was that the person who heard and believed his word would receive divine life as a present possession. Jesus had described this experience to Nicodemus the Pharisee as being born all over again, not by natural procreation, but "from above" (Jn 3:3-10). Here John speaks of being "born of God" (1 Jn 2:29; 3:9), of being therefore "children of God" (3:1-2, 10). The "last hour" for the world is not "last" for the child of God. He faces the future with confidence, not because he knows in detail what it will bring but because he is sure of his present relationship to the Father (3:2). In early Christian expectation this final appearing of Jesus Christ was to be preceded by times of trouble and stress for the church. There would be persecutions from the outside, while even within the household of faith many would turn from Christ to follow false prophets and teachers.[2] These calamities were frequently expected to cluster around one man or one world system that would come upon the scene as the virtual embodiment of ultimate evil—a "desolating sacrilege" (Mk 13:14), or a "man of lawlessness" (2 Th 2:3, 8-9), or a "beast rising out of the sea" (Rv 13:1), or a counterfeit Christ— an anti-Christ. In this section of 1 John, the life situation of the author and his readers comes vividly to life as the concept of "anti-Christ" is boldly applied to a group of teachers that has very recently been in their midst: "They went out from us, but they were not of us; for if they had been of us, they would have continued with us; but they went out, that it might be plain that they all are not of us" (2:19). This is the primary clue to a very important fact: *The church or churches to which John writes have been torn by a schism.* A sizable group has

---

2. Cf. Mt 24:10-12; 1 Tm 4:1 ff.; 2 Pt 3:3; Rv 2-3.

left the church, and John addresses himself to those who remain. The hints within the first cycle that some kind of Gnosticism threatens the church here assume a more definite shape. The schismatics have been guilty of lying; they have sinned against the truth by denying that Jesus is the Christ (2:21-22). They have been guilty of murder, through hatred of their brethren. To violate the commandment of love is to disdain the life that God gives and to dwell in the realm of death (3:14-15). To rend the church by such apostasy and hatred is to commit "mortal sin" for which there is no forgiveness (5:16). He who is truly born of God does not sin in this way. He who commits mortal sin thereby proves that he is not a child of God but belongs to the devil (3:7-10).

The tendency of Gnostic teaching was to lay claim to an esoteric body of knowledge that went far beyond the basic tenets of the gospel. Those who professed such knowledge exalted themselves above ordinary Christians, whom they relegated to "second-class citizenship" within the church. They themselves were the "knowers"; the rest of the church, mere "believers." In response to such a divisive doctrine, John assures his readers that "you have been anointed by the Holy One, and you *all* know" (2:20); "the anointing which you received from him abides in you, and you have no need that any one should teach you; as *his anointing teaches you about everything*, and is true, and is no lie, just as it has taught you, abide in him" (2:27). All who have been baptized and anointed by the Holy Spirit of truth possess the only knowledge that matters, the knowledge of God, both Father and Son, that means eternal life. In this sense there are no differentiated levels of spiritual attainment. All Christians are the children of God; all share a common hope in him. Anyone, whether inside or outside the church, who repudiates this unity of God's family, identifies himself as no Christian at all, but an anti-Christ. In attempting to exclude his brothers from the knowledge of God, he succeeds only in excluding himself from the divine life.

Thus John speaks harshly against those who would tamper with the essentials of Christian truth. Relentlessly he brings to bear against them the tests of righteousness and love. This treatise of 1 John lacks most of the qualifying clauses and lists of extenuating circumstances that usually go with ethical instruction. In the crisis faced here, everything is either light or darkness, truth or error, life or death, good or evil. Few gray areas exist to shade these contrasting zones of white and black. One fact above all, however, should be remembered: The righteousness and love which mark the child of God do not mean that he is perfect or altogether without sin—at least not until that day when "we shall be like him [i.e., Christ], for we shall see him as he is" (3:2). Though the Gnostics may have indulged themselves in extravagant pretension of sinlessness, John warns his readers against self-deceit of this kind: "If we say we have no sin, we deceive ourselves, and the truth is not in us" (1:8). Jesus himself was the only sinless one (3:5). "All wrongdoing is sin" (5:17), and there are many sins which are not mortal. As these continually afflict the child of God, they must be confessed and forgiven (1:9). John closes out his second cycle with a word of assurance: "If our heart condemn us, God is greater than our heart and knows all things" (3:20). The righteousness that God requires is summed up in the twofold commandment "that we should believe in the name of his Son Jesus Christ and love one another" (3:23). This formulation sets the "new commandment" of love into its true perspective. It is not only the highest expression of righteousness but also a corollary of the gospel message that God sent his Son into the world to take away sin—a message that demands faith as its proper response. Thus the three strands of righteousness, love, and faith become interwoven into a strong cord that sustains and assures the child of God, giving him the victory that John celebrates in his third cycle.

Third Cycle: Believing the Truth (4:1-5:21)

The theme of this last section of 1 John is *faith*. The practical tests of "abiding in God" are doctrinal as well as ethical. He who claims to know God must demonstrate the life that is within him not only by loving his brother and keeping God's commandments but also by assenting to a creed. The Johannine creed is short and specific. It is embodied in the doctrinal affirmation that introduces this last cycle: "Jesus Christ has come in the flesh" (4:2).

Several times through the last two chapters of 1 John the creed reappears in different forms:

"God sent his only Son into the world" (4:9).
"The Father has sent his Son as the Savior of the world" (4:14).
"Jesus is the Son of God" (4:15; 5:5).
"Jesus is the Christ" (5:1).
"The Son of God has come" (5:20).

This is the event of which John testifies. This is what every Christian must believe and confess. Its fullest development is found in 5:6-7, in which the whole Johannine witness to Jesus' career is epitomized in remarkably few words:

This is he who came by water and blood, Jesus Christ, not with the water only but with the water and the blood. And the Spirit is the witness, because the Spirit is the truth.

Here is the "Gospel According to John" reduced to its essentials: the ministry of Jesus from his baptism to his death upon the cross, revealed and interpreted by the Holy Spirit of truth. Nowhere else does the thought of 1 John run as closely parallel to that of the fourth Gospel as it does here.

The distinctive contribution of the epistle to the task of understanding Johannine thought, however, lies in the clearer picture it gives of the life situation that called it forth. While the purpose of John's Gospel can only be defined as that of introducing Christians into a fuller comprehension of the Christ event, the purpose of the epistle is a more specific one: to defend this understanding of Christ against a serious doctrinal deviation. The Gnostics did not content themselves with neglecting the moral life (1:6) nor even with cutting themselves off from the Christian community (2:18 ff.). They also denied that Jesus Christ had come in the flesh (4:1-6). Their doctrine of God did not allow them to accept the idea that God had really become man. A human Jesus was conceivable to them; so was a divine Christ as revealer of God. But that the two could be united in one historical personality—this was inconceivable. Hence John's distinctive terminology: "in the *flesh*," "*Jesus* is the son

of God," *"Jesus* is the Christ." In describing the spirit of anti-
Christ, John emphasizes that it does not confess *"Jesus"* (4:3),
not that it denies "Christ" or "God" or "the Son." We know
that the church of John's day was already threatened by a
Docetic teaching that denied the reality of Christ's human nature and of his sufferings. The divine Christ, it was taught,
came upon the human Jesus at his baptism but left him before
his violent death upon the cross. Jesus was a man; Christ was
God. Jesus suffered, but Christ was incapable of experiencing
pain.

A late-second-century document, that ironically bears John's
name, exemplifies this point of view:

> And my Lord stood in the middle of the cave and gave light
> to it and said, "John, for the people below in Jerusalem
> I am being crucified and pierced with lances and reeds and
> given vinegar and gall to drink. But to you I am speaking,
> and listen to what I speak" (*Acts of John,* 97).

> "This Cross then (is that) which has united all things by
> the Word and ... has also compacted all things into [one].
> But this is not that wooden Cross which you shall see when
> you go down from here; nor am I the (man) who is on the
> Cross..." (*ibid.,* 99).

It is perhaps against speculations of this kind that John insists
Jesus came "not with the water only but with the water and the
blood" (1 Jn 5:6). Similarly, in the fourth Gospel, such phrases
as "the Word became flesh" (1:14), the references to "eating the
flesh" and "drinking the blood" of the Son of man (6:53 ff.),
and the deliberate mention of the blood and water from Jesus'
side at the crucifixion (19:34) may exhibit a parallel awareness
of the Docetic danger.

John develops his third cycle along much the same lines
as the first two. Following the basic statement of belief in 1 John
4:1-6, the ethical implications of *love* (4:7-5:2) and *righteousness*
(5:3-21) are developed, each section drawing to a close on a
strong note of assurance and confidence in God (4:16-18; 5:13-21).

When the tests of life have been applied over and over again,
John ends the treatise as he began. Having started by inviting

his readers into that communion with the Father and the Son that he had known as a witness, he concludes that "we are in him who is true, in his Son Jesus Christ. This is the true God and eternal life" (5:20). It is this central reality of "life in God" that binds together the Gospel and 1 John.

Second and Third John

Second and Third John are true letters in a sense in which 1 John is not. Virtually all of the content of *Second John*, however, is paralleled somewhere in the longer 1 John. The mutual inter-relation of righteousness and love, for example, is summed up concisely in verses 5-6: the new commandment is "that we love one another" (v. 5); love is then defined as following his com-mandments, and once more John reiterates that "this is the com-mandment, as you have heard from the beginning, that you follow love" (v. 6). Thus John's thought moves in a never-ending circle: love, righteousness, and again love. The doctrinal test recommended to uncover the anti-Christs is "the coming of Jesus Christ in the flesh" (v. 7). The only new feature introduced in 2 John is that these things are specifically summed up, perhaps for brevity's sake, as "the doctrine of Christ" (vv. 9-10). This becomes the test of life and fellowship: "Any one who goes ahead and does not abide in the doctrine of Christ does not have God; he who abides in the doctrine has both the Father and the Son" (v. 9). A teacher who comes without this doctrine is not even to be greeted or received into one's house, much less into a place of authority in the church (v. 10). The situation clearly parallels that of 1 John in which "Many false prophets have gone out into the world" (1 Jn 4:1). Discernment is needed, and John supplies a practical, if simplified, rule to follow in the matter of receiving missionaries.

Second John thus appears to be a brief précis or abstract of 1 John written for one particular church. The "elect lady" (v. 1) is clearly a church, and "her children" are its individual members, while "the children of your elect sister" (v. 13) are the members of John's own church—tradition suggests Ephesus. If this tradition is correct, 2 John may have been sent from Ephesus to another church in Asia Minor, while 1 John, like the Book of Revelation, may have been a circular distributed to all of Asia Minor. Perhaps 2 John was written first, and briefly, because John hoped to explain things more fully in person (2 Jn 12). Then, when he was unable to come, and found that the problem of heresy was widespread, 1 John was written in lieu of a personal visit "so that our joy may be complete" (2 Jn 12; 1 Jn 1:4).

Third John is not written to a church but to a certain Gaius, otherwise unknown. Its tone is friendly and intimate. Superficially, it seems to contradict the second epistle in that emphasis is laid not on rejecting false teachers but on receiving the true messengers of God. John remembers Jesus' words to his disciples after the washing of their feet: "Truly, truly, I say to you, he who receives any one whom I send receives me; and he who receives me receives him who sent me" (Jn 13:20).

Gaius is to do good to fellow Christians who come to him as traveling strangers, for itinerant missionaries were dependent upon the Christian hospitality that John commends: "You will do well to send them on their journey as befits God's service. For they have set out for his sake and have accepted nothing from the heathen. So we ought to support such men, that we may be fellow workers in the truth" (3 Jn 6-8).

Not everyone in the church exhibited this attitude. A certain Diotrephes, "who likes to put himself first" (v. 9), has not only denounced John and denied his authority but "refuses himself to welcome the brethren, and also stops those who want to welcome them and puts them out of the church" (v. 10). Though Diotrephes is not accused of a specific doctrinal error, he is characterized here as a schismatic. His sin, like that of the Gnostic teachers in 1 John, is against the unity of the church. It is the sin of hatred and division among the brethren. Diotrephes seems to fall under the condemnation of Cain, a condemnation that John has already pronounced elsewhere: "Any one who hates his brother is a murderer, and you know that no murderer has eternal life abiding in him" (1 Jn 3:15). The life that Christians have in God is not to be regarded lightly. As Jesus was reunited with the Father, John says, we his disciples have been united to the Son and the Father. The very life of the Christian depends upon this relationship; to deny it is to forfeit one's own life. This is what Diotrephes and the Gnostics have done. But those who maintain this relationship, who "abide in God," are friends of God and of Jesus Christ. Jesus had declared to his disciples: "No longer do I call you servants, for the servant does not know what his master is doing; but I have called you *friends*, for all that I have heard from my Father I have made known to you" (Jn 15:15).

John's closing word to Gaius echoes this word "friends" and applies it to the people of God with confidence in Jesus' promise: "Peace be to you. The *friends* greet you. Greet the *friends*, every one of them" (3 Jn 15). It would be hard to find a more appropriate expression for the new way of life made possible because the Son of God has come.

The witness of John in his Gospel and three epistles is perhaps the fullest expression of the New Testament message. The good news is that God's Word has come into our midst. God has spoken in his Son Jesus, and because he has spoken, a new situation confronts the world. Since the Son has finished his work, men can know God as children and as "friends." This is the unique gift, and the awesome responsibility, of which the New Testament speaks.

REVIEW QUESTIONS
MATERIAL FOR COMMENT AND DISCUSSION

MARSH—John's "difference". (cf. also Davies) Is it possible that John knew about and used the synoptics or their sources as material for his own gospel? If such is the case, why is his gospel so "different" from theirs? In particular what could be behind John's "different" chronology? Is chronology *per se* important to the evangelists? Give Mark's version of the early episodes in Christ's public life and contrast how Luke recounts the same episodes. Speculate on the "why" of Luke's adjusted chronology. The cleansing of the Temple is placed differently in the synoptics and John. What seems to be Mark's theological reason for his placement? John's theological reason for his? Is a theology of the Cross implied in both placements? Explain. Are the conflicting John/synoptic dates for the Last Supper and the Crucifixion theologically compatible? Comment. What is typology and was it a good historiographical tool for the evangelists? Explain. Was symbolism also a useful tool? Show how the symbolism of Cana tells an important historical truth about Jesus and his mission. Though the synoptics are rich in episode and John selective, do they both use episodes for much the same purpose? Discuss and illustrate. The miracles in John are called "signs". Using the Lazarus episode as an example, illustrate its sign-value. How are the discourses in John related to his signs? Their overall theme? Some say John freely constructed these discourses. If so, could they be considered *reliable* reflections of Jesus and his teachings? Comment.

MANSON—Jesus as *Logos*. (cf. also DePinto) In using the term *Logos* to describe Jesus, John could more likely be pushing a theory than explaining a fact. Comment. How did the Stoics understand the term *Logos*? When John uses the term is he in any way like the Stoics? How does Philo use the term? Is his understanding similar to John's? Explain. What qualities does Wisdom in the Old Testament, especially when personified, have in common with John's *Logos?* What effect did "words" have for the ancients? for Jews? In comparison, how effective was God's word? Would it be "natural" for John as a Jew to refer to Jesus as God's word? Explain. Where in the Old Testament does Manson think John more probably finds the basis for his *Logos* doctrine? A possible secondary source? How does Jesus as Word differ from the word spoken by the Old Testament prophets? If in Manson's view the synoptics contain something analogous to the *Logos* doctrine, how is it expressed? When the Word became flesh what happened to our knowledge of God? Explain. Would the kind of Messiah Jesus turns out to be illustrate that even in that office he can fittingly be called the Word of God? Explain and illustrate. How does Manson relate Jesus the son of Joseph to the *Logos?* Discuss his summary remarks on the *Logos.*

DE PINTO—Wisdom and the Word. (cf. also Manson) Why according to the Old Testament can the Word be considered to be involved with God in the creation of the world? Show some of the similarities and parallels that De Pinto sees as existing between biblical Wisdom and the Johannine Jesus. The Old Testament prophetic literature was especially understood as God's Word; is John's Jesus even more so God's prophetic Word? Explain. The Law in the Old Testament was also spoken of as the Word of God. Why? Could John possibly have been thinking about Law-as-Word when he calls Jesus the Word? Explain. Why should the *embodied* Word be any more helpful to man than the Word God gave us in the Old Testament? How is the embodied Word made present and effective in our lives?

BROWN—John and Qumran. (cf. also Schnackenburg on "Morality"). Why do many scholars draw comparisons between the Johannine Writings and the Qumran literature? What is meant by saying both are dualistic; in what sense? Would the Old Testament or an extrabiblical source more likely account for Qumran's dualism? What affinities does Qumran seem to have with Iranian Zoroastrianism? The differences? Comment on the similarities between John's dualism and Qumran's. Compare what the two theologies have to say about: creation—the two spirits as leaders of good and evil—the struggle between light and darkness. Comment on the similarities and dissimilarities of John and Qumran in each area. Some say that the Qumran system treats man as morally determined to walk either in light or darkness. How deterministic was Qumran? Why is John certainly not deterministic? How does a Qumran sectarian know he is a "son of light"; how does he live in the light? In John how does one become a "son of light" and how does he remain in this light? Granted that in many ways John and Qumran are alike, comment on the big difference Christ makes in John's theology. Discuss the various uses of the terms "truth" —"brotherly love"—"living water"—as employed by the two theologies. Could John the Baptist possibly be a connecting link between Qumran and John? Discuss.

DAVIES—Jesus' Signs. (cf. also Marsh, Vawter) What are signs in the biblical sense? Why, for example, did the prophets use them? How does Jesus in John use them? How does Davies interpret the meaning of the following signs and episodes, with their accompanying discourses and dialogues: The Wedding at Cana? The cleansing of the Temple? The Jesus-Nicodemus meeting? (Why does man need a new birth? Why is Jesus as judge called the "light"? Does his "judging light" condemn man?) Davies' interpretation of the two healings: the nobleman's son; the man at the pool? The Feeding of the five-thousand? Jesus at the Feast of Tabernacles? (Could he be using the rituals of this feast to sign forth who and what he is? Explain. The Jews are very critical of Jesus at this feast. What do they have against him? How does Jesus answer their criticism? Why is Jesus' coming a time of judgment for this world? Is a choice that says "either take Jesus or lose all" fair? Comment.) The man born blind? (Jesus is and gives light; yet men judge him adversely. Why?) The good Shepherd? (What does the shepherd imagery tell us about Jesus and the state of Judaism in John's time?) The raising of Lazarus? (Why the delay to help Lazarus? The deeper meaning of the sign? Is there a prophecy of Jesus' own death here?) The anointing at Bethany and the triumphant entry into Jerusalem? (What were the saving implications of these events? Discuss the enigmatic concept that the new *life* comes about through Jesus' *death*). Relate the earlier signs in John to the sign of Jesus' death. Why is his death more salutary and effective than his earlier signs?

BROWN—The "Egō Eimi" passages. What are Bultmann's four classifications of the "egō eimi" phrase in ancient Jewish and pagan writings? What are John's three ways of using the phrase? (The absolute use with no predicate; some examples? The use where a predicate may be understood; some examples? The use with a predicate nominative; some examples? Does the latter type especially depict Jesus in his relationship to man? Explain. Do Jesus' discourses and use of Old Testament symbolism seem to corroborate this latter "egō eimi" function?) Where does Brown find the most likely source of this phrase, especially in its absolute sense and why? (E.g., when God is reassuring his people? when he reveals himself or is telling them something? when he stresses his unicity or existence? when he proclaims his divine name? Explain.) Comment especially on the frequent reference to Jesus' *name* in John. Could this be a subtle paraphrase of "egō eimi"? Could there be a connection between the "I" style of Old Testament Wisdom and John's Jesus? Are there synoptic parallels to the absolute use of "egō eimi" as found in John?

SCHELKLE—Theology of Man and the World. (cf. also Brown on "Qumran", Feuillet, Barrosse, Grossouw, Michaels) The Bible sees life, light, and truth as great "goods" for man. Comment particularly on the biblical rationale behind the value of human life. Does John present the concept of life as an even more valuable and profound good? What kind of life is now promised man through Christ? How is man's yearning for this deeper, more spiritual life fulfilled? What does the Bible generally have to say about light as a "good" for man? Is man because of his human plight in special need of a saving light? Explain. Why can John's Jesus provide a better light than that promised by gnostic and qumran "redeemers"? Man seeks truth as a necessary good. What is truth for John; what kind of unique truth does Christ offer man? What is meant by worshipping "in spirit and in truth"? How do greek, gnostic, and qumran notions of truth contrast to truth in John? According to John how did the world become so evil? What is its biggest sin? What are the general effects that flow from this sin? Are these evil effects the product of some uncontrollable dualism? Comment. How is the world ultimately saved from evil? Why is man's salvation essentially .God's work?

FEUILLET—Participation in God's life. (cf. also Schelkle, Barrosse, Vawter) If John speaks of salvation in terms of man's acquiring divine knowledge and a life of union with God, is he not very close to a variety of hellenistic religions and philosophical systems? Comment. How does John's "mysticism" differ from these other systems (as to its origin? as to its being more concerned about man's sin and his forgiveness?) Is a "mysticism" analogous to John's discoverable in the synoptics? Comment especially on the "mystical" implications inherent in the synoptic idea of the Kingdom of God, the salvific blessings, Jesus' words as recorded in Mt 11:25-30. Many note that John's Jesus when compared to the synoptics speaks differently; could this mean that the "mysticism" we find in John is more John than Jesus? Comment.

BARROSSE—Relationship of Love to Faith. (cf. also Schelkle, Feuillet) According to John what in essence is Christian faith? Some examples? Is it largely an intellectual process? Can man within himself initiate an act of faith? Paul and John seem to speak differently of Christian faith. Why? How is man's faith related to God's love? Why does one presuppose the other? Speculate why God's all-powerful love in a sense is *dependent* on man's faith. There are selfish loves opposed to God's love. What, e.g., is love of darkness? How can man as a creature of God even think of embracing such a love? What is love for the glory of men? Why does this love frustrate God's desire to give us himself? What is love for one's own life? Such a love would seem natural to man; how could it be opposed to a love for God? Why according to John is it impossible to love both God *and* the "world"? What is divine glory? What is love for the glory of God? What is love for the light? Why is it impossible according to John to love God while refusing Christ our love?

VAWTER—Spirit; Eschatology. (cf. also Davies, Feuillet, Brown on "Johannine Sacramentary") Why is it incorrect to say, as some do, that the Spirit plays a subordinate role in John? What role does he play; who is he? In treating of the Spirit how are Luke, John, and Paul alike; how different? What is meant by the expressions—"the Spirit is life"—"the Spirit is truth"—"the Spirit is paraclete"? What functions does he perform under these titles? What is eschatology? *Future* (i.e. final) eschatology? *Realized* eschatology? Why in view of John's teaching about the Spirit would his eschatology almost have to be realized? Why did the Church embrace both final and realized eschatology? Where do Christians "meet" or "realize" the Spirit and why? Do the sacraments feature in this meeting with the Spirit? Is Jesus in a sense still working his "signs" and are they efficacious? Explain. How did Christian worship and daily living take on an eschatological character? Does John's understanding of the judgment have a *realized* aspect to it? Comment.

SCHNACKENBURG—Christian Morality. (cf. also Brown on "Qumran", Feuillet, Grossouw, Michaels) John's morality is said to be Christological. What does this mean? Is John dualistic in his moral outlook? In what sense? Again, recall his affinities with the moral doctrine of Qumran. Where according to Schnackenburg does he especially differ from Qumran? Relate the Christian moral life to *belief* in Christ. What for John is the *worst* sin? Why is he so hard on disbelievers? Allowing for man's weakness and ignorance one would think he should be more tolerant of disbelief. Comment. Is John's moral doctrine "belief" ethics or "love" ethics? Would "communion" ethics be a better way to describe it? Comment. What is so *new* about Jesus' commandment to love the brethren? How selfless a love is implied here? If it is *that* selfless, who but Jesus could keep such a commandment? Does brotherly love "earn" grace or "reveal" grace? Comment. Does brotherly love extend beyond the brethren? In view of the seeming lack of "specifics", comment on the *practicality* of Christian morality according to John.

GROSSOUW—Johannine Spirituality. (cf. also Feuillet, Barrosse, Schnackenburg on "Morality") In what sense is John's spirituality "unworldly"? Does this mean he is "aloof" from everyday concerns? What did the Greeks understand by the *kosmos* (world); what did they make of the problem of evil? How does the Old Testament view of the world and evil differ from the Greeks? What is the general gnostic attitude toward the world and evil? What kind of "redemption" were the gnostics looking for? Why do some say John had a gnostic-dualist view of the "world"? Do you think this is true? Comment. Could John by using dualist terms perhaps be trying to correct gnostic ideas rather than to expound them? Discuss. Are John's views on spirituality even when addressed to historical persons (e.g., the Samaritan woman, Nicodemus, the disciples, etc.) aimed at all Christians? Discuss. How does the postresurrection Christian develop a "spiritual life" and *must* it be Christo-centric? Explain. Can the postresurrection Christian really "know" or "see" Christ? Discuss. Why according to John is Christ so essential in developing an authentic spiritual life; why isn't *deism* enough? Can our spiritual love for God in the Johannine system exist apart from the world and people? Comment. Why is *agape* so difficult to give those who are not "brothers"? Is brotherly love mainly ьa *moral* obligation? Comment.

BROWN—John's Sacramentary. (cf. also Vawter, Schnackenburg on "Ecclesiology.") What is the case for saying John is "nonsacramentalist"? Why do nonsacramentalists posit an ecclesiastical redactor for the gospel? Describe generally the views of the "ultrasacramentalist" school. If John underwent redactional or editorial modifications involving the insertion of more pronounced sacramental symbolism in his work, does this necessarily mean he was originally non or antisacramentalist? Explain. What does Brown say about the school that sees any "sacramentalism" in John as peripheral at best and present mostly as an antidote to Docetism? What are some useable rules for arguing a possible sacramental reference in John? Using these rules why is it doubtful that the foot-washing scene in chapter 13 refers to the eucharist? Brown mentions two clear criteria for judging sacramental symbolism in John. Are such criteria to be found in the pool episode in chapter 5? the cure of the blind man in chapter 9? Jesus' baptism at the Jordan in chapter 1? the Cana episode in chapter 2 with reference to marriage and the eucharist respectively? the cleansing of the Temple in chapter 2? the allegory of the vine in chapter 15?

SCHNACKENBURG—Johannine Ecclesiology. (cf. also Brown on the "Johannine Sacramentary") John's gospel is mainly a Christological document with little or no stress on ecclesiology. Would you agree or disagree? Discuss. Does John have anything to say about baptism or the eucharist, and if so, would this indicate some ecclesiological interest? Explain. Does the "polemic" of the epistles have any ecclesiastical implications? Explain. Jesus speaks of sharing his "work" with the disciples once he has been exalted and glorified. In light of the sayings and metaphors of Jesus that define his work (e.g., Jesus is a shepherd, he has a present and future flock, he gives a postresurrectional mission to Peter, he prays for unity, other disciples, etc.) can one fairly find reference to a Christian church? Discuss. Could any ecclesiological implications be drawn from Jesus' use of the "vine and branches" allegory? Explain. Is the unity Jesus seeks between himself and the believer only an individual, subjective thing? Does the religious activity depicted or implied in the gospel and the epistles presuppose that Jesus continues his saving function through a church or community of some sort? Discuss. Are there any ecclesiastical implications to the "missionary" interest of John; to his frequent defensive stance?

MICHAELS—The Three Epistles. (cf. also Schelkle, Schnackenburg on "Morality", Grossouw) Many summarize the overall theme of First John in the word koinōnia. What do they mean and is the word also a good one to summarize John's gospel? Comment. In what sense is First John a more practical document than the gospel? What are the tests that indicate whether or not we really possess "new life" and walk in the "true light"? Recall the main theses of gnosticism as described in this essay. Could First John be a refutation of some form of gnosticism? Explain. Why is belief in God and living undisturbed by sin (though seen as consistent by gnostics) viewed as totally inconsistent by John? When John warns us against the anti-Christ and his activity is he also teaching us something about the false premises of gnosticism? Comment. How does John assure his Christians that *they* have sufficient *gnosis*? Is John's "creed" anti-gnostic, anti-docetist? Explain. How do we discern a true Christian teacher and missionary?